REVIEWS

"Author Diane Weber Bederman serves up an essential reality check about the 'Islamophobia' industry's aim to shut down all criticism of Islam, while propagating the farcical view of Islam as a "race". This engaging exposé captures the urgency in understanding the threat to all freedoms by a doctrine that has insidiously infiltrated every layer of Western society.

Christine Douglass-Williams
International award-winning journalist and best-selling author of The Challenge of Modernizing Islam", #1 Amazon best seller in International Institutions category

"As the memory of the 9/11 attacks twenty years ago recedes, Diane Weber Bederman's important book *The Islamophobia Industry* serves as a crucial wakeup call to a Western world that, in the name of tolerance and inclusion, is succumbing to an even more insidious, internal threat – the erosion of our rights and freedoms as the value system of Islam grows in influence and power."

Mark Tapson
Shillman Journalism Fellow
David Horowitz Freedom Center

Publisher: Canadian Centre for the Study of Extremism (CCSE)

Editor: Rick Gill

FOREWORD

Tom Quiggin, MA, CD

Islamophobia is the weapon used by Islamists to silence criticism of their political ideology. An Islamist is anyone who would impose a given interpretation of Islamic religious law and culture over society. For current Islamist groups such as the Muslim Brotherhood, Hizb ut Tahrir, the Taliban, ISIS, Al Qaeda, Boko Haram or Jamaat E Islami, this means a politicized form of Islam. In short, it is a theocratic ideology that has a distinctive relationship with confrontation and violence.

The Islamists must silence discussion of their ideolog. It is so misogynistic, anti-democratic and brutal that any public debate would expose it as being in direct confrontation with individual or collective human rights.

This use of Islamophobia results in a situation where facts are no longer permissible in the public realm. Only that which is seen as being politically correct can be put forward.

To say that something is politically correct, is to say that it is not correct. If an idea or belief is 'correct,' it does not need the world 'politically' in front of it. Something is politically correct only if it can ignore most of reality and be seen only through a narrow and forcibly imposed political lens.

Islamophobia, and political correctness, are used for enforcing ideological orthodoxy. They are wielded now in much the same way that *politicheskaya korrektnost* (political correctness) was used in the Soviet Union or during the Communist Chinese Cultural Revolution.

In this book, the author points out that moral and cultural relativism are our enemies, especially when it is insisted that all cultures are somehow equal and that all values are the same. Taking advantage of this, the author argues that an industry, called Islamophobia, is an attack on our liberty while it infiltrates and influences Western values and democracy.

Freedom of speech remains our single most important right. Without freedom of speech, all other rights and freedoms will erode to the point of irrelevance. As such, the Islamophobia industry must be stopped now.

PREFACE

Why did I decide to write a book about Islam at a time when saying anything negative about Islam is considered irrational and racist?

While we have gone about our daily business, Islam has been quietly promoting itself in our everyday lives. Islam has accomplished this by silencing any criticism about its value system; a system that is diametrically opposed to all things Western. With credible facts, you can speak up and not be intimidated by calls of racism or anti-Islamism.

Islam has infiltrated every aspect of our lives from government to media to education. And we, the people of the West, because of our love of tolerance, inclusion and accommodation allow this to happen.

We analyze the effects of China on our culture. We criticize Christianity and Judaism, Buddhism and Sikhism without a word. However, we have stood by as Islam crept into all our institutions.

This book reveals the value system of Islam. The #IslamophobiaIndustry wants one thing, and one thing only - our silence. It is an attack on our freedom of speech. We must not let ourselves be silenced by any ideology.

We are committing suicide by democracy. Will the West bend the knee, or will we protect and defend our freedom–loving way of life?

Diane Weber Bederman, Toronto, September 2021

ACKNOWLEDGEMENTS

Thank you to Rick Gill who took my manuscript and turned it into a book, no easy task.

And thank you to Tom Quiggin for making all of this possible.

INTRODUCTION

"Democracy... while it lasts is more bloody than either aristocracy or monarchy. Remember, democracy never lasts long. It soon wastes, exhausts, and murders itself. There is never a democracy that did not commit suicide."

~ John Adams

There is a story about a lobster who found himself in a pot. A big pot. Of warm water. It was lovely. And he lay back. In the pot, relaxed, and closed his eyes. He began to drift off and as he drifted away, the water slowly got warmer and warmer, and then hot. He was so relaxed and acclimated that he did not notice, until it was too late. He had allowed himself to be lulled. To death. A lobster; an Empire. If one does not pay attention to one's surroundings, all can be lost.

We are not paying attention. Whether it be from compassion or apathy or ignorance, we have been lulled into accepting ideologies and values that conflict with ours. Our intentions have been good, but good intentions have been known to pave the road to perdition. Unintended consequences are catching up to us. Western culture is in decline but there is time to prevent the fall.

Empires have risen and fallen over the millennia. For many reasons. The Roman Empire had strong political government and economic prosperity for several centuries. And fell. The British Empire collapsed. War depleted her treasury. The Ottoman Empire is gone. The capital of the Eastern Roman Empire, Constantinople, was conquered by the Ottoman Army, under the command of Ottoman Sultan Mehmed II on 29th May 1453. With this conquest Ottomans became an Empire and one of the most powerful empires. World War I ended the Empire. But not its aspirations.

Today, one might classify the West as an Empire; of democratic countries firmly rooted in the Judeo/Christian ethic that underpins all their constitutions. We begin with the values that all people are born with equal intrinsic value and all life is sacred.

This ethic requires discipline; the ability to repress and supress one's instincts, particularly those that relate to vengeance and sex. It requires giving up some freedoms for the sake of community; a living social contract described by philosophers Thomas Hobbes, John Locke, and Jean-Jacques Rousseau as an agreement that makes it possible for citizens to "give up certain of their rights and freedoms, handing them over to a central authority, which in return, will ensure the rule of law within the society and the defense of the realm against external enemies."[1]

Who are today's external enemies? Moral and cultural relativism are our enemies, today. Our belief that all cultures are equal and all moral values are the same.[2] We can look back to the early 20th century when Franz

---

[1] Rabbi Jonathan Sacks, "Biblical Insights into the Good Society," Biblical Insights into the Good Society (November 30, 2011), http://www.rabbisacks.org/biblical-insights-into-the-good-society-ebor-lecture-2012/.
[2] Elizabeth Lewis, "Franz Boas, Father of American Anthropology," ThoughtCo.com (ThoughtCo, part of the Dotdash publishing family, December 10, 2020), https://www.thoughtco.com/franz-boas-4582034.

Boas brought forward his now well-known theory of cultural relativism which held that all cultures were essentially equal but simply had to be understood in their own terms. Comparing two cultures was tantamount to comparing apples and oranges. This marked a decisive break with the evolutionary thinking of the period, which attempted to organize cultures and cultural artifacts by an imagined level of progress.[3] Boas was pushing back on the ethnocentrism; the practice of viewing and judging someone else's culture based on the values and beliefs of one's own.

Boas promoted the idea that no culture is better than another or more evolved. He taught his views during his nearly four-decade career teaching anthropology at Columbia University, where he built the first anthropology program in the country and trained the first generation of anthropologists in the U.S. who shared these views everywhere for decades.

If we follow his teachings then we must accept all values, all cultures, in our Western societies; from honor killings to caste systems which define some people as superior to others, to sex selection abortion.

Are we really prepared to do that in the name of tolerance, accommodation and inclusion? In the name of diversity or multiculturalism?

Winston Churchill knew all too well about democracy and Western Culture.

---

[3] Nicki Lisa Cole, "Cultural Relativism Explains Why Breakfast Differs around the World," ThoughtCo.com (ThoughtCo, part of the Dotdash publishing family, August 17, 2019), https://www.thoughtco.com/cultural-relativism-definition-3026122.

"Many forms of Government have been tried and will be tried in this world of sin and woe. No one pretends that democracy is perfect or all-wise. Indeed, it has been said that democracy is the worst form of Government except all those others that have been tried from time to time."

The West, the best and the worst of it, is under attack. There are other value systems that want to spread their wings. Colonize for want of a better word, today.

Plato warned us "Dictatorship naturally arises out of democracy, and the most aggravated form of tyranny and slavery out of the most extreme liberty."

Extreme tolerance, inclusion and accommodation can be linked to extreme liberty: accepting that which is incompatible in the name of freedom.

There is an industry at work, today, taking advantage of our liberty, infiltrating and influencing Western values and democracy. It is the #IslamophobiaIndustry, aided and abetted by billions of dollars from countries like Qatar and Saudi Arabia. The industry has taken advantage of media, education, propaganda and government to spread its values; values that Islam has clearly stated are not compatible with the West. It is an Industry that strives to silence critics of its ideology. The industry has upended the rules of engagement.

Abdur-Rahman Muhammad, a former member of the International Institute of Islamic Thought (IIIT) said, "Islamophobia is nothing more than a thought terminating cliché conceived in the bowels of Muslim think tanks for the purpose of beating down critics."[4]

---

[4] Matthew Vadum, "Lifting the Veil on the 'Islamophobia' Hoax," Capital Research Center (Capital Research Center,

Council of American Islamic Relations (CAIR) founder Omar Ahmad had stated how CAIR could eventually gain influence in Congress: "This can be achieved by infiltrating the American media outlets, universities and research centers," going on to suggest how this would give them an entry point that would allow them to pressure U.S. policymakers.[5] In Canada, CAIR has re-branded as the National Council of Canadian Muslims (NCCM).

And here we are, silenced. Afraid to criticize Islam; the religion and the political ideology for fear of being labeled a racist or Islamophobe. No other religion or culture has been able to silence us; prevent us from criticizing it, comparing, and contrasting one to another. There was a time when we were taught the importance of critical thinking.

Franklin D. Roosevelt stated: "Democracy cannot succeed unless those who express their choice are prepared to choose wisely. The real safeguard of democracy, therefore, is education."

The West is in decline, from fear of the other. It is education that will free us from this irrational fear. We must not let ourselves be intimidated by the #IslamophobiaIndustry which is destroying freedom of speech all over the world. Remarkable. Communism could not do it. Neither could Fascism. Nazism failed.

November 30, 2015),
https://capitalresearch.org/article/islamophobia-hoax/.
[5] Professor Arnon Gutfeld, "The Saudi Specter over the American Education System," Jewish Political Studies Review, Volume 29, Numbers 1-2 (Jerusalem Center for Public Affairs, September 3, 2018), https://jcpa.org/article/saudi-specter-over-american-education-system/.

Islamophobia has brought pundits, politicians, and professors to their knees. Those responsible for maintaining our culture have been silenced.

Looking back one can see that banning and criminalizing "hate speech" took hold with the Salman Rushdie "affair" thirty years ago. In 1988 Rushdie, a Muslim born in India, published The Satanic Verses, a novel whose main story was inspired in part by the life of Muhammad. The book, which won the Whitbread Award for novel of the year and was a finalist for the Booker Prize, also drew condemnation from the Islamic world for what was perceived to be its irreverent account of Muhammad. In many countries with large Muslim populations, the novel was banned and on February 14, 1989, Ayatollah Khomeini, the spiritual leader of Iran, issued a fatwa requiring the author's execution. A fatwa is an "Islamic legal pronouncement, issued by an expert in religious law (mufti), pertaining to a specific issue, usually at the request of an individual or judge to resolve an issue where Islamic jurisprudence (fiqh), is unclear."[6] In this case a bounty was offered for Rushdie's death and for several years he was forced to live under police protection. At that moment, criticism of Islam became dangerous throughout the West. Rushdie issued a public apology and voiced his support for Islam which he later recanted. The heat around The Satanic Verses eventually cooled and in 1998, Iran declared it would not support the fatwa.[7]

---

[6] "What Is a Fatwa?" Islamic Supreme Council of America (Islamic Supreme Council of America, 2021), https://wpisca.wpengine.com/?p=106.

[7] Biography.com, ed., "Salman Rushdie - Biography," Biography.com (A&E Networks Television, May 21, 2021),

But I think most of us were unaware of the danger to freedom because of that fatwa. Islam revealed its agenda and we ignored it or did not recognize it or refused to believe the seriousness. Ayaan Hirsi Ali has also suffered under a fatwa for her views on Islam. Born into a devout Somali Muslim family Ayaan Hirsi Ali was elected to the Dutch parliament. In 2004 she worked with filmmaker Theo van Gogh to create Submission, a film depicting Islam as a religion that sanctions the abuse of women. Several weeks after the film aired on Dutch television, van Gogh was murdered; shot and stabbed, with a knife pinning to his body a letter that called for the death of Hirsi Ali.[8]

At what point will we awaken to attacks on our basic freedoms? Freedoms that we have taken for granted for far too long.

When the killings took place at Charlie Hebdo, should that not have been a wake-up call about attacks on our basic freedoms to criticize the other? Remember, we were all Charlie Hebdo in France, in January 2015, when the lives of 17 people, including 11 journalists and security personnel at the Paris offices of Charlie Hebdo, a satiric magazine, were murdered. For how long did we remember? Muslim terrorists murdered people for the crime of making fun of Mohamed. Putting a turban on him with a bomb in it, representing the murder of non-Muslims by Muslims. This was not to be allowed, anywhere in the world. Keep that in mind. It was a

---

https://www.biography.com/writer/salman-rushdie.
[8] Virginia Gorlinski, "Ayaan Hirsi Ali - Biography," ed. Encyclopaedia Britannica, Encyclopædia Britannica (Encyclopædia Britannica, inc., February 11, 2021), https://www.britannica.com/biography/Ayaan-Hirsi-Ali.

warning to anyone and everyone that one cannot belittle or demean Islam or the Prophet on pain of death. This was not the first attack for the gall of poking fun at Mohammed.[9]

A series of cartoons, some depicting the Prophet Mohammed as a terrorist with a bomb, were first published by Danish newspaper Jyllands-Posten in 2005. Later, Charlie Hebdo was sued by Muslim groups for publicly "insulting" Islam. Francois Hollande testified in favour of freedom of expression. In 2008 a video from Osama bin Laden threatened the EU over reprinting of the cartoon, which he claimed was part of a "new Crusade" against Islam led by the Pope. In 2011 Charlie Hebdo's Paris offices were burned in an apparent arson attack on day after it published an issue with the Prophet Mohammed as "editor-in-chief". He is depicted on the front page saying: "100 lashes if you don't die of laughter."

The fear of criticizing Islam is so strong that a former cartoonist at Charlie Hebdo, Delfeil de Ton, after the 2015 massacre of his colleagues, accused Charlie Hebdo's late editor Stéphane Charbonnier of "dragging" the staff into the slaughter by satirizing Mohammed.[10]

---

[9] Foreign Staff, "Prophet Mohammed Cartoons Controversy: Timeline," The Telegraph (Telegraph Media Group, May 4, 2015), https://www.telegraph.co.uk/news/worldnews/europe/france/11341599/Prophet-Muhammad-cartoons-controversy-timeline.html.

[10] Giulio Meotti, "France Quietly Reintroducing the Crime of Blasphemy," Gatestone Institute (Gatestone Institute, February 9, 2020), https://www.gatestoneinstitute.org/15526/france-blasphemy-

In February 2020, five years after the Charlie Hebdo massacre, Franz-Olivier Giesbert, an influential commentator, and former editor of Le Figaro, accused Justice Minister Belloubet of appeasing Islamists, and compared her actions to those of the Vichy regime that collaborated with Hitler.[11]

That did not stop the attacks. Late October 2020, French teacher Samuel Paty, 47, was targeted for showing cartoons of the Prophet Muhammad to his students. He was beheaded. His killer, 18-year-old Abdullakh Anzorov, a teenage refugee of Chechen origin, was shot dead by police. Six others, including two more students were arrested.[12] A young Tunisian man killed three people inside the basilica in the southern city of Nice, beheading one woman. But this series of bloodletting began September 25 when a young Pakistani refugee injured two people outside the former Charlie Hebdo newsroom office in Paris.[13]

Following the beheading of Samuel Paty, French Minister of Education Jean Michel Blanquer shared that 800 Islamist "incidents" had taken place in French schools.[14,15]

---

censorship.

[11] Giulio Meotti, "France Quietly Reintroducing the Crime of Blasphemy," Gatestone Institute (Gatestone Institute, February 9, 2020), https://www.gatestoneinstitute.org/15526/france-blasphemy-censorship.

[12] "France Teacher Attack: Seven Charged over Samuel Paty's Killing," BBC News Europe (BBC News Services, October 22, 2020), https://www.bbc.com/news/world-europe-54632353.

[13] Elaine Ganley, "French Muslims, Stigmatized by Attacks, Feel under Pressure," AP News (The Associated Press, November 1, 2020), https://apnews.com/article/paris-france-emmanuel-macron-islam-europe-ea5e15bb651bbe443b27bc19948cae6b.

We should not be surprised. In 2015, Islamic State announced that French schools must be attacked and invited its followers to "kill the teachers". According to Gilles Kepel, an expert on Islamism, "The school, for the supporters of political Islam, has become a citadel to tear down."[16]

And yet we remain silent. There are no world-wide protests about the negative influence of Islam on our freedom of expression or speech. We are silent, like the lambs. As if silence would end the onslaught.

There will be no attacks on Islam and certainly not on Mohammed while attacks on Christianity and Judaism and Jesus and Mary are rampant all over the West. But not Islam in the West. Absolutely not!

Islamophobia is bringing on a new Dark Age. The historical Dark Ages took place following the fall of the Western Roman Empire around 475 CE until 1000 CE. The Dark Ages was seen as a period of religious struggle between Christian factions. It was a time when Catholics

---

[14] valeursactuelles.com, "800 Signalements Pour 'Radicalisme Islamiste' à L'ÉCOLE Depuis L'assassinat De Samuel Paty," Valeurs actuelles, December 16, 2020, https://www.valeursactuelles.com/societe/800-signalements-pour-radicalisme-islamiste-a-lecole-depuis-lassassinat-de-samuel-paty/.

[15] Giulio Meotti, "The Religious Transformation of French Schools," Gatestone Institute (Gatestone Institute, January 23, 2021), https://www.gatestoneinstitute.org/16972/france-schools-religion.

[16] Giulio Meotti, "The Religious Transformation of French Schools," Gatestone Institute (Gatestone Institute, January 23, 2021), https://www.gatestoneinstitute.org/16972/france-schools-religion.

were warned against reading. This concept of a "Dark Age" was created by the Italian scholar Francesco Petrarca (Petrarch) and was originally intended as a sweeping criticism of the character of Late Latin literature. Later historians expanded the term to include not only the lack of Latin literature, but a lack of contemporary written history and material cultural achievements in general. Popular culture has further expanded on the term as a vehicle to depict this time frame as a time of backwardness. Darkness. Islam spread its wings during this time conquering land until the time of the Crusades.

Islam is spreading its wings, again. And Darkness.

In the name of tolerance, inclusion, diversity and accommodation we have allowed a culture that is incompatible with western values to take hold and then silence us from criticizing it as we have criticized communism, fascism and Nazism. How do I know that Islam is not compatible with the West? Islamic scholars and organizations have said so.

We must not give in to fear. We must not let others silence us. Silence is collusion.

In this book, I will take you on a journey of discovery. Why do citizens in the West, recipients of one of the greatest cultures in recorded history, choose to silence themselves about Islam, and how did it happen?

"Civilizations die from suicide, not murder."

~ Arnold Toynbee

CHAPTER 1: WHAT'S IT ALL ABOUT? WHAT IS ISLAMOPHOBIA?

French intellectual Jean-François Revel cautioned us about the danger of complacency in his book *"How Democracies Perish"*:[17]

> *"Democracy tends to ignore, even deny, threats to its existence because it loathes doing what is needed to counter them. It awakens only when the danger becomes deadly, imminent, evident. By then, either there is too little time to save itself, or the price of survival has become crushingly high."*

So, what is Islamophobia? Here is a little history of that word.

The neologism "islamophobia" did not simply emerge *ex nihilo* from nowhere. It was invented, deliberately, by a Muslim Brotherhood front organization, the International Institute for Islamic Thought (IIIT), which is based in Northern Virginia.

Abdur-Rahman Muhammad, a former member of the International Institute of Islamic Thought (IIIT) said, "Islamophobia is nothing more than a thought terminating cliché conceived in the bowels of Muslim think tanks for the purpose of beating down critics".[18] He

---

[17] Revel Jean François, How Democracies Perish: Jean-Francois Revel; with the Assistance of Branko Lazitch; Trans. from the French by William Byron (London: Weidenfeld and Nicolson, 1983).

also went on to say, "They (Muslim think tanks) study such movements as the gay movement and modeled islamophobia after homophobia and they use it like a bat to beat down the critics and to stifle any kind of debate and to stymie their critics."

Raheel Reza, a Muslim Pakistani-Canadian journalist, author, public speaker, media consultant, anti-racism activist, and interfaith discussion leader explained that "the term Islamophobia was created in the 1990s, when groups affiliated to the U.S. Muslim Brotherhood[19] decided to play victim for the purpose of beating down critics."[20] It is also in sync with a constant push by the OIC (Organization of Islamic Cooperation) to turn any criticism of Islam or Muslims into racism and bigotry."

Dr. Qanta Ahmed, a staunch defender of Israel, but also a deeply committed Muslim, wrote, "Islamophobia, a word designed to deter scrutiny of extremist ideology."[21]

---

[18] Matthew Vadum, "Lifting the Veil on the 'Islamophobia' Hoax," Capital Research Center (Capital Research Center, November 30, 2015), https://capitalresearch.org/article/islamophobia-hoax/.

[19] The Editors of Britannica, "Muslim Brotherhood," Encyclopædia Britannica (Encyclopædia Britannica, inc., September 11, 2020), https://www.britannica.com/topic/Muslim-Brotherhood.

[20] Raheel Raza, "Raheel Raza: M-103 Won't Build a more united Canada. It will turn Canadians against each other," nationalpost.com (National Post, February 27, 2017), https://nationalpost.com/opinion/raheel-raza-m-103-wont-build-a-more-united-canada-it-will-canadians-against-each-other.

[21] Dr. Qanta Ahmed, "My Grief for the Victims of the New Zealand Mosque Attack," The Spectator (The Spectator (1828) Ltd, March 14, 2019),

She is an Associate Professor of Medicine at the State University of New York Stony Brook, and the author of In the Land of Invisible Women an account of her experience living and working in the Kingdom of Saudi Arabia. An Op-Ed contributor to the Dutch National Trouw, she has also been published in the Huffington Post, The Jerusalem Post, The Guardian, The Wall Street Journal, The Christian Science Monitor, The New York Post, The New York Daily News, Pakistan's The Daily Times and the World Policy Journal.

Back in 2004, Kofi Annan, the seventh Secretary-General of the United Nations from January 1997 to December 2006, asserted at a conference entitled "Confronting Islamophobia" that the word Islamophobia had to be coined to "take account of increasingly widespread bigotry."[22,23] There was a fear in the air that Islam was being attacked for no rational reason.

The United Nations has taken up the call; working with the Organization of Islamic Cooperation[24] to prohibit all speech that Muslims consider offensive. Pakistan's ambassador Maleeha Lodhi said Islamophobia was

---

https://www.spectator.co.uk/article/my-grief-for-the-victims-of-the-new-zealand-mosque-attack.

[22] Kofi Annan, "Secretary-General Addressing Headquarters Seminar on Confronting Islamophobia, Stresses Importance of Leadership, Two-Way Integration, Dialogue," United Nations (United Nations, December 7, 2004), https://www.un.org/press/en/2004/sgsm9637.doc.htm.

[23] "Islamophobia," en-academic.com (Academic Dictionaries and Encyclopedias, 2021), https://en-academic.com/dic.nsf/enwiki/110470.

[24] "Organization of Islamic Cooperation (OIC)," Organization of Islamic Cooperation (OIC) (Organization of Islamic Cooperation (OIC), 2021), https://www.oic-oci.org/home/?lan=en.

"today the most prevalent expression of racism and hatred against 'the other.'[25]

In preparation for the celebration of the Organization of Islamic Cooperation's (OIC) 50th anniversary, November 2019, in Jeddah, Muslim leaders, Yousef Al-Dhobei, Dr. Al-Othaimeen, Dr. Saud Kateb and Tariq Bakhit demanded the introduction of an international law to criminalize all acts of Islamophobia.

Its secretary-general, Dr. Yousef Al-Othaimeen told in Arab News called for a global crackdown on individuals or groups responsible for "insulting religions or prophets."

Dr. Yousef Al-Othaimeen told Arab News: "There are laws against anti-Semitism and racism. So, we request a law against mocking religions."

In a report released by the OIC, he said that modernization and the Internet revolution had turned the world into a "global village" where religions and cultures should coexist, and races and nations must live side by side as neighbors.

"Islamophobia is a sentiment of excessive fear against Islam that is transformed into acts of intolerance and discriminations against Muslims and even violent crimes against people with Islamic attires...These issues are of great importance, to be worked on in collaboration not only with governments, but also with people and non-profit organizations, to prove to everyone that Islam is

---

[25] Melanie Phillips, "The Dangerous Drive to Correlate Islamophobia with Anti-Semitism," JNS.org (Jewish News Syndicate, July 4, 2019), https://www.jns.org/opinion/the-dangerous-drive-to-correlate-islamophobia-with-anti-semitism/.

the voice of mercy, moderation and coexistence with Muslims and non-Muslims," he added.

So, what is the universal working definition of Islamophobia?

According to the Oxford English Dictionary Islamophobia is "Dislike of or prejudice against Islam or Muslims, especially as a political force."

Edward Said, former professor of literature at Columbia University, a public intellectual, and a founder of the academic field of postcolonial studies, brought the term into mainstream in his paper *Orientalism Reconsidered* when he brought Islamophobia and Anti-Semitism together.[26]

The term Islamophobia made its way into our collective consciousness with the publication of the Runnymede Trust's report in 1997,[27] because of Islam being seen as a single monolithic bloc, static and unresponsive to new realities.

It is Islamophobic to see Islam as separate and other; as not having any aims or values in common with other cultures; as not affected by them; as not influencing them. To see Islam as inferior to the West – barbaric, irrational, primitive, sexist, is Islamophobic. To see Islam as violent, aggressive, threatening, supportive of terrorism, engaged in 'a clash of civilisations' is

---

[26] Edward W. Said, "Orientalism Reconsidered," Cultural Critique, no. 1 (1985): pp. 89-107, https://doi.org/10.2307/1354282.

[27] "[Report] Islamophobia: A Challenge for Us All," Runnymede Trust, 1997, https://www.runnymedetrust.org/companies/17/74/Islamophobia-A-Challenge-for-Us-All.html.

Islamophobic. To see Islam as a political ideology, used for political or military advantage is Islamophobic. Criticisms made by Islam of 'the West' and rejected out of hand is Islamophobic. Hostility towards Islam used to justify discriminatory practices towards Muslims is Islamophobic. The exclusion of Muslims from mainstream society is Islamophobic. Anti-Muslim hostility accepted as natural and 'normal,' is Islamophobic.

The British All-Party Parliamentary Group (APPG) proposed the following one-sentence definition of Islamophobia:

> *"Islamophobia is rooted in racism and is a type of racism that targets expressions of Muslimness or perceived Muslimness."*[28]

The definition, the result of six months of consultations, was endorsed by hundreds of Muslim organizations, London Mayor Sadiq Khan, as well as several political parties, including Labour, the Liberal Democrats, and the Scottish Conservatives.

The National Police Chiefs' Council, which represents the leaders of law enforcement in England and Wales, expressed concern with the broadened definition. Its chair, Martin Hewitt, said:

> "We take all reports of hate crime very seriously and will investigate them thoroughly. However, we have some concerns about the proposed

---

[28] Soeren Kern, "Britain's Back-Door Blasphemy Law," Gatestone Institute (Gatestone Institute, June 8, 2019), https://www.gatestoneinstitute.org/14351/britain-blasphemy-law.

definition of Islamophobia made by the All-Party Parliamentary Group on British Muslims. We are concerned that the definition is too broad as currently drafted, could cause confusion for officers enforcing it and could be used to challenge legitimate free speech on the historical or theological actions of Islamic states. There is also a risk it could also undermine counter-terrorism powers, which seek to tackle extremism or prevent terrorism".

Richard Walton, a former head of Counter-Terrorism Command of the Metropolitan Police, wrote: "If the Government accepts the APPG definition of Islamophobia, all of these [anti-terrorism] powers are more likely to be challenged by anti-Prevent campaigners and their supporters who would seek to label police officers 'Islamophobic' (and, therefore, racist)...Whole government departments, the entire police service, intelligence agencies, the Crown Prosecution Service (CPS), judiciary and HM Prison and Probation Service could be branded and labelled 'institutionally Islamophobic' by anti-Prevent campaign groups. It would be an allegation that would be impossible to refute, owing to the indistinct and imprecise nature of the APPG definition..."[29]

To equate Islam with race, language had to be abused. Racism needed a new definition. "While it is true that Islam is not a race but a religion, the director of the anti-

---

[29] Judith Bergman, "UK: The Push to End Free Speech," Gatestone Institute (Gatestone Institute, September 17, 2019), https://www.gatestoneinstitute.org/14329/britain-criticism-of-islam.

racism   think-tank   Runnymede   Trust,   Omar
Khan, explained:

> "*Defining Islamophobia as anti-Muslim racism
> properly locates the issue as one in which groups
> of people are ascribed negative cultural and
> racial attributes which can lead to a wide range
> of experiences, either as an unconscious bias,
> prejudice, direct or indirect discrimination,
> structural inequality or hate incidents.*"[30]

The definition is not in conformity with the Equality Act
2010, which defines "race"[31] as comprising color,
nationality and national or ethnic origins — not religious
practice.

And yet, the Muslim Brotherhood refers to Islam as a
religion and a way of life.[32]

But why should facts matter?

Canada passed Motion 103 to combat Islamophobia.
Liberal MP Iqra Khalid, who brought the Motion forward,
was the former President of the York chapter of the
Muslim Student's Association which is associated with
the Muslim Brotherhood. I will discuss the Muslim
Brotherhood in another chapter. The Motion, passed
March 23, 2017, by a margin of 201-91, calls on the

---

[30] Khan, Omar. "Islamophobia Is Anti-Muslim Racism." London
UK: Runnymede Trust, 2018.
[31] Expert Participation, "Equality Act 2010," Legislation.gov.uk
(Statute Law Database, 2010),
https://www.legislation.gov.uk/ukpga/2010/15/section/9.
[32] Bryony Jones and Susannah Cullinane, "What Is the Muslim
Brotherhood?" CNN (Cable News Network, July 3, 2013),
https://www.cnn.com/2013/07/03/world/africa/egypt-
muslim-brotherhood-explainer/index.html.

government to "condemn Islamophobia and all forms of systemic racism and religious discrimination."

Motion 103 passed despite the fact there was concern raised when the Motion came to the floor of Parliament about the definition of Islamophobia[33] because 26 different definitions of the term Islamophobia had been provided by different witnesses who appeared before the committee discussing the Motion. "The concerns raised, regarding the dangers of an over-broad definition, or of attempting to condemn 'Islamophobia' without defining which thoughts and actions are thereby also being condemned, were widespread," reads the Conservative report. The Committee to define Islamophobia was unable to establish a working definition.[34] Although they did not know the definition, the government still voted for it.[35]

People concerned about possible attacks on free speech were told that this is as a non-binding motion, not a Bill.

---

[33] Maura Forrest, "M-103 Report Makes Few Recommendations about Islamophobia," nationalpost.com (National Post, February 1, 2018), https://nationalpost.com/news/politics/m-103-report-makes-few-recommendations-about-islamophobia.

[34] Miranda Gallo and Samer Majzoub, "When Will Canadians Get the Anti-Islamophobia Measures They Want?," HuffPost Canada (HuffPost Canada, February 8, 2018), https://www.huffingtonpost.ca/miranda-gallo/canadians-support-m-103-recommendations-why-wont-the-government_a_23355447/.

[35] Diane Weber Bederman, "Is It Time to Repeal Islamophobia?," The Bederman Blog (Diane Weber Bederman, January 18, 2019), https://dianebederman.com/is-it-time-to-repeal-islamophobia/.

Passing of the motion will not change Canadian law and it will not amend the Charter of Rights and Freedoms, which protects free speech.

Concerns were shared that Islamophobia is not defined in the motion. Not to worry. As a motion calling on the Government to study the matter further, a parliamentary committee can tackle a definition.

Concern was also shared that accusations of hate crimes could arise from the Motion. Canadians were assured that the Courts will always protect free speech. This motion does not prevent criticism of Islam; so, they said. One can be critical of the institution without hating or discriminating against the individuals who practice the faith.

So, one need never worry about being called an Islamophobe. It is more about religious discrimination; hate crimes. Certainly, nothing to do with free speech.

Canada updated the definition of Islamophobia[36] in 2019:

> "Islamophobia – Includes racism, stereotypes, prejudice, fear or acts of hostility directed towards individual Muslims or followers of Islam in general. In addition to individual acts of intolerance and racial profiling, Islamophobia can lead to viewing and treating Muslims as a

---

[36] Rachel Ehrenfeld, "Canada Officially Defines Islamophobia," ACD (American Center for Democracy and the Economic Warfare Institute, July 3, 2019), https://news.acdemocracy.org/canada-officially-defines-islamophobia/?fbclid=IwAR0Co9OXfzQZiGCuulHllSMOzhqCHDf MB4hvgcVbsl0Vne37Y-02ElhfMK8.

greater security threat on an institutional, systemic and societal level."

Except, Islam is not a race.

The province of Ontario has declared January 29 as a "Day of Remembrance and Action Against Islamophobia."

Here is part of the motion:[37]

"In the aftermath of the shooting (The attack on a mosque in Quebec, January 29, 2017), the Prime Minister of Canada condemned the act as terrorism and stated in the House of Commons that the six victims were "gunned down by ignorance and hatred, fuelled by Islamophobia and racism". The leader of the Federal Opposition and the Premier of Quebec also condemned the shooter's actions as an act of terror. The Commissioner of the Royal Canadian Mounted Police called the shooter a criminal extremist and warned that "caustic" political debate can have deadly consequences."

The Ontario Human Rights Commission states the following with respect to Islamophobia:

"Islamophobia can be described as stereotypes, bias or acts of hostility towards individual Muslims or followers of Islam in general. In addition to individual acts of intolerance and

---

[37] Rima Berns-McGown, "Day of Remembrance and Action on Islamophobia Act, 2019," Legislative Assembly of Ontario (Government of Ontario, 2019), https://www.ola.org/en/legislative-business/bills/parliament-42/session-1/bill-83.

racial profiling, Islamophobia leads to viewing
Muslims as a greater security threat on an
institutional, systemic and societal level."

The Ontario Human Rights Commission called on "governments and communities, and each one of us, to ask again, what we can do, what we must do, to eliminate Islamophobia."

The cities of Toronto, Mississauga, Brampton, Markham and Hamilton have also designated January 29 as a Day of Remembrance and Action on Islamophobia. Many municipalities across Canada commemorate the events of January 29 with their Muslim community partners.

The province of Saskatchewan has done the same.[38] National Council of Canadian Muslims promoted the idea to reflect on what happened in the Quebec Mosque where a man had shot and killed six Muslims in a mosque in Quebec City January 29,2017.

All this despite the fact that a Statistics Canada report[39] released on April 30, 2019, pointed out that after "a notable increase in hate crimes against the Muslim population in 2015, police reported 20 fewer in 2016 for a total of 139...Similarly, after an increase in 2015, hate

---

[38] CJME News, "Sask. to Adopt Day against Islamophobia," 980 CJME (Rawlco Radio Ltd, March 20, 2019), https://www.cjme.com/2019/03/26/sask-to-adopt-anti-islamophobia-day/.
[39] Amelia Armstrong, "Police-Reported Hate Crime in Canada, 2017," Statistics Canada: Canada's national statistical agency / Statistique Canada : Organisme statistique national du Canada (Government of Canada, April 30, 2019), https://www150.statcan.gc.ca/n1/pub/85-002-x/2019001/article/00008-eng.htm.

crimes against Catholics also decreased, from 55 to 27 in 2016," the report notes...In contrast," Statistics Canada found, "hate crimes against the Jewish population grew from 178 to 221 incidents" during the same reporting period.

According to the 2018 Public Report on the Terrorism Threat to Canada:

> *"The principal terrorist threat to Canada and Canadian interests continues to be that posed by individuals or groups who are inspired by violent Sunni Islamist ideology and terrorist groups, such as Daesh or al-Qaida (AQ)."*[40]

Perhaps I digress.

I had the pleasure of meeting Kamran Bokhari, author of *Political Islam in the Age of Democratization*. In it he wrote:

> *"Islamists and many Muslims are unlikely to accept Western practice of confining religion to the private sphere or to dilute their worldview so much that they cease to believe that Islam has a certain role to play in public affairs..."*[41]

Does that not mean Islam is a political force as well as a religion? If so, then decreeing dislike or prejudice against

---

[40] Public Safety Canada, "2018 Public Report on the Terrorism Threat to Canada," Public Safety Canada (Government of Canada, April 29, 2019), https://www.publicsafety.gc.ca/cnt/rsrcs/pblctns/pblc-rprt-trrrsm-thrt-cnd-2018/index-en.aspx#s11.

[41] Kamran Bokhari and Farid Senzai, in *Political Islam in the Age of Democratization* (Basingstoke, UK: Palgrave Macmillan, 2013), pp. 194.

Islam as a political force is Islamophobia. Interesting, as we have no such qualms about criticizing any other religion or political system or ideology.

In 2021, the National Council of Canadian Muslims shared 61 recommendations[42] concerning Islamophobia. Advocates have called for all levels of government — federal, provincial, territorial, municipal — to come together for a National Action Summit on Islamophobia.

The recommendations include: a special envoy for Islamophobia; public awareness campaigns in cities; an investigation into national security agencies and how they deal with white supremacist groups; a National Support Fund for survivors of hate-motivated crimes; instituting a provincial Hate Crimes Accountability Unit in all provinces.

Mustafa Farooq, CEO of NCCM said, "Acts of violence, Islamophobia, need to be confronted through new measures. We need a cross jurisdictional approach here. It's not just going to be a federal response. It's going to be a provincial response…We need everyone in Canada to come together, our leaders to come together and bring us real policy change." Farooq said he's looking forward to seeing promised federal legislation aimed at quashing online hate. The NCCM helped the government craft the soon-to-be proposed bill.[43]

---

[42] "NCCM Recommendations - National Summit on Islamophobia." Ottawa: National Council of Canadian Muslims (NCCM), July 19, 2021.
[43] Rachel Gilmore, "What Is the Government Doing about Islamophobia in Canada? Here's What We Know - National," Global News (Global News, June 9, 2021), https://globalnews.ca/news/7934835/london-attack-islamophobia-muslim-hate-government-action/.

To put Islamophobia in Canada in perspective, hate crimes against the Muslim population rose slightly in 2019, from 166 to 181 incidents (+9%). There are slightly more than 1 million Muslims in Canada. Compare this to hate crimes against the Jewish population, declined from 372 incidents to 296 incidents in 2019 (-20%). There are 329,500 Jews in Canada.[44]

The report came out after a Muslim family was struck down by a white, male, Christian 20-year-old driver in his truck. The event was declared a terrorist attack on the scene. At the memorial for the family in London, Ontario, Dr. Munir El-Kassem, an Islamic cleric who once served as the *chaplain of the London Police Service*, drew a parallel between the Palestinian-Israel conflict and the tragedy that descended on London. He concluded his remarks by saying, "Whatever is happening in Jerusalem and Gaza, is related to whatever happened in London, Ontario."

He blamed the Jews for an attack by a white, male Christian for an attack on a Muslim family.[45]

I am sharing an article by Canadian journalist John Robson from The National Post that speaks to the danger of Islamophobia.[46]

---

[44] Statistics Canada, "Canada Day... by the Numbers," Statistics Canada (Government of Canada, September 28, 2017), https://www.statcan.gc.ca/eng/dai/smr08/2017/smr08_219_2017.

[45] Diane Weber Bederman, "Why Are Esteemed Jewish Elders Bending the Knee to Cancel Culture and the #IslamophobiaIndustry?," The Bederman Blog (Diane Weber Bederman, July 7, 2021), https://dianebederman.com/why-are-esteemed-jewish-elders-bending-the-knee-to-cancel-culture-and-the-islamophobiaindustry/.

"London's prestigious Saatchi Gallery just covered up some paintings that offended religious sensibilities."

Whose, you might ask? Muslims. It seems some Muslims were offended by a painting by "SKUstyle."

The "offending" images, superimposing Arabic script on naked people, "were meant to represent the conflict between America and Islamic extremists."

This modern art included the "shahada" or "declaration of faith": "There is no god but God. Muhammad is the messenger of God."

"According to The Times the dispute was perfectly civil and principled. 'The gallery rejected calls to remove the paintings on the grounds it wanted visitors to see the works and come to their own conclusions.' But then the artist asked that they be covered as 'a respectful solution that enables a debate about freedom of expression versus the perceived right not to be offended,' and the gallery agreed. Submission. Dhimmitude. The exact response demanded by Islam.

Notes had been sent to the gallery suggesting that the painting was unacceptable. Usama Hasan, head of Islamic studies at the British think-tank Quilliam, had opined that "the paintings were not only offensive but blasphemous and sacrilegious. 'They are really

---

[46] John Robson, "John Robson: YES, Offending Muslim Sensibilities Is RUDE. but It Shouldn't Be Dangerous," nationalpost.com (National Post, May 16, 2019), https://nationalpost.com/opinion/john-robson-yes-offending-muslim-sensibilities-is-rude-but-it-shouldnt-be-dangerous?fbclid=IwAR0f4P_AVkjZmN-ea2cl2qvUI1RNC4RZrtGfNltX45MAtShvZOHrzBV4iEg.

dangerous,' he said. 'It's The Satanic Verses all over again.'

For those unfamiliar with the Satanic Verses, the authored, Salman Rushdie,[47] was accused of blasphemy and unbelief by Islam and a fatwa was placed on his head. A death threat that came with a $6 million bounty on his head.

As Robson noted "such notes from Christians usually go straight into the wastebasket." But not these. These "notes" require a response.

And Robson wrote "And while you can dump a crucifix in urine and make out like a bandit, you can't … you know … do anything that offends a Muslim."

It is Islamophobia: submission by law.

When it comes to degrading, demeaning, disrespectful artwork of Jesus, where is the call for limiting free speech? Where is the cry for tolerance? Where are Peter Stockland[48] and Amira Elghawaby[49]? Where is Canada's Prime Minister, Justin Trudeau?

Russell Oliver painted Jesus as a slaughtered lamb's head. He tells The Creators Project, "The Monstrosity of

---

[47] Index on Censorship, "Thirty Years on: The Salman Rushdie Fatwa Revisited," Index on Censorship (Index on Censorship, June 9, 2021), https://www.indexoncensorship.org/2019/02/student-reading-list-salman-rushdie-fatwa/.

[48] "Peter Stockland - Senior Writer," Cardus.ca (Cardus Institute, August 6, 2021), https://www.cardus.ca/who-we-are/our-team/pstockland/.

[49] "Amira Elghawaby: Authors: Toronto Star," thestar.com (Toronto Star Newspapers Ltd., 2021), https://www.thestar.com/authors.elghawaby_amira.html.

Christ is my critique of Christianity as a cult of human sacrifice—one of scapegoating and vicarious redemption."

Similarly, Cosimo Cavallaro's six-foot chocolate statue of Jesus remarks on the tie between Christianity and global consumer trends.

As Cavallaro tells The Creators Project, "My Sweet Lord is the symbolic representation of the intermingling of Christian religion with industry, tread, globalization, and our addiction to the sinful sweet sacrament of chocolate." These pieces are not without their negative reactions; My Sweet Lord was described by the head of the Catholic League, Bill Donohue as "One of the worst assaults on Christian sensibilities ever.

Then there is this depiction. Jesus Christ with Mickey Mouse ears.

One of the most famous controversial depictions of Christ must be Andres Serrano's Piss Christ, a photograph of a plastic, crucified Christ figure, submerged in the artist's urine. By using raw, human waste to represent and stand beside divine concepts, Serrano makes Biblical reference to the mortal body and blood of Christ.

We are told when it comes to these representations: "Whether you accept, understand—or even enjoy—these depictions or not, the controversial images continue to remind us that, as a tolerant society, we must protect a freedom of speech, opinions, and beliefs of both believers and non-believers. After all, artistic representation has arguably a longer history than any religion or faith."[50]

March 23, 2019, the Organisation of Islamic Cooperation (OIC) urged the UN Secretary General to convene a special session of the UN General Assembly to declare Islamophobia as a form of racism and to assign a special rapporteur for monitoring and combating the menace in the western countries.[51]

Millions have died to protect Western Culture. Yet here we are, willingly giving up our responsibility to compare and contrast, critique Islam. The late, great journalist, George Jonas wrote "Don't let Western civilization—the best and most humane form of civilization developed by mankind—perish by default."

---

[50] Anna Marks, "When Artists Take the Piss out of Christ, It's Complicated," Vice.com (Vice Media Group, May 16, 2016), https://www.vice.com/en/article/8qv3gp/contemporary-controversial-artists-depictions-of-christ.

[51] News Desk, "OIC Urges UN to TACKLE Islamophobia, Declare It a Form of Racism," The Express Tribune Pakistan (The Express Tribune, March 23, 2019), https://tribune.com.pk/story/1935888/3-oic-urges-un-tackle-islamophobia-declare-form-racism?fbclid=IwAR3Y2N9Q8I_X1aLw-CWiUlw0RJo5oxkKK0-Rga-MJVp1-ECYlckc3YzjY7U.

CHAPTER 2: WHATEVER HAPPENED TO CRITICAL THINKING?

"Every part of thinking should be questioned, doubted, and tested"

~ Descartes

If Islamophobia is not an attack on free speech, why are so many voices critical of Islam, the religion, silenced when criticism of Christianity and Judaism are di rigeur? Think about that. If one substituted Buddhism, Zoroastrianism, Christianity, Judaism, Jehovah's Witnesses for Islam, would you be accused of a phobia for asking questions about these religions? And what of the world religion courses that are offered in secondary and graduate schools? There was a time when world religion courses encouraged questions.[52] I know, because I studied world religions.

> "One was encouraged to ask questions! Learn logic and reasoning skills. Study one's religion and others. Study opposing views. Study related fields in both the sciences and philosophy, including the philosophy of religion. Find reasons for your beliefs that satisfy not only you but would be persuasive to others. Seek the truth, whatever it may be, regardless of what you wish

---

[52] Fergus Duniho, "The Importance of Critical Thinking in Religion," For the Love of Wisdom (Fergus Duniho, May 26, 2019), https://fortheloveofwisdom.net/57/religion/critical-thinking/.

or hope to be true. Don't just bash other views or defend your own. Seek not only to criticize but to understand. Humbly acknowledge when you are wrong."[53]

Could it be that Islam does not believe in questioning? That it is blasphemous: "O you who have believed, do not ask about things which, if they are shown to you, will distress you. But if you ask about them while the Qur'an is being revealed, they will be shown to you. Allah has pardoned that which is past; and Allah is Forgiving and Forbearing." [Qur'an 5:101, Sahih International translation]

"A people asked such [questions] before you; then they became thereby disbelievers." [Qur'an 5:102, Sahih International translation]

And then there is German philosopher Martin Heidegger (1889–1976) who wrote, "Questions are the piety, the prayer of human thought."

Deep questions drive our thought underneath the surface of things, force us to deal with complexity.[54] Questions of purpose force us to define our task. Questions of information force us to look at our sources of information as well as at the quality of our information. Questions of interpretation force us to

---

[53] Fergus Duniho, "The Importance of Critical Thinking in Religion," For the Love of Wisdom (Fergus Duniho, May 26, 2019)

[54] "The Role of Socratic Questioning in Thinking, Teaching, and Learning," The Role of Socratic Questioning in Thinking, Teaching, and Learning (Foundation for Critical Thinking, 2019), https://www.criticalthinking.org/pages/the-role-of-socratic-questioning-in-thinking-teaching-amp-learning/522.

examine how we are organizing or giving meaning to information and to consider alternative ways of giving meaning. Questions of assumption force us to examine what we are taking for granted. Questions of implication force us to follow out where our thinking is going. Questions of point of view force us to examine our point of view and to consider other relevant points of view. Questions of relevance force us to discriminate what does and what does not bear on a question. Questions of accuracy force us to evaluate and test for truth and correctness. Questions of precision force us to give details and be specific. Questions of consistency force us to examine our thinking for contradictions. Questions of logic force us to consider how we are putting the whole of our thought together, to make sure that it all adds up and makes sense within a reasonable system of some kind.

The goal of critical thinking is to establish a disciplined "executive" level of thinking to our thinking, a powerful inner voice of reason, to monitor, assess, and re-constitute — in a more rational direction — our thinking, feeling, and action. Socratic discussion cultivates that inner voice by providing a public model for it. [55]

The intellectual roots of critical thinking are as ancient as its etymology, traceable, ultimately, to the teaching practice and vision of Socrates,[56] one of the greatest

---

[55] Richard Paul, Linda Elder, and Ted Bartell, "A Brief History of the Idea of Critical Thinking," A Brief History of the Idea of Critical Thinking (Foundation for Critical Thinking, 1997), https://www.criticalthinking.org/pages/a-brief-history-of-the-idea-of-critical-thinking/408.

[56] "Socratic Questions," Socratic Questioning (Changing Works, 2021),

educators, who taught the importance of asking questions drawing out answers from his pupils.

Twenty-five hundred years ago he discovered by a method of probing questioning that people could not rationally justify their confident claims to knowledge... He established the importance of asking deep questions that probe profoundly into thinking before we accept ideas as worthy of belief.... In the Renaissance (15th and 16th Centuries), a flood of scholars in Europe began to think critically about religion, art, society, human nature, law, and freedom. They proceeded with the assumption that most of the domains of human life needed searching analysis and critique. Among these scholars were Colet, Erasmus, and Moore in England. They followed up on the insight of the ancients.... Francis Bacon, in England, was explicitly concerned with the way we misuse our minds in seeking knowledge: "Idols of the market-place" (the ways we misuse words), Descartes wrote: "Every part of thinking should be questioned, doubted, and tested."

"The critical thinking of these Renaissance and post-Renaissance scholars opened the way for the emergence of science and for the development of democracy, human rights, and freedom for thought.... Locke defended a common-sense analysis of everyday life and thought. He laid the theoretical foundation for critical thinking about basic human rights and the responsibilities of all governments to submit to the reasoned criticism of thoughtful citizens. William Graham Sumner wrote in 1906 "Criticism is the examination and test of propositions of any kind which

http://changingminds.org/techniques/questioning/socratic_q uestions.htm.

are offered for acceptance, in order to find out whether they correspond to reality or not." Ludwig Wittgenstein; "We have increased our awareness not only of the importance of concepts in human thought, but also of the need to analyze concepts and assess their power and limitations."

It is questions that fuel political discussion and debate, and determine, to a large extent, what is available for comment and analysis, and what is left unsaid.[57] Questions play a vital, and often unnoticed, role in the political landscape. By asking a question, a person asserts their right to be a part of the discussion and to have their concerns considered. Secondly, asking questions is a familiar and effective way of getting information. This is, once again, a simple but powerful function of questions: it could indeed be viewed as their primary function. When we ask questions we are often, perhaps typically, trying to find things out. In doing so, we gather information about topics and issues that interest or concern us, whether it be out of pure curiosity, or for practical or political reasons... Questions facilitate informed decision-making.

Critical theorists Michael Scriven and Richard Paul endeavor to encapsulate in one definition the wide expanse of critical thinking's many definitions:

> *"Critical thinking is the intellectually disciplined process of actively and skillfully conceptualizing, applying, analyzing, synthesizing, and/or*

---

[57] Lani Watson, "Good Democracy Needs Good Questions," Open for Debate (Cardiff University, October 9, 2017), https://blogs.cardiff.ac.uk/openfordebate/2017/09/25/good-democracy-needs-good-questions/.

evaluating information gathered from, or generated by, observation, experience, reflection, reasoning, or communication, as a guide to belief and action. In its exemplary form, it is based on universal intellectual values that transcend subject matter divisions: clarity, accuracy, precision, consistency, relevance, sound evidence, good reasons, depth, breadth, and fairness."[58,59]

There are good reasons for teaching comparative religions.

William A. Graham wrote: "Why study religion in the twenty-first century?" Is this because religion, whether as an agent of stability or instability, of progress or retrogression, of peace or conflict, or simply of diverse kinds of change everywhere in the world, will long continue to be a critical factor in individual, social, and political life around the world, and we need to understand it? By "religion," I mean the myriad ways in which human beings around the globe and across the centuries have dealt with the meaning of life and the values by which to order one's personal life, one's family life, one's social organization, and one's dealing with other human beings—both within and outside of one's

---

[58] Michael Scriven and Richard Paul, "Defining Critical Thinking," Defining Critical Thinking (Foundation for Critical Thinking, 1987), https://www.criticalthinking.org/pages/defining-critical-thinking/766.

[59] Shane Anderson, "Critical Thinking in Religious Education," Religious Educator 18, no. 3 (2017): pp. 69-81, https://rsc.byu.edu/vol-18-no-3-2017/critical-thinking-religious-education.

own particular religious, national, racial, ethnic, linguistic, or socioeconomic group.

There are courses on Comparative Religion. Because we are encouraged to compare and contrast.[60] Except Islam.

I doubt anyone has been called racist for critiquing Buddhists or Confucianism, or made to feel terrible for commenting on Communism, socialism, Marxism, fascism, capitalism, liberalism; what have I left out? Ahh, yes Italians. We have had no problem talking about the Mafia. No fear of "blowback" from Italians when commenting on the Mafia. Some of the most watched, critically acclaimed movies are about the Mafia; The Godfather Series and on television; the Sopranos. And I have yet to hear about "blowback" on Hindus for the sin of criticizing their caste system.

Yet, we, in the West, in the name of tolerance, tolerating the intolerable, have agreed; been coerced, to keep our comments about Islam to ourselves; for fear of offending or releasing a backlash. And that silence made it possible for thousands of young children to be molested in Britain by Pakistani Muslims.[61,62]

---

[60] Shane Anderson, "Critical Thinking in Religious Education," *Religious Educator* 18, no. 3 (2017): pp. 69-81, https://rsc.byu.edu/vol-18-no-3-2017/critical-thinking-religious-education.

[61] Diane Weber Bederman, "#Rotherham: Where Are the #MeToo Feminists?" The Bederman Blog (Diane Weber Bederman, January 6, 2018), https://dianebederman.com/rotherham-where-are-the-metoo-feminists/.

[62] "Rotherham Child Sexual Exploitation Scandal," en.wikipedia.org (Wikipedia, the free encyclopedia, August 7,

While we have succumbed to silence regarding criticism of Islam; religion or political force, we are told we must allow Muslims to criticize the West. To do otherwise is Islamophobic.

I have read comments made by Imams in Canada and around the world. It seems there is no prohibition against insulting the West, insulting our way of life, in our own homes. But in the West, Muslims, with the help of Progressives, have promoted the concept of Islamophobia; the irrational fear of Islam. Our elites have decided that we must not insult Islam. All over the West we are being frightened and bullied into silence about Islam in the name of Islamophobia.

2021),
https://en.wikipedia.org/wiki/Rotherham_child_sexual_exploi tation_scandal.

CHAPTER 3: IN THE BEGINNING. AND SO IT BEGAN. WHAT IS THE MUSLIM BROTHERHOOD?

"The Ikhwan[63,64] [Muslim Brotherhood] must understand that their work in America is a kind of grand jihad[65] in eliminating and destroying Western civilization from within and 'sabotaging' its miserable house by their hands and the hands of the believers so that it is eliminated, and God's religion made victorious over all other religions."[66]

The rise of Islamophobia and charges of Islamophobia, did not begin in a vacuum. Like all well planned attacks, the seeds were planted long ago.

For 100 years the West was made ready for "Islamophobia." Not just to accept Islam, but to silence those opposing the ideology.

---

[63] "Muslim Brotherhood - Al-Ikhwan Al-Muslimin - Al-Ikhwan ('The Brothers')," Muslim Brotherhood (Federation of American Scientists (FAS), January 8, 2002), https://fas.org/irp/world/para/mb.htm.

[64] "Muslim Brotherhood," Encyclopædia Britannica (Encyclopædia Britannica, inc.), accessed August 9, 2021, https://www.britannica.com/topic/Muslim-Brotherhood.

[65] "Jihad - Definition," Merriam-Webster.com dictionary (Merriam-Webster), accessed August 9, 2021, https://www.merriam-webster.com/dictionary/jihad.

[66] Akram, Mohamed. "1991 Explanatory Memorandum on the General Strategic Goal for the Group [Muslim Brotherhood] in North America [Translated] Government Exhibit, U.S. v HLF, Et Al." U.S. Government, May 19, 1991. Document available at: http://www.investigativeproject.org/documents/misc/20.pdf

The latest attempt at resurrecting Islam began in Egypt in 1928 with the founding of the Muslim Brotherhood, by Hassan al-Banna, for the purpose of reuniting the Muslim nation [*ummah*] following the fall of the Ottoman Empire in World War I.[67]

> *"We want a Muslim individual, a Muslim home, a Muslim people, a Muslim government and state that will lead the Islamic countries and bring into the fold the Muslim Diaspora and the lands robbed from Islam and will then bear the standard of jihad and the call [da'wah] to Allah. [Then the] world will happily accept the precepts of Islam… The problems of conquering the world will only end when the flag of Islam waves and jihad has been proclaimed."*

> *"The goal is to establish one Islamic state of united Islamic countries, one nation under one leadership whose mission will be to reinforce adherence to the law of Allah… and the strengthening of the Islamic presence in the world arena… The goal… is the establishment of a world Islamic state."*

> *"And if prayer is a pillar of the faith, then jihad is its summit… and death in the path of Allah is the summit of aspiration."*

Just to be clear, here is the motto of the Muslim Brotherhood:

---

[67] Jonathan D. Halevi, "Where Is the Muslim Brotherhood Headed?," Jerusalem Center for Public Affairs, June 20, 2012, https://jcpa.org/the-muslim-brotherhood-a-moderate-islamic-alternative-to-al-qaeda-or-a-partner-in-global-jihad/.

"Allah is our objective, the Prophet is our leader, the Qur'an is our law, jihad is our way, dying in the way of Allah is our highest hope."

We know the intent of the modern-day Muslim Brotherhood because in 2004 Federal investigators in the USA found "An Explanatory Memorandum on the strategic Goal for the Group in North America,"[68] written by Mohamed Akram, May 19, 1991, in the home of Ismael Elbarasse, a founder of the Dar Al-Hijrah mosque in Falls Church, Virginia. Elbarasse was a member of the Palestine Committee, which the Muslim Brotherhood had created to support Hamas in the United States. This memorandum, derived from the general strategic goal of the Group in America which was approved by the Shura Council and the Organizational Conference in the year 1987, speaks to the "Enablement of Islam in North America, meaning: establishing an effective and a stable Islamic movement led by the Muslim Brotherhood..."

A new legal doctrine was also introduced in the 1990s by two notable Islamic figures, Shaykh Dr. Taha Jabir Al-Alwani of Virginia, and Shaykh Dr. Yusuf al-Qaradawi of Qatar. Titled *"Fiqh al-Aqalliyyat"* (the minorities' jurisprudence), the doctrine focuses on aspects of daily life for the Muslim minority in the West so that Muslims can live in harmony with the Westerners while still abiding by the dictates of Islam. The Brotherhood seeks allies and partners within the European society that will increase its ability to make its *da'wah* (proselytizing)

---

[68] Akram, Mohamed. "1991 Explanatory Memorandum on the General Strategic Goal for the Group [Muslim Brotherhood] in North America [Translated] Government Exhibit, U.S. v HLF, Et Al." U.S. Government, May 19, 1991. Document available at: http://www.investigativeproject.org/documents/misc/20.pdf

effective. The Brotherhood does not see the West as an amalgamation of nation-states like the Westerners do, but rather as one single entity. This is consistent with the Brotherhood's idea that Islam is a religion which will eventually encompass the entire globe. Therefore, Muslims living in the West do not need to emigrate back to Dar al-Islam, countries where Muslims can practice their religion as the ruling sect because the whole world is destined to become Dar al-Islam.

Today's Brotherhood sits on the teachings of al-Banna.

In his book "The Way of Jihad" Hassan al-Banna wrote[69] that:

> "All Muslims must make Jihad. Jihad is an obligation from Allah on every Muslim and cannot be ignored nor evaded. Allah has ascribed great importance to jihad and has made the reward of the martyrs and the fighters in His way a splendid one. Only those who have acted similarly and who have modelled themselves upon the martyrs in their performance of jihad can join them in this reward. Furthermore, Allah has specifically honoured the Mujahideen (those engaged in struggle) with certain exceptional qualities, both spiritual and practical, to benefit them in this world and the next. Their pure blood is a symbol of victory in this world and the mark of success and felicity in the world to come..."

---

[69] "The Way of Jihad : Complete Text by Hassan Al-Banna, Founder of the Muslim Brotherhood," The Way of Jihad : Complete text by Hassan Al-Banna, founder of the Muslim Brotherhood (Militant Islam Monitor, January 16, 2005), http://www.militantislammonitor.org/article/id/379.

"Islam is concerned with the question of jihad and the drafting and the mobilisation of the entire Umma into one body to defend the right cause with all its strength than any other ancient or modern system of living, whether religious or civil. The verses of the Qur'an and the Sunnah of Muhammad (PBUH) are overflowing with all these noble ideals and they summon people in general (with the most eloquent expression and the clearest exposition) to jihad, to warfare, to the armed forces, and all means of land and sea fighting...

"Why Do the Muslims Fight? ...jihad is used to safeguard the mission of spreading Islam. This would guarantee peace and the means of implementing the Supreme Message. This is a responsibility which the Muslims bear, this Message guiding mankind to truth and justice... The Muslims in war had only one concern and this was to make the name of Allah Supreme, there was no room at all for any other objective...

"Many Muslims today mistakenly believe that fighting the enemy is jihad asghar (a lesser jihad) and that fighting one's ego is jihad akbar (a greater jihad). The following narration [athar] is quoted as proof: "We have returned from the lesser jihad to embark on the greater jihad." They said: "What is the greater jihad?" He said: "The jihad of the heart, or the jihad against one's ego." This narration is used by some to lessen the importance of fighting, to discourage any preparation for combat, and to deter any *offering of jihad in Allah's way. This narration is not a saheeh (sound) tradition...*

"My brothers! The ummah that knows how to die a noble and honourable death is granted an exalted life in this world and eternal felicity in the next. Degradation and dishonour are the results of the love of this world and the fear of death. Therefore, prepare for jihad and be the lovers of death. Life itself shall come searching after you."

Since its founding in 1928[70] the Brotherhood has evolved into a transnational, Pan-Islamic ideological network – known as the Global Muslim Brotherhood (GMB) – which is allegedly active in more than 80 countries worldwide. Muslim Brotherhood affiliates emphasize the need for grassroots work via coordinated and guided "civil society" groups in fields like education, welfare, medical services, and religious institutions, known as the *da'wah* (proselytization) system.

I can understand the desire of al-Banna to regain the empire. Why not? History is filled with peoples who wanted to take over the known world.

Hassan al-Banna stated:

"Islam does not recognize geographical boundaries, nor does it acknowledge racial and blood differences, considering all Muslims as one Umma [global community of Muslims]. The Muslim Brethren [Muslim Brotherhood] believe that the caliphate is a symbol of Islamic Union

---

[70] "Muslim Brotherhood," Encyclopædia Britannica (Encyclopædia Britannica, inc.), accessed August 9, 2021, https://www.britannica.com/topic/Muslim-Brotherhood.

and an indication of the bonds between the nations of Islam. They see the caliphate and its re-establishment as a top priority..."[71]

Today the Muslim Brotherhood in America echoes the call of al-Banna:

"The process of settlement is a 'Civilization-Jihadist Process' with all the word means. The Ikhwan [Muslim Brotherhood] must understand that their work in America is a kind of grand jihad in eliminating and destroying the Western civilization from within and "sabotaging" its miserable house by their hands and the hands of the believers so that it is eliminated and God's religion is made victorious over all other religions."[72]

Without this level of understanding, we are not up to this challenge and have not prepared ourselves for Jihad yet. It is a Muslim's destiny to perform Jihad and work and work where ever he is and wherever he lands until the final hour comes, and there is no escape from that destiny.

---

[71] zhyntativ, "Hasan Al-Banna and His Political Thought of Islamic Brotherhood," (Ikhwanweb :: The Muslim Brotherhood official English website, May 13, 2008), https://web.archive.org/web/20100107010100/http:/www.ikhwanweb.com/article.php?id=17065.

[72] Prof. Arnon Gutfeld, "The Saudi Specter over the American Education System," Jerusalem Center for Public Affairs, May 23, 2019, https://jcpa.org/article/saudi-specter-over-american-education-system/.

Saudi wealth, from its oil billions, helped to spread the Muslim Brotherhood ideology globally beginning in the 1960's.[73,74]

In America

Lorenzo Vidino, the Director of the Program on Extremism at George Washington University wrote: "The Muslim Brotherhood is the oldest and arguably the most influential contemporary Islamist movement. While not shunning violence as a political tool, it advocates a bottom-up, gradual Islamisation of society. Starting with the reformation of individuals, this would eventually lead to the formation of a purely Islamic society and, as a natural consequence, political entity. The Brotherhood has a presence in some ninety countries worldwide (seems the number of countries is in question) and in each country the movement has taken different forms, adapting to the local political conditions. Brotherhood linked entities in each country work according to a common vision but in complete operational independence, making the Brotherhood a global informal movement."[75]

---

[73] Prof. Arnon Gutfeld, "The Saudi Specter over the American Education System," Jerusalem Center for Public Affairs, May 23, 2019.

[74] John Mintz and Douglas Farah, "In Search Of Friends Among The Foes," The Washington Post (The Washington Post Company, September 11, 2004), http://www.washingtonpost.com/wp-dyn/articles/A12823-2004Sep10.html.

[75] Lorenzo Vidino, "The Muslim Brotherhood in the United Kingdom," The Muslim Brotherhood in the United Kingdom (Program on Extremism at George Washington University, December 2015), https://extremism.gwu.edu/sites/g/files/zaxdzs2191/f/downlo

In 2004 John Mintz and Douglas Farah wrote in the Washington Post: "Muslim Brotherhood supporters make up the U.S. Islamic community's most organized force. They run hundreds of mosques and dozens of businesses engaging in ventures such as real estate development and banking. They also helped set up some of the leading American Islamic organizations that defend the rights of Muslims, promote Muslim civic activism and seek to spread Islam."[76]

Universities were targeted. Qatar provided financial assistance for the Muslim Students' Association (MSA) founded in 1963. MSA built their headquarters complex on former farmland in suburban Indianapolis. With 150 chapters, the MSA is one of the nation's largest college groups. There is North American Islamic Trust (NAIT) 1971, the Islamic Society of North America (ISNA) 1981, the International Institute of Islamic Thought (IIIT) 1981, the Islamic Association for Palestine (IAP) 1981, the Islamic Association of Palestine founded in 1981 and Hamas founded by the Brotherhood in 1987, the United Association for Studies and Research (UASR) 1989, The Occupied Land Fund and the Media Office, the American Muslim Council (AMC) 1990, the Muslim American Society (MAS) 1992, the Muslim Arab Youth Association (MAYA), the Council on American-Islamic Relations (CAIR) 1994, and others.[77] Then there is ICNA's

ads/MB%20in%20the%20UK.pdf.

[76] John Mintz and Douglas Farah, "In Search Of Friends Among The Foes," The Washington Post (The Washington Post Company, September 11, 2004)

[77] Tom Quiggin, "Muslim Brotherhood Front Organizations, U.S. and Canada," Gatestone Institute (Gatestone Institute, January 31, 2017), https://www.gatestoneinstitute.org/9770/muslim-

charitable arm, ICNA (Islamic Circle of North America) Relief, a donor to the Al-Khidmat Foundation,[78] a Pakistani JI (Jamaat-e-Islam) charity that, according to JI's own website, openly funds the Gaza-based terrorist group, Hamas.[79]

In fact, nearly all prominent Islamic organizations in the United States are rooted in the Muslim Brotherhood.

In Europe

In Britain, there three categories of individuals and organizations operating inside the UK that can be referred to as "Muslim Brotherhood." In decreasing degrees of intensity, these are the pure Brothers, Brotherhood affiliates, and organisations influenced by the Brotherhood.[80] Their goals include spreading their religious and political views to British Muslim

---

brotherhood-front-organizations.

[78] Cliff Smith, "'Steele Dossier' Law Firm Peddles Misinformation for Jamaat-e-Islami Linked Charity," The Sunday Guardian Live (Information TV Pvt Ltd., June 27, 2020), https://www.sundayguardianlive.com/news/steele-dossier-law-firm-peddles-misinformation-jamaat-e-islami-linked-charity.

[79] Central Information Department, "JI Donates Rs. 6 m to Palestinians - Internet Archive Wayback Machine," 'JI donates RS. 6 M TO Palestinians' - JI media news (Jamaat-e-Islami Pakistan, August 17, 2006), https://web.archive.org/web/20071003065109/http://www.jamaat.org/news/2006/aug/17/1001.html.

[80] Lorenzo Vidino, "The Muslim Brotherhood in the United Kingdom," The Muslim Brotherhood in the United Kingdom (Program on Extremism at George Washington University, December 2015), https://extremism.gwu.edu/sites/g/files/zaxdzs2191/f/downloads/MB%20in%20the%20UK.pdf.

communities; becoming the official or de facto representatives of British Muslim communities in the eyes of the government and the media; and supporting domestic and international Islamist causes with local Muslim communities and British policy-makers and public.[81]

Sheikh Yusuf Qaradawi, a staunch Islamist, who in the past was a candidate for the Muslim Brotherhood leadership, issued a fatwa in April 2003, describing how Islam would conquer Europe and defeat Christianity by exploiting Western liberalism and democracy. It would be made possible, he promised, by spreading Islam until it was strong enough to take over the entire continent. He wrote that "it is eminently clear that the future belongs to Islam, and that the religion of Allah will be victorious and will, by the grace of Allah, conquer all other religions." His prediction was based on an Islamic tradition according to which the prophet Muhammad said that one of the signs of redemption in Islam would be the initial conquest of Constantinople and then the conquest of Rome.

According to Saudi Crown Prince Mohammed bin Salman, there are more than 500 Muslim Brotherhood-affiliated organizations in Europe.[82] The umbrella group

---

[81] Lt. Col. (ret.) Jonathan D. Halevi, "Where Is the Muslim Brotherhood Headed?," Jerusalem Center for Public Affairs, June 20, 2012, https://jcpa.org/the-muslim-brotherhood-a-moderate-islamic-alternative-to-al-qaeda-or-a-partner-in-global-jihad/.

[82] Brig.-Gen. (res.) Yossi Kuperwasser, Ehud Rosen, and Eitan Fischberger, "The Security Implications of Muslim Migration," Jerusalem Center for Public Affairs (Jerusalem Center for Public Affairs, March 26, 2019), https://jcpa.org/immigration-

for the Muslim Brotherhood is the Federation of Islamic Organizations in Europe (FIOE) consisting of member organizations from 28 countries. FIOE maintains a strong link to the main Muslim Brotherhood-affiliated organizations in Europe, as well as Hamas. One of FIOE's stated goals is the appointment of Muslims to influential positions in Europe. This is indicative of their aspiration to become powerful players on the continent, and how far they intend to spread their influence.

Students have their own organization. The Forum of European Muslim Youth and Student Organisations (FEMYSO) presents itself as the "de facto voice of Muslim Youth in Europe." FEMYSO claims it "developed useful links with the European Parliament, the European Commission, the Council of Europe, the Organization for Security and Co-operation in Europe (OSCE), the United Nations, and a host of other significant organizations at the European and international level."[83]

Imam Mazin Abdul Adhim, a London, Ontario-based Imam and a senior cleric of Hizb ut-Tahrir, called upon the Muslim Ummah (Nation) to unite in order to establish the global Islamic state, also known by its Arabic name the Caliphate. He teaches:

> *"What our identity is? We are Muslims, strewn about all across the planet without anybody who represents us. We are Muslims who are actually belong to the Khilafah [Caliphate]. The Khilafah*

to-europe/the-security-implications-of-muslim-migration/.

[83] Brig.-Gen. (res.) Yossi Kuperwasser, Ehud Rosen, and Eitan Fischberger, "The Security Implications of Muslim Migration," Jerusalem Center for Public Affairs (Jerusalem Center for Public Affairs, March 26, 2019), https://jcpa.org/immigration-to-europe/the-security-implications-of-muslim-migration/.

[Caliphate] represents us and it was destroyed in 1924. We are responsible for working to re-establish it. So, this is the first thing. We must work to establish the Khilafah [Caliphate]." [84]

[84] Anthony Furey, "Pro-Shariah Caliphate Lecture Held at Ontario College," torontosun.com (Postmedia Network Inc., January 7, 2016), https://torontosun.com/2016/01/06/mohawk-college-distances-itself-from-refugee-crisis-speaker.

CHAPTER 4: WHY SHOULD I CARE ABOUT CAIR?

"CAIR's vision is to be a leading advocate for justice and mutual understanding. CAIR's mission is to enhance understanding of Islam, protect civil rights, promote justice, and empower American Muslims."[85]

All about CAIR

CAIR[86],[87] stands for the Council on American-Islamic Relations. According to its website, CAIR exists "to promote a positive image of Islam and Muslims in America." It annually issues reports on the status of American Muslim civil rights; reports[88] on its website date back to 1996.

CAIR was founded in 1994[89] following a meeting of the US Muslim Brotherhood's Palestine Committee, in

---

[85] "CAIR: About Us," CAIR.com (Council on American-Islamic Relations (CAIR), May 6, 2020), https://www.cair.com/about_cair/about-us/.

[86] Brady, Andrea. "Profile: The Council on American Islamic Relations." New York NY: Anti-Defamation League, August 21, 2015.

[87] "The Council on American-Islamic Relations (CAIR): CAIR Exposed." Washington, DC: The Investigative Project on Terrorism, April 8, 2008.

[88] "CAIR Civil Rights Reports," CAIR (Council on American-Islamic Relations (CAIR), August 26, 2020), https://www.cair.com/resources/cair-civil-rights-reports/.

[89] Ilhan Omar, "PolitiFact - Ilhan Omar Misstates the Facts About CAIR's Founding," ed. Angie Drobnic Holan, PolitiFact.com (The Poynter Institute, April 15, 2019),

Philadelphia, which the Department of Justice has described as a covert organization established to support Hamas.[90]

In 2007, CAIR was listed as an unindicted co-conspirator in the case that found Holy Land Foundation responsible for siphoning more than $12 million to Hamas. A 2009 ruling by US District Court Judge Jorge A. Solis determined that CAIR is Hamas. In 2014, CAIR was designated a terrorist organization by the United Arab Emirates.[91]

More information on CAIR is available from the Investigative Project on Terrorism (IPT).[92]

CAIR states their aim, today, is fighting what they call the "Islamophobia Network."[93] In April 2019, the Council on

---

https://www.politifact.com/factchecks/2019/apr/15/ilhan-omar/ilhan-omar-misstates-facts-about-cairs-founding/.

[90] Jerusalem Post Staff, "CAIR Report Claims Jewish Funders Supporting 'Islamophobia Network'," The Jerusalem Post | JPost.com (Palestine Post Ltd., May 27, 2019), https://www.jpost.com/American-Politics/CAIR-report-claims-Jewish-funders-supporting-Islamophobia-Network-590747?fbclid=IwAR3IJ2LkjxIZdXI1HuYWrJeH7r3F98sFvtUOQpf_3hZvsqjMbcKqHSlbcXE.

[91] "Council on American Islamic Relations (CAIR) (Profile)," InfluenceWatch.org (Capital Research Center, April 24, 2020), https://www.influencewatch.org/non-profit/council-on-american-islamic-relations-cair/.

[92] "The Council on American-Islamic Relations (CAIR): CAIR Exposed." Washington, DC: The Investigative Project on Terrorism, April 8, 2008.

[93] James Simpson, "CAIR's New 'Islamophobia' Report: A Partnership with the SPLC," Capital Research Center (Capital Research Center, July 1, 2019), https://capitalresearch.org/article/cairs-new-islamophobia-

American-Islamic Relations (CAIR) released a report,[94] "Hijacked by Hate: American Philanthropy and the Islamophobia Network." CAIR claimed "traditional American charities, foundations, and philanthropic institutions are being used to anonymize and funnel money from powerful donors to the Islamophobia Network." And claimed: "This decentralized group of actors is known as the Islamophobia Network, a close-knit family of organizations and individuals that share an ideology of extreme anti-Muslim animus, and work with one another to negatively influence public opinion and government policy about Muslims and Islam."[95]

The report claims that more than 1,096 mainstream foundations funded 39 groups. They state that "Islamophobia" is a $1.5 billion enterprise that needs to be stopped with education, auditing, and implementing policies to halt the funding of certain non-profit groups that CAIR deems to be Islamophobic.

CAIR has been receiving help against this "Islamophobic Network" fight since 2008. "The Silicon Valley

report-part-1/?fbclid=IwAR22sHdXccQMBu_vc90czgSJd0NPKOPtQeC_rPLQ-UhmrbsnYTSdWwH3Tag.

[94] Barzegar, Dr. Abbas, and Zainab Arain. "Hijacked by Hate: American Philanthropy and the Islamophobia Network." Washington DC: Council on American-Islamic Relations (CAIR), May 6, 2019.

[95] Jerusalem Post Staff, "CAIR Report Claims Jewish Funders Supporting 'Islamophobia Network'," The Jerusalem Post | JPost.com (Palestine Post Ltd., May 27, 2019), https://www.jpost.com/American-Politics/CAIR-report-claims-Jewish-funders-supporting-Islamophobia-Network-590747?fbclid=IwAR3IJ2LkjxIZdXI1HuYWrJeH7r3F98sFvtUOQpf_3hZvsqjMbcKqHSlbcXE.

Community Foundation (SVCF) has granted $330,524 to two Islamist organizations, the Council on American-Islamic Relations (CAIR) and Islamic Relief.... SVCF is America's largest community foundation, with assets of more than $8 billion.[96] Its corporate partners include some of the country's biggest tech companies[97] -- its largest donation was $1.5 billion from Facebook founder Mark Zuckerberg".[98],[99]

Despite their calls to stop Islamophobia, CAIR's national executive director Nihad Awad,[100] has a long history of supporting designated terror-group Hamas. As the Investigative Project on Terrorism documented, Awad declared "I am a supporter of the Hamas movement," and revealed that he supports Israel's extinction and replacement with an Islamist state, saying: "they [Jews]

---

[96] John Shinal, "When Silicon Valley Execs Suddenly Make Billions, They Turn to This Man to Help Them Give It Away," CNBC.com (CNBC LLC, June 10, 2017), https://www.cnbc.com/2017/06/10/silicon-valley-community-foundation-got-huge-on-tech-industry-giving.html.

[97] "Our Corporate Partners," Silicon Valley Community Foundation (Silicon Valley Community Foundation, November 11, 2020), https://www.siliconvalleycf.org/our-corporate-partners.

[98] John Shinal, "When Silicon Valley Execs Suddenly Make Billions, They Turn to This Man to Help Them Give It Away," CNBC.com

[99] Judith Bergman, "Facebook Still Championing Blasphemy Laws," Gatestone Institute (Gatestone Institute, February 19, 2019), https://www.gatestoneinstitute.org/13583/facebook-blasphemy-laws.

[100] "Profile: Nihad Awad`," The Investigative Project on Terrorism (The Investigative Project on Terrorism, 2010), https://www.investigativeproject.org/profile/113/nihad-awad.

have been saying 'next year to Jerusalem'; we say 'next year to all Palestine.'"

In Canada, CAIR-CAN became the National Council of Canadian Muslims (NCCM) in 2013. NCCM Executive Director Ihsaan Gardee stated:

"We remain the same organization our constituents and partners have come to rely on to represent a broad and diverse spectrum of Canadian Muslims."[101]

---

[101] "CAIR.CAN Evolves – Introducing the National Council of Canadian Muslims (NCCM)," NCCM (National Council of Canadian Muslims (NCCM) / Conseil National des Musulmans Canadiens (CNMC), July 6, 2013), https://www.nccm.ca/introducing-the-national-council-of-canadian-muslims-nccm/.

CHAPTER 5: WHAT DO INDIA AND CHINA HAVE TO DO WITH THE #ISLAMOPHOBIAINDUSTRY?

"Remember the call from the Party: spread China's voice, support the country's development, safeguard national interests, promote Chinese culture and make new contributions to fulfilling national rejuvenation and building a community with a shared future for mankind."

~ Opening ceremony of the 10th National Congress of Returned Overseas Chinese and their Relatives in Beijing, Aug. 29, 2018

Yes, I know. It might seem odd to turn to China and India in a book about Islamophobia and the silencing of the West. Both are very important to the story. Let's talk about China, first.

China is under attack on a regular basis from leaders all over the world. COVID-19 increased that criticism. China is filled with Chinese people - a race. One would think that criticizing the Chinese government would be racist. But it isn't. Journalists regularly investigate China's policies and how they interfere with freedom-loving countries. While we are encouraged to talk about the influence of China and its ideology on our economy, education, media, propaganda, and our governments and its use of soft power, the same tactics as Islam, we are discouraged from criticizing Islam. Islam calls itself a race. But it isn't. It is an ideology and a religion.

So why is it acceptable to criticize China but not Islam when Islam is trying to influence the West in the same way as China?

According to the first-ever annual report of the National Security and Intelligence Committee of Parliamentarians, (NSICOP), released April 9, 2019, China is a threat to Canada's national security.[102] Although this report is about Canada, other countries are under the same influence.

> *"China is known globally for its efforts to influence Chinese communities and the politics of other countries. The Chinese government has a number of official organizations that try to influence Chinese communities and politicians to adopt pro-China positions, most prominently the United Front[103] Work Department."*

President Xi Jinping has overseen what one leading academic expert calls a "massive expansion" in China's use of soft power overseas, much of it under the auspices of the United Front Work Department, a shadowy offshoot of the Chinese communist party.

---

[102] Terry Glavin, "Terry Glavin: It's Official – China Is a Threat to Canada's National Security," nationalpost.com (National Post, a division of Postmedia Network Inc., April 10, 2019), https://nationalpost.com/opinion/terry-glavin-its-official-china-is-a-threat-to-canadas-national-security.

[103] Tom Blackwell, "How China Uses Shadowy United Front as 'Magic Weapon' to Try to Extend Its Influence in Canada," thestarphoenix.com (The Star Phoenix, a division of Postmedia Network Inc., December 31, 2019), https://thestarphoenix.com/news/how-china-uses-shadowy-united-front-as-magic-weapon-to-try-to-extend-its-influence-in-canada/wcm/120d977b-2aa6-4e67-8029-666cc14e9549.

The United Front began in pre-revolutionary China, used by the party to co-opt non-communist groups into its struggle for power. In recent years, it has been increasingly deployed to win over overseas Chinese — and the broader societies around them.

"United Front work has taken on a level of significance not seen since the years before 1949," Anne-Marie Brady, a political scientist at New Zealand's University of Canterbury, told a U.S. conference last year. "(China) is increasingly able to use its soft-power 'magic weapons' to help influence the decision-making of foreign governments and societies."[104]

Charles Burton, a political scientist at Ontario's Brock University, who closely monitors China-related rights issues, pointed out that the problem is with the United Front Work Department. The *Department* engages with persons of Chinese origin who have Canadian citizenship and encourages them to serve the interests of the motherland, when in fact the motherland should be Canada.[105]

It appears the Chinese government has *infiltrated our education system.*

The Confucius Institutes were founded by the Chinese government and are managed by China's Ministry of Education to spread Communist ideas. It offers its services to teach Mandarin to schoolchildren and is now entrenched at three school boards and on nine university and college campuses across Canada.[106,107,108]

---

[104] Tom Blackwell, "How China Uses Shadowy United Front as 'Magic Weapon' to Try to Extend Its Influence in Canada,", December 31, 2019.
[105] Tom Blackwell, December 31, 2019.

Consul General Fang Li had urged locals to come out in support of the institute.

To encourage such leanings, the United Front's tools include both the Confucius Institutes, and the less-well-known Chinese Students and Scholars Associations[109] at post-secondary institutions across Canada — and in numerous other countries. The associations are sometimes dispatched to counteract protests against visiting Chinese dignitaries, promote the homeland and monitor the activities of Chinese students.

The Chinese Institutes are in America, as well. According to Judicial Watch, they provide a platform to disseminate Chinese Communist Party propaganda, encourage censorship and restrict academic freedom. The University of Arizona (UA), a taxpayer-funded institution with an enrollment of about 44,000, paid

---

[106] "13 Confucius Institutes (CIs) in Canada," Confucius Institute of Toronto (Confucius Institute of Toronto, 2021), https://confuciusinstitutetoronto.weebly.com/.

[107] "Chinese Students and Scholars Association (UTCSSA)," Ulife - Chinese Students and Scholars Association (UT CSSA) - University of Toronto (Office of the Vice-Provost Students, University of Toronto, 2021), https://www.ulife.utoronto.ca/organizations/view/id/1832.

[108] "Chinese Student and Scholars Association," Chinese Student and Scholars Association at the University of Calgary (UCCSSA) (Campus Labs, 2021), https://suuofc.campuslabs.ca/engage/organization/chinese-students-and-scholars-association.

[109] "Chinese Students and Scholars Association (CSSA)," Chinese Students and Scholars Association (CSSA) (Students' Society of McGill University, 2021), https://ssmu.ca/clubs/religion-culture-clubs/chinese-students-and-scholars-association-at-mcgill-university-cssa/.

$100,000 to launch a Confucius Institute on its Tucson campus more than a decade ago and subsequently dedicated nearly $2 million and other public resources to keep it going. The University dedicated at least $1.9 million to the Communist installation through various campus clubs and organizations. From 2012 to 2019 the records show that there were more than 400 university approved events and classes with the Confucius Institute.

The original agreement[110] between the Arizona Board of Regents and the People's Republic of China was originally written in Chinese and English. It is signed by former UA President Robert N. Shelton on behalf of the board and Lin Xu, identified in the document as chief executive of the Confucius Institute Headquarters (Hanban), People's Republic of China. The contract allotted UA employees paid positions within the Confucius Institute and provides the Chinese establishment with offices, classrooms, equipment, operating supplies and funding, instructors, guest lecturers, administrative services and other assorted resources. It also provides the Confucius Institute with exclusive rights to intellectual concepts, trademarks and inventions.[111]

---

[110] Mary Alice Murphy, ed., "Does Anyone Believe That This Was Just a Casual Partnership?" The Grant County Beat, October 18, 2019, https://www.grantcountybeat.com/columns/informational/immigration-matters/53850-does-anyone-believe-that-this-was-just-a-casual-partnership.

[111] "Public University Gives Chinese Communists Funding, Exclusive Rights to Intellectual Concepts, Trademarks, Inventions," Judicial Watch (Judicial Watch, Inc., October 17, 2019), https://www.judicialwatch.org/corruption-

In 2019, the U.S. government, threatened to withhold generous Department of Defense (DOD) language program funding to schools with Confucius Institutes.[112]

According to the department of Education in America, China provided $111,756,254 to U.S. universities in the first half of 2019 alone.[113]

Michel Juneau-Katsuya, former Asia-Pacific chief for the Canadian Security Intelligence Service, also documented ties between the leaders of a number of Chinese Canadian groups and China, arguing in a presentation to the Toronto school board the groups *"are following Beijing's request, not the Canadian constituents."*

> *"While insinuating their ideologies in our western schools, China's Education Minister Yuan Guiren, a former president of Beijing Normal University, stated: "Never let textbooks promoting Western values appear in our classes."[114]*

---

chronicles/public-university-gives-chinese-communists-funding-exclusive-rights-to-intellectual-concepts-trademarks-inventions/.

[112] Lum, Thomas, and Hannah Fischer. "IF11180 Confucius Institutes in the United States: Selected Issues - Version 5 (Updated)." Congressional Research Service - In Focus. Government of the United States, March 18, 2021. https://crsreports.congress.gov/product/pdf/IF/IF11180

[113] Alex VanNess, "DOE Launches Investigations into Harvard and Yale," Clarion Project (Clarion Project Inc., February 13, 2020), https://clarionproject.org/harvard-and-yale-doe-launches-investigations/.

[114] Giulio Meotti, "The West Needs to Wake up to China's Duplicity," Gatestone Institute (Gatestone Institute International Policy Council, March 28, 2020),

Canadian veteran foreign-affairs reporter, Jonathan Manthorpe, has written about this influence in his book, *Claws of the Panda: Beijing's Campaign of Influence and Intimidation in Canada*:

> *"In most cases...they are espionage outstations for Chinese embassies and consulates through which they control Chinese students, gather information on perceived enemies and intimidate dissidents."* [115]

Kenny Chiu, a losing 2015 federal Conservative candidate in B.C. stated:

> *"There are many immigrants coming to Canada who are actually very proud of the development that has occurred in the motherland."* [116]

In August 2018, Xi made a direct appeal to ethnic Chinese residents of countries like Canada — what Beijing calls the "overseas Chinese" — urging them to:

> *"...remember the call from the Party and the people, spread China's voice, support the country's development, safeguard national interests."* [117]

---

https://www.gatestoneinstitute.org/15804/china-duplicity.

[115] Jonathan Manthorpe, *Claws of the Panda: Beijing's Campaign of Influence and Intimidation in Canada* (Toronto, Ontario: Cormorant Books, 2019).

[116] Tom Blackwell, "How China Uses Shadowy United Front as 'Magic Weapon' to Try to Extend Its Influence in Canada," thestarphoenix.com (The Star Phoenix, a division of Postmedia Network Inc., December 31, 2019), https://thestarphoenix.com/news/how-china-uses-shadowy-united-front-as-magic-weapon-to-try-to-extend-its-influence-in-canada.

Canada's Chinese-language media, with the exception of Falun Gong's Epoch Times and one or two other newspapers, toe Beijing's line, says Cheuk Kwan, head of the Toronto Association for Democracy in China.[118] Most of the Chinese-language media in Canada are now owned by businesses tied to Beijing, offering positive coverage of China, while Chinese Canadian community groups have largely fallen under the sway of the "motherland."

Charles Burton says one of the United Front's key goals is to soften opinions around issues like Chinese companies' acquisition of Canadian natural resources and technology.

It's difficult to map exactly how the United Front Work Department deploys its resources in places like Canada but its influence has been helped by immigration in the last two decades made up increasingly of people raised under Communist rule on the Chinese mainland. Burton believes a "substantial" portion of Chinese diplomatic staff in Canada are likely United Front operatives, interacting with Chinese Canadian leaders, politicians, students and others. China's Overseas Affairs Office — under Xi, is now officially part of the United Front.

"An organization (United Front Work Department) that once had another purpose has

---

[117] Tom Blackwell, "How China Uses Shadowy United Front as 'Magic Weapon' to Try to Extend Its Influence in Canada," thestarphoenix.com, December 31, 2019

[118] "About - Toronto Association for Democracy in China," Toronto Association for Democracy in China, 2021, https://www.tadc.ca/about/.

gradually been taken over to serve China's national interest."

Cheuk Kwan of the Toronto Association for Democracy in China also points out the influence of China through the United Front Work Department in Canada.[119] Dozens of Chinese Canadian groups had voiced support for the China-backed government in Hong Kong singling out violent "extremists" among the demonstrators.

"We support the rule of law and stability in Hong Kong, oppose the violent acts of a small number of extremists, oppose any Hong Kong independence movement ... and support the Hong Kong government maintaining law and order," the letter in Ming Pao newspaper said. "Hong Kong is China's inalienable sovereign territory; Hong Kong's affairs are China's internal affairs; and we oppose any foreign interference."

Cheuk Kwan pointed out "These are basically fake organizations ... They are what I call the mouthpieces of the Chinese consulate. This is a very clearly United Front effort by the Chinese government ... If it's not instituted directly, then indirectly."[120]

Fenella Sung, spokesman for Vancouver's Friends of Hong Kong, said the letter seems typical of the United Front. She pointed especially to its appeal to ethnic nationalism, with statements that Chinese Canadians are

---

[119] Tom Blackwell, "Open Letter From Chinese-Canadian groups boosts Hong Kong Government, blasts protesters," nationalpost.com (Postmedia Network Inc., July 9, 2019), https://nationalpost.com/news/open-letter-from-chinese-canadian-groups-boosts-hong-kong-government-blasts-protesters.

[120] Tom Blackwell, nationalpost.com, July 9, 2019

"all sons of China and members of the Chinese people," and "blood is thicker than water."[121] She added there is "not a word about being Canadians, as if they have nothing to do with Canada. The text of the ad could be used anywhere in the world."

A training manual for United Front cadres, obtained by the Financial Times newspaper, notes with approval that the number of politicians of Chinese descent elected in Toronto had almost doubled between 2003 and 2006.[122]

Chinese Canadian politicians, meanwhile, have to be cognizant that recent Chinese immigrants are mostly products of the mainland Communist regime, said Kenny Chiu, a losing 2015 federal Conservative candidate in B.C.

> "A lot of people don't think of the long arm of influence of China in Canada, because they're under the influence, to put it mildly ... Outsiders like me, who is a Hong Kong immigrant ... we see very clearly that this is a United Front effort, a very subtle, soft-power kind of advance into Canadian society."

China wants to be an Empire. Fei-Ling Wang, author of "China Order: Centralia, the World Empire and the Nature of the Chinese Power" wrote:

> "Tianxia is a long-standing Chinese political tradition and practice that is revitalized and

---

[121] Tom Blackwell, nationalpost.com, July 9, 2019

[122] Jamil Anderlini, Lucy Hornby, and James Kynge, "Inside China's Secret 'Magic Weapon' for Worldwide Influence," Financial Times (The Financial Times Ltd., October 26, 2017), https://www.ft.com/content/fb2b3934-b004-11e7-beba-5521c713abf4.

encouraged in today's People's Republic. The Chinese dream of Tianxia, or the China Order, presupposes a hierarchical world empire system."[123]

Sounds very much like the idea of the *Umma* in Islam.

Why is there no backlash when critiquing China? No shaming for those who criticize China's alleged influence over our education, our policies and economy?

On June 19, 2019, David Mulroney, Canada's ambassador to China from 2009 to 2012, shared his concern about China's influence on Canada.[124] He questions Canada's commitment of $256 million over five years for the Beijing-based Asian Infrastructure Investment Bank, a pledge Canada made despite China's obsession with shutting down the free flow of information that real investment banks require. Yet where is our concern about the Sharia-compliant parallel economy that is available in Canada, despite the fact that is discriminates against Jewish citizens and their companies?

Mulroney questions the growth of what I would call empire building on the part of China, reminiscent of America's Manifest Destiny and Britain's Empire. He asks

---

[123] Fei-Ling Wang, *The China Order: Centralia, World Empire, and the Nature of Chinese Power* (Albany, NY: State University of New York Press, 2017).

[124] David Mulroney, "Opinion: Ottawa Seems to Be out of Ideas on Devising a New Kind of China Policy," The Globe and Mail (The Globe and Mail Inc., June 20, 2019), https://www.theglobeandmail.com/opinion/article-ottawa-seems-to-be-out-of-ideas-on-devising-a-new-kind-of-china-policy/.

why it is "building a blue-water navy and why it is militarizing rocks and shoals in the South China Sea." He also wrote:

> "We need to put more money into domestic security, enabling us to combat Chinese interference more effectively. And we shouldn't be afraid to name and shame perpetrators when we discover examples of meddling; Beijing won't like it, but it will also probably tone down its more egregious activities."

Mulroney shared concerns about bullying, by China:

> "It is in America's interest and it is in the interest of a lot of other countries to see China pull back from hostage diplomacy and bullying... The only way to counter that is through collective action and that is a long, hard slog."

In the fall of 2019 Daryl Morey, general manager of the basketball franchise Houston Rockets, sent out a tweet: "Fight for Freedom. Stand with Hong Kong," defending the rights of people in Hong King to protest the government of China. China was not happy. It is important to know that the NBA, the National Basketball Association has a big presence in China: the Houston Rockets in particular The Basketball Commissioner, Adam Silver, said he recognized that the "views expressed" by Morey had "offended" many in China, which was "regrettable." China was not willing to accept that statement. Many Chinese companies associated with the NBA pulled out.[125]

---

[125] Jordan Valinsky, "How One Tweet Snowballed into the NBA's Worst Nightmare," CNN (Cable News Network, October 11, 2019), https://www.cnn.com/2019/10/09/business/nba-

Money was at stake. Chinese state broadcaster CCTV:

> "Any remarks that challenge national sovereignty and social stability are not within the scope of freedom of speech."[126]

China was attempting to exert her power over the West by silencing dissent. The West pushed back. There were no calls of racism or some kind of irrational fear of the Chinese.

Liao Yiwu, a Chinese writer exiled in Berlin, wrote in Le Point International, April 6, 2019:

> "The West is so tolerant, passive, accommodating and naive towards Beijing. Westerners... are seduced like an old man in front of a young girl.... Europe shows all its weakness.[127] It does not realize that the Chinese offensive threatens its freedom and values."

Where is the equal concern about Islam's influence in Canada and the West? CAIR, Council of American Islamic Relations, founder Omar Ahmad had stated how CAIR could eventually gain influence in Congress: "This can be achieved by infiltrating the American media outlets, universities and research centers," going on to suggest

---

china-hong-kong-explainer/index.html.

[126] Scott Stinson, "Stinson: NBA's Adam Silver Tries Compromise to Smooth Things over with China over pro-Hong Kong Tweet," torontosun.com (Postmedia Network Inc., October 9, 2019), https://torontosun.com/sports/basketball/nba/stinson-nbas-adam-silver-tries-compromise-to-smooth-things-over-with-china-over-pro-hong-kong-tweet.

[127] Giulio Meotti, Gatestone Institute International Policy Council, March 28, 2020)

how this would give them an entry point that would allow them to pressure U.S. policymakers.[128] The very same objectives of China.

If we were to remove the words Chinese and China and replace with Islam and Muslims, we would be accused of Islamophobia.

And then there is India. There is a caste system in India. We have no problem criticizing this Hindu caste system. There are no accusations of "Hinduphobia."

I was first introduced to the Dalit[129] in India by the esteemed journalist, Stephanie Nolan, of the Globe and Mail who wrote about this group of people many years ago. It was her article that informed me about a group of people treated as "Untouchables;" not because of their actions, but by dint of birth. By birth! I remember the articles and the horror I felt. She was writing about the discrimination based on caste and gender that continues to bedevil India. It seems few want to talk about it.

Amrit Dhillon, a New Delhi journalist wrote about the Dalit, again in the Globe and Mail.[130] Did you know that there are 160 million Dalit in India? That "the Dalits (earlier known as "untouchables") of India were

[128] Prof. Arnon Gutfeld, "The Saudi Specter over the American Education System," Jerusalem Center for Public Affairs, May 23, 2019, https://jcpa.org/article/saudi-specter-over-american-education-system/.

[129] Sagarika Ghose, "The Dalit in India," Social Research 70, no. 1 (2003): pp. 83-109.

[130] Amrit Dhillon, "Why Not a Museum for the Dalits of India?" The Globe and Mail (The Globe and Mail Inc., September 30, 2016), https://www.theglobeandmail.com/opinion/why-not-a-museum-for-the-dalits-of-india/article32150225/.

exploited, demeaned and oppressed by the Hindu upper castes for 2,000 years?"

Did you know they had foods they were forced to eat, clothes they were told to wear and that they had musical instruments they had to fashion for themselves because they were not allowed to play certain kinds of instruments?

Or "Dalit women, for example, had to wear their sari in a particular way and were allowed to wear only certain ornaments, such as tin bangles. Dalits had to wear a bell around their necks, which they had to ring to alert any oncoming Brahmin of their presence lest it pollute him"?

Can any of you imagine someone being called a racist for being against this behaviour? Did anyone call Ms. Nolen a xenophobe? No. Has there been a campaign of Hinduphobia to stop us from speaking of this treatment?

No.

CHAPTER 6: WHAT DID ISLAM LEARN FROM NAZISM?

"What is there to separate the Muslims in Europe and around the world from us Germans? We have common aims. There is no more solid basis for cooperation than common aims and common ideals. For 200 years, Germany has not had the slightest conflict with Islam."

~ Heinrich Himmler

I am sharing the way anti-Semites spread the hate for Jews prior to the Holocaust. It is a pattern that has been followed by Islamic leaders to spread Islamophobia and silence the west. In both cases government, universities, education and media worked to spread their values. Islam has infiltrated our institutions to affect our views on Islam; what we can and cannot say.

Over the centuries anti-Semitism had reared its ugly head in Christian Europe and, by the 1800's, the people in Germany and Austria were bathed in its rhetoric.

The land had been well-prepared for anti-Semitism, long before the rise of National Socialism. In 1793, Johann Gotlieb Fichte (1762–1814), the father of both German nationalism and German anti-Semitism, characterized the Jews as a state within a state that would undermine the German nation. The only way in which he could concede giving rights to Jews would be "to cut off all their heads in one night and to sew new ones on their shoulders, which should contain not a single Jewish idea."

In the latter half of the 19th century Paul de Lagarde shared his views on Jews. He was a theologian and orientalist a professor of oriental languages at the University of Göttingen in 1869. Politically, he was a conservative and a virulent anti-Semite. His writings have been said to epitomize the "Germanic ideology" that fed into Nazism. He stated:

> *"Every Jew is proof of the enfeeblement of our national life and the worthlessness of what we call the Christian religion." And later "One would need a heart as hard as crocodile hide not to feel sorry for the poor exploited Germans and – which is identical – not to hate the Jews and despise those who – out of humanity! – defend these Jews or who are too cowardly to trample these usurious vermin to death. With trichinae and bacilli, one does not negotiate, nor are trichinae and bacilli to be educated; they are to be exterminated as quickly and thoroughly as possible."*

The Mittelstand - the middle class - small farmers, peasants, artisans and small businessmen feared the rapidly changing society that was turning forward to industrialization and away from the land. They embraced the "Jewish Conspiracy" rhetoric of Berliner Adolph Stocker (1835–1909). He was a German court chaplain to Kaiser Wilhelm I, a politician, a leading anti-Semite, and a Lutheran theologian who founded the Christian Social Party. In 1879 Stocker had shared his views at a Christian Social meeting:

> *"Modern Jewry is a great danger to German national life. The Jews are a people within a people, a state within a state, a separate tribe*

within a foreign race who pitted their unbroken Semitic character against Teutonic nature, their rigid cult of law or their hatred of Christians against Christianity."

In universities in the 1880's the cry was heard, "The Jews are our misfortune." In the fall of 1880, the Anti-Semites petition was circulated by two schoolteachers depicting the Jews as exploitative masters, who would destroy the German fatherland. "Jews are alien people", they said.

"Their thinking and feeling are completely alien to the German Volk. If the German people are not to be destroyed and fall into economic slavery by the Jews, steps need to be taken to liberate the German people from this Jewish danger."

By the spring of 1881, there were 225,000 signatures, mostly Prussian; 9000 from Bavaria, and 4000 university students.

Eugene Karl Duhring (1833–1921), a philosopher and economist at the University of Berlin wrote *The Jewish Question as a Racial, Moral and Cultural Question* in 1877. He described the Jews as a "counter-race" separated from all humanity, whom neither conversion nor assimilation could affect because their basic nature was evil and unchangeable. He was highly respected amongst his students.

Duhring was idealized by Georg von Schonerer (1842–1921) who formulated Pan-Germanism. Guido von List (1848–1919), another vehement Jew hater was an associate of Schonerer. He contributed to Pan German ideology; "What the Jew believes is all one, in his race lies the swinishness"

In the agricultural areas, the peasants advanced the notion that Germany "repeal, by legal means, Jewish emancipation by placing the Jews under alien legislation." Jews were described as an octopus with claws in every sphere of German life. This belief morphed into the description of Jews as "beasts of prey" and "cholera bacilli." In 1892, all the rhetoric turned the Conservative Party toward antisemitism as a political tool to win elections. Antisemitism was given the imprimatur of rationality. "We fight the multifarious and obtrusive Jewish influence that decomposes our people's life."

The Agrarian League started its antisemitic output in 1894:

> "Jewry has become altogether too mighty in our country and has acquired a decisive say in the press, in trade and on the exchanges."

> "Agriculture and Jewry must fight to the death, until one or other lies lifeless-or at least powerless-on the ground."

By the beginning of the 20th century, each year "tens of thousands of antisemitic pamphlets were sent free to all officials of the state and members of the upper ten thousand." They were in every library. By the 1920's, there were approximately 430 antisemitic associations and societies, including the List Society, the Austrian Alpine Association, The German Language Club, the German Social Party, and the Thule Society which spread Volkist racial propaganda which was based on nineteenth century Romanticism; a belief that the true German was spiritually connected to the very soil of the homeland, rooted in the ground itself, unlike the wandering materialistic Jew.

Rudolph Hess (1894–1987), one of Hitler's closest followers, was a member. There were as many as 700 anti-Semitic periodicals. Anti-Semitic bills were introduced into state and national legislatures. Anti-Semitism was in the printed word, in speeches, and in music. The air was saturated with hatred of the Jew.[131]

Just as Germany and Europe were prepared for Hitler, Islamophobia prepared the west for the infiltration of Islamic values in all of our institutions.

---

[131] Lucy S. Dawidowicz, "The War against the Jews: 1933-1945," The War Against the Jews: 1933-1945 (Amazon.ca, March 1, 1986), https://www.amazon.ca/War-Against-Jews-1933-1945/dp/055334532X.

CHAPTER 7: WHO IS PROMOTING THE TERM ISLAMOPHOBIA?

"To disseminate, promote and preserve the Islamic teachings and values based on moderation and tolerance, promote Islamic culture and safeguard Islamic heritage..."

"To protect and defend the true image of Islam, to combat defamation of Islam and encourage dialogue among civilisations and religions."

~ Organization of Islamic Cooperation Charter[132]

"Islam is perfect, there is nothing to be added or changed."

~ Abu Bakar Bashir[133], former head of Jemaah Islamiah (JI)

The #IslamophobiaIndustry is silencing Western Culture by taking advantage of our values of inclusion, accommodation and tolerance: our need to care for the other; in order to attack anyone, any organization that dares to criticize Islam. This was no mean feat. This has been done by promoting the term Islamophobia: the fear of Islam is irrational.

This is not a new concept.

---

[132] "Organization of Islamic Cooperation (OIC) Charter," OIC Charter (Organization of Islamic Cooperation (OIC), 2021), https://www.oic-oci.org/page/?p_id=53&p_ref=27&lan=en.
[133] "Abu Bakar Ba'asyir: The Radical Indonesian Cleric Linked to Bali Bombings," BBC News (BBC, January 8, 2021), https://www.bbc.com/news/world-asia-pacific-10912588.

Islamophobia had been promoted by the Nazis. Throughout the war years, the Nazi Propaganda Ministry repeatedly instructed the press to promote a positive image of Islam. Urging journalists to give credit to the "Islamic world as a cultural factor," Goebbels in the autumn 1942 instructed magazines to discard negative images of Islam, which had been spread by church polemicists for centuries, and instead to promote an alliance with the Islamic world, which was described as both anti-Bolshevik and anti-Jewish. References to similarities between Jews and Muslims, as manifested in the ban of pork and the ritual circumcision, were to be avoided. In the coming months, the Propaganda Ministry decreed that magazines should depict the U.S. as "the enemies of Islam" and stress American and British hostility toward the Muslim religion."[134]

In 1941, the Wehrmacht distributed the military handbook *Der Islam* to train the troops to behave correctly towards Muslim populations.

Heinrich Himmler while expressing disdain for Christianity, found Islam "very admirable."

> *"What is there to separate the Muslims in Europe and around the world from us Germans? We have common aims. There is no more solid basis for cooperation than common aims and common ideals. For 200 years, Germany has not*

---

[134] David Motadel, "The Swastika and the Crescent," wilsonquarterly.com (Woodrow Wilson International Center for Scholars, December 2, 2014), https://www.wilsonquarterly.com/quarterly/fall-2014-the-great-wars/the-swastika-and-the-crescent/.

had the slightest conflict with Islam. The Nazis had found commonality with Islam."

This Nazi-Arab alliance thrived, complete with tens of thousands of Islamic and Arab volunteers arduously fighting in the trenches, coordinating diplomatic and strategic affairs through the Arab Higher Committee, broadcasting nightly incendiary hate messages beginning with words "Oh Muslims," and undertaking all things calculated to advance a German victory, which promised an Arab state in Palestine and a disappeared Jewish population. No wonder the Arab marketplaces were filled with placards that exhorted, "In Heaven, Allah is your ruler. On Earth, it is Adolf Hitler."[135]

But the words of Hitler mattered most. Islam for Hitler was a *Männerreligion*; a religion of men; and hygienic too. He had spoken of soldiers of Islam receiving a warrior's heaven, a real earthly paradise with houris and wine flowing. Islam, he had intoned, was a cult which glorifies the heroism, and which opens up the seven Heavens to bold warriors alone. Islam, he claimed, was much more suited to the 'Germanic temperament' than the Jewish filth.[136]

Here we are, in the 21st century, believing that we have learned from the past, yet we are repeating words of hate that had led to the Shoah but from a different

---

[135] Edwin Black, "When the Holocaust Came to the Middle East," History News Network, May 30, 2018, https://historynewsnetwork.org/article/169158.
[136] Dominic Green, "Why Hitler Wished He Was Muslim," The Wall Street Journal (Dow Jones & Company, January 16, 2015), https://www.wsj.com/articles/book-review-ataturk-in-the-nazi-imagination-by-stefan-ihrig-and-islam-and-nazi-germanys-war-by-david-motadel-1421441724.

source. At the same time as we are admonished against saying anything negative about that source. We are bringing the past into the present:

Mohamed Gad El-Zoghby, an Egyptian researcher and a poet with a master's degree in Shari'a and law from Ain Shams University, was asked in a February 9, 2019 interview on Safa TV (Saudi Arabia/Egypt) who was worse: Adolf Hitler or Imam Khomeini. He answered:

> "Objectively speaking, Hitler wins. But as far as we're concerned, we should erect a statue of Hitler for what he did to the Jews."[137]

In Germany, a journalist, Michael Stürzenberger, was handed a six-month suspended jail sentence[138] for posting on his Facebook page a historical photo of the Grand Mufti of Jerusalem, Haj Amin al-Husseini, shaking the hand of a senior Nazi official in Berlin in 1941. The prosecution accused Stürzenberger of "inciting hatred towards Islam" and "denigrating Islam" by publishing the photograph.

Journalist Giulio Meotti[139] wrote that Turkey is leading the ideological persecution of the "Islamophobes."

---

[137] Safa TV (Saudi Arabia), "Egyptian Researcher Mohamed Gad El-Zoghby: We Should Erect a Statue of Hitler Because of What He Did to the Jews," MEMRI.org (Middle East Media Research Institute (MEMRI), February 15, 2019), https://www.memri.org/tv/egyptian-researcher-gad-zoghby-should-erect-statue-hitler-because-did-jews-holocaust-khomeini-worse.

[138] J. Daniels, "[Translation] EILT: Six Months Imprisonment for PI-NEWS Author Michael Stürzenberger," PI-NEWS (Politically Incorrect), August 18, 2017, http://www.pi-news.net/2017/08/eilt-sechs-monate-haft-fuer-pi-news-autor-michael-stuerzenberger/.

Under the auspices of Turkish diplomat Volkan Bozkir, President of the 75th Session of the United Nations General Assembly, the UN celebrated the "International Day against Islamophobia" and Secretary General Antonio Guterres himself strongly denounced an "epidemic of Islamophobia". Turkey's PM Erdogan was promoting his global campaign of victimization by "Islamophobia", while in fact it is the critics of extremist Islam who are in danger and frequently killed. In an official visit to Paris on January 5, 2018, Erdogan stated to the leaders of the French Council for Muslim Worship, without fear of punishment, from any quarter, "The Muslims of France are under my protection".[140]

This conference was organized by the Organisation of Islamic Cooperation (OIC), an entity made up of 56 mainly Muslim countries, plus "Palestine". In the OIC, states such as Pakistan punish "blasphemy" with death; Saudi Arabia flogs and jails liberal bloggers such as Raif Badawi, and Turkey fills its jails with writers and journalists, to mention just a few of members.[141]

Jasmin Zine[142], Professor of Sociology & the Muslim Studies Option, Wilfrid Laurier University, is an

[139] Editors, "Writings by Giulio Meotti," Gatestone Institute, 2021, https://www.gatestoneinstitute.org/author/Giulio+Meotti.
[140] Giulio Meotti, "Erdoganistan: The New Islamic Superpower?," Gatestone Institute, March 28, 2021, https://www.gatestoneinstitute.org/17202/erdogan-turkey-islamic-superpower.
[141] Judith Bergman, "Killing Free Speech," Gatestone Institute, September 21, 2018, https://www.gatestoneinstitute.org/12975/killing-free-speech.
[142] Editors, "Jasmin Zine | Professor, Sociology and Muslim

education consultant who has developed award winning curriculum materials that address Islamophobia and anti-Muslim racism and has worked with the Office for Democratic Institutions and Human Rights at the Organization for Security and Cooperation in Europe (ODHIR/OSCE), the Council of Europe, and the United Nations Educational, Scientific and Cultural Organization (UNESCO) on developing international guidelines for educators and policy-makers on combating Islamophobia and discrimination against Muslims. She is part of the "Islamophobia Research and Documentation Project," an initiative designed to buttress the claim that Muslims are targets of wholesale discrimination and harassment in the West. She gave a keynote speech on "Islamophobia, Anti- Muslim Racism, and the Weaponizing of Free Speech" at "The Road Traveled: 9th Annual International Islamophobia Conference"[143]held at the University of California Berkeley. She is hard at work defending Islam as it spreads throughout the West, by invoking the term "Islamophobia."[144] Zine defines "Islamophobia" as "fear and hatred of Islam and Muslims that translates into

Studies Option" (Wilfrid Laurier University, 2021), https://www.wlu.ca/academics/faculties/faculty-of-arts/faculty-profiles/jasmin-zine/index.html.

[143] "The Road Traveled: 9th Annual International Islamophobia Conference," University of Canlifornia at Berkley (UCB) Center for Race & Gender, 2018, https://www.crg.berkeley.edu/events/the-road-traveled-9th-annual-international-islamophobia-conference/.

[144] Robert Spencer, "Canada: Muslim Professor Who Claims She Was Assaulted at Conference Has Long Record of 'Islamophobia' Propagandizing," Jihad Watch, April 15, 2019, https://www.jihadwatch.org/2019/04/canada-muslim-prof-who-claims-she-was-assaulted-at-conference-has-long-record-of-islamophobia-propagandizing.

individual, ideological and systemic forms of oppression."

Pay attention to the language that she employed. "Anti-Muslim Racism." "Racism?" The greatest accomplishment by the #IslamophobiaIndustry is the Orwellian twisting of language. Turning a religion, an ideology, into a race. We have worked hard to remove attacks on people based on race. One is born into one's race. It is not a choice. One cannot opt out of race.

To push the narrative that Islam is a race silences all discussion. This abuse of language is not an accident. In 2017 Sociologist, writer and Montreal-based activist Dalila Awada speaking to CUPE[145] said:

> "The first step to combatting Islamophobia, she instructed, is to recognize it as racism. Anti-Muslim racism shows itself in different ways, whether it is physical or verbal aggression "or a family not being able to rent an apartment because the man's name is Mohammed and not Mark." The next step is to ask questions about institutions that perpetuate this racism. "We need to go beyond words like diversity and dialogue, as if they are magic formulas that solve all problems."

Amy Lai[146], lawyer and author of The Right to Parody[147], a book on free speech and higher education, under

---

[145] Dalila Awada, "Society Must Fight Islamophobia, Says Awada," ed. CUPE, Canadian Union of Public Employees, October 5, 2017, https://cupe.ca/society-must-fight-islamophobia-says-awada.
[146] PEN Canada, "Amy Lai Wins 2021 PEN Canada/Ken Filkow Prize for Freedom of Expression," PEN Canada, July 22, 2021,

contract with the University of Michigan Press wrote: "Freedom of speech has long been held as a fundamental right in the Western world. The view that free speech enables a "marketplace of ideas," often used with reference to John Stuart Mill's *On Liberty*, has its roots in a number of earlier works. For example, Enlightenment philosopher John Locke contended that freedom of conscience is an inalienable right in all humans, which, when guided by reason, enables them to resist state coercion and pursue the truth. Free speech is essential not only to the pursuit of truth but also to democratic governance. Twentieth-century philosopher John Rawls considered free speech to be one of the basic liberties that enables citizens to participate in the lawmaking in a democracy. For moral philosopher Immanuel Kant, it is congenial to the self-development of individuals as much as it is important for a functional society."

Note the statement that "Free speech is essential not only to the pursuit of truth but also to democratic governance." As I explain in the chapter about Shirk, according to several Muslim scholars, liberalism (democracy), is a religion and is in conflict with the teachings of Islam. Free speech is not innate in Islam. Neither is democracy.

Pascal Bruckerner wrote, "the word 'Islamophobia' amalgamates two very different concepts: the

---

https://pencanada.ca/news/amy-lai-wins-2021-pen-canada-ken-filkow-prize-for-freedom-of-expression/.
[147] Amy Tak-Yee Lai, "The Right to Parody: Comparative Analysis of Copyright and Free Speech," in SearchWorks catalog (Cambridge University Press, 2019), https://searchworks.stanford.edu/view/12863816.

persecution of believers, which is a crime; and the critique of religion, which is a right."[148]

Melanie Phillips, British journalist, author, and public commentator, provides another perspective on Islamophobia. She wrote: "The term Islamophobia was coined to suppress the rational, legitimate and necessary acknowledgement of the dangers within the Islamic world."[149]

The Organisation of Islamic Cooperation, The Collective Voice of the Muslim World wields both religious and political power. It describes itself as:

> "...the second largest inter-governmental organization after the United Nations with a membership of 57 states spread over four continents. The Organization is the collective voice of the Muslim world... espousing all causes close to the hearts of over 1.5 billion Muslims of the world."[150]

OIC reached out to media, academics, and experts and engaged with Western governments to raise awareness, support the efforts of Muslim civil society bodies in the

---

[148] Pascal Bruckner, "There's No Such Thing as Islamophobia," ed. Brian C. Anderson, trans. Alexis Cornel, CityJournal.org (Manhattan Institute, January 8, 2020), https://www.city-journal.org/html/theres-no-such-thing-islamophobia-15324.html.

[149] Melanie Phillips, "How Jews Claiming 'Islamophobia' Are Helping Embolden Ant-Semitism," MelaniePhillips.com, April 14, 2019, https://www.melaniephillips.com/how-jews-claiming-islamophobia-are-helping-embolden-antisemitism.

[150] Editors, "History - Organisation of Islamic Cooperation (OIC)" (The Organisation of Islamic Cooperation (OIC), 2021), https://www.oic-oci.org/page/?p_id=52&p_ref=26&lan=en.

West, and engage all in developing plans and programs to counter Islamophobia. The OIC called on the United Nations and other international and regional organizations to adopt March 15 as the "International Day of Solidarity Against Islamophobia."[151] It also requested the OIC Secretary-General Yousef Al-Othaimeen to engage the management of social media platforms -- including Facebook, Twitter and Instagram -- in order to filter or ban any content that encourages hatred and violence against Muslims.

Here is a document from the OIC: The Organisation of Islamic Co-operation "Challenges of Countering Islamophobia Initiative:[152]

> *"One of the biggest threats to global peace and security in our present time is the scourge of Islamophobia. It is a matter of great concern not only to the Muslim world but also to humanity itself that the issue of Islamophobia is growing at an alarming rate. Today the Muslims are faced with a formidable challenge to counter an orchestrated campaign that is active in defaming Islam and distorting its sacred values of peace, tolerance and acknowledging the other, that lies at the basis of the Islamic faith. The danger is*

---

[151] Ali Murat Alhas, "OIC Calls for Global Action against Islamophobia," Anadolu Ajansı (Anadolu Agency, March 22, 2019), https://www.aa.com.tr/en/middle-east/oic-calls-for-global-action-against-islamophobia/1426137.

[152] Sarah, "Challenges of Countering Islamophobia - The OIC Initiative," IqraSense.com | Islamic Blog (Unknown, February 16, 2018), http://www.iqrasense.com/islamic-outreach/challenges-of-countering-islamophobia-the-oic-initiative.html.

being exacerbated by media misreporting and provocations under the pretext of freedom of expression.

"Islam has been a pioneer in championing democratic freedoms. Freedom of expression is sacrosanct but it cannot be a license to hurt and abuse the sentiments and feelings held sacred by people of different faiths. To ignore or negate this fundamental value would be at the peril of civilized existence

"The negative reports emanating from the West have more than often been the result of ignorance and insufficient knowledge of Islam and Muslims. Many reports have been on hearsay and distorted information."

The director of the information department of the OIC, Maha Mustafa Aqeel, also said part of the OIC's media strategy is to counter "Islamophobia":

"Our strategy focuses on interacting with the media, academics, and experts on various relevant topics, in addition to engaging with Western governments to raise awareness, support the efforts of Muslim civil society bodies in the West, and engage the latter in developing plans and programs to counter Islamophobia."[153]

OIC has also added the "Voice of Wisdom," an electronic platform to combat hate speech on social media.

---

[153] Arab News Editors, "European-Islamic Media Forum Calls for Clampdown on Hate Speech in Western Press," Arab News (Saudi Research & Publishing Company, June 30, 2018), https://www.arabnews.com/node/1330536/saudi-arabia.

According to the OIC's Charter,[154] one of the objectives of the organization is:

> "To disseminate, promote and preserve the Islamic teachings and values based on moderation and tolerance, promote Islamic culture and safeguard Islamic heritage," as well as "To protect and defend the true image of Islam, to combat defamation of Islam and encourage dialogue among civilisations and religions."

Despite the statements of Islamic scholars regarding liberalism and democracy (which I write about in Chapter 13 on *Shirk*), the OIC has had help from Presidents of the United States of America, whether by chance or by design, including William Clinton and Barack Obama. Their comments helped to silence anyone who had concerns about the compatibility of Islam with western ideals. The problem is not a clash of cultures. Rather the discord can be traced to social issues.

President Clinton said not only was the West not at war with Islam, but the West could fully embrace Islam: "The traditional values of Islam-devotion to faith and good works, to family and society-are in harmony with the best of American ideals. Therefore, we know our people, our faiths, our cultures can live in harmony with each other."

Under President Obama, August 2009, references to terrorism did not contain the terms Islam, Muslim or

---

[154] Editors, "OIC Charter" (The Organization of Islamic Cooperation (OIC), 2021), https://www.oic-oci.org/page/?p_id=53&p_ref=27&lan=en.

Jihad. He promoted an explanation for Muslim unrest as based in "colonialism, by which the West denied rights and opportunities to Muslims; the Cold War, which caused the West to treat Muslims as proxies and to disregard their aspirations; modernization and globalization, which breed Western hostility toward Islam. Thus, in Obama's conception, Muslim extremism is driven by legitimate grievances. The logic that follows is that once those grievances are addressed, the extremism will subside."[155]

Calls of Islamophobia rang out following attacks on Muslims. In March 2019, following the attack on two mosques in Christchurch, New Zealand. The Organisation of Islamic Cooperation (OIC) urged the UN Secretary General to convene a special session of the UN General Assembly to declare Islamophobia as a form of racism[156] and to assign a special rapporteur for monitoring and combating the menace in the western countries. Racism. Yet Islam is not a race: it is a religion and a political ideology. It was decided that the "OIC must play a proactive role in countering demonization and denigration of Islam and Muslims and adopt a comprehensive strategy in this regard."

We are permitted, if not encouraged, to criticize other countries and their ideologies. We have no calls of racist

---

[155] Gorka, Katharine C. "The Flawed Science Behind America's Counter-Terrorism Strategy." Washington: Council on Global Security, October 2014.
[156] News Desk, "OIC Urges UN to Tackle Islamophobia, Declare It a Form of Racism," The Express Tribune Pakistan (The Express Tribune, March 23, 2019), https://tribune.com.pk/story/1935888/3-oic-urges-un-tackle-islamophobia-declare-form-racism.

or xenophobic when we criticize India's caste system or report on China's soft power infiltration into Canada, and the potential infiltration into government via the 5G network from Huawei, or the influence of Russia in Western politics. We have all witnessed the two-year investigation into the alleged Russian interference in the 2016 American elections.

But Islam? No.

We are told over and over that we must not insult Islam.

And we obey.

CHAPTER 8: WHO IS SPREADING ISLAM? AND HOW?

"In war, the first casualty is truth."

~ Aeschylus

The plan to spread Islam is brilliant: embedding its philosophy, ideology, religious beliefs into every corner of western democracy; particularly targeting education and public relations; propaganda. The method of extending Islam morphed over time.

Mohamed Akram's blueprint for the advancement of the Islamic movement which he shared in his "Explanatory Memorandum On the General Strategic Goal in North America" [157] stressed the need to form a coalition of groups coming from the worlds of education; religious proselytization; political activism; audio and video production; print media; banking and finance; the physical sciences; the social sciences; professional and business networking; cultural affairs; the publishing and distribution of books; children and teenagers; women's rights; vocational concerns; and jurisprudence.

The following 29 groups[158] are the organizations they believed could collaborate effectively to destroy America from within – "if they all march according to one plan":

---

[157] Akram, Mohamed. "1991 Explanatory Memorandum on the General Strategic Goal for the Group [Muslim Brotherhood] in North America [Translated] Government Exhibit, U.S. v HLF, Et Al." U.S. Government, May 19, 1991. Document available at: http://www.investigativeproject.org/documents/misc/20.pdf
[158] "Muslim Brotherhood (MB)," DiscoverTheNetwork.org - A Guide to the Political Left (Internet Archive Wayback Machine,

- Islamic Society of North America (ISNA);
- ISNA Fiqh Committee (now known as the Fiqh Council of North America);
- ISNA Political Awareness Committee;
- Muslim Youth of North America;
- Muslim Students Association of the U.S. and Canada;
- Association of Muslim Scientists and Engineers;
- Islamic Medical Association (of North America);
- Islamic Teaching Center;
- Malaysian Islamic Study Group;
- Foundation for International Development;
- North American Islamic Trust;
- Islamic Centers Division;
- American Trust Publications;
- Audio-Visual Center;
- Islamic Book Service;
- Islamic Circle of North America;
- Muslim Arab Youth Association;
- Islamic Association for Palestine;
- United Association for Studies and Research
- International Institute of Islamic Thought;

April 23, 2020),
https://web.archive.org/web/20200423074744/http://www.discoverthenetworks.com/groupProfile.asp?grpid=6386.

- Muslim Communities Association;

- Association of Muslim Social Scientists (of North America);

- Islamic Housing Cooperative;

- Muslim Businessmen Association;

- Islamic Education Department;

- Occupied Land Fund (later known as the Holy Land Foundation for Relief and Development);

- Mercy International Association;

- Baitul Mal Inc., and

- Islamic Information Center (of America).

The state of Qatar has been busy spreading the word of Allah throughout Europe. It has funded 140 mosques and Islamic centers in Europe with €71 million. The country with the most of the projects (50) was Italy, where Rome's Al Houda Centre received €4 million.[159,160]

The Muslim Cultural Complex of Lausanne, Switzerland, received $1.6 million.[161] Qatar, in

[159] Damien McElroy, "Qatar 'Spent Huge Sums on Muslim Brotherhood Groups in Europe'" (The National, July 5, 2021), https://www.thenationalnews.com/world/qatar-spent-huge-sums-on-muslim-brotherhood-groups-in-europe-1.845510.

[160] Giulio Meotti, "Qatar: 'A Wolf in Sheep's Clothing'," Gatestone Institute, April 9, 2019, https://www.gatestoneinstitute.org/14042/qatar-europe-islamism-finance.

[161] Sylvain Besson, "L'argent Du Qatar Inonde L'islam Suisse Et Paie Tariq Ramadan," Tribune de Genève (Tamedia Publications romandes S.A., April 3, 2019), https://www.tdg.ch/suisse/argent-qatar-inonde-lislam-suisse-

2015, donated a new £11 million building at Oxford's St Antony's College[162], where Tariq Ramadan, grandson of Muslim Brotherhood founder Hasan al-Banna, [was] a professor.

In France, the emirate financed the Islamic Center of Villeneuve-d'Ascq and the Lycée-Collège Averroès,[163] France's first state-funded Muslim faith school. Lycée-Collège Averroès became the center of a scandal when one of its teachers resigned after writing that the school was "a hotbed of anti-Semitism and 'promoting Islamism' to pupils".[164,165]

Qatar has also financed the Great Mosque of Poitiers[166], which is in the vicinity of the site of the Battle of Tours

paie-tariq-ramadan/story/13748479.

[162] Editors, "New Building by Zaha Hadid Unveiled at Oxford University's Middle East Centre" (University of Oxford, May 26, 2015), https://www.ox.ac.uk/news/2015-05-26-new-building-zaha-hadid-unveiled-oxford-university%E2%80%99s-middle-east-centre.

[163] Romain Gubert, "Comment Le Qatar Finance L'islam De France" (Le Point International, April 4, 2019), https://www.lepoint.fr/monde/comment-le-qatar-finance-l-islam-de-france-04-04-2019-2305782_24.php.

[164] Stéphanie Maurice, "Le Lycée Averroès S'accroche à Sa 'Normalité'" (Libération, February 24, 2015), https://www.liberation.fr/societe/2015/02/22/le-lycee-averroes-s-accroche-a-sa-normalite_1207940/.

[165] Rory Mulholland, "Teacher Quits French Muslim SCHOOL Accusing It Of 'Promoting Islamism'," The Telegraph (Telegraph Media Group, February 8, 2015), https://www.telegraph.co.uk/news/worldnews/europe/france/11398672/Teacher-quits-French-Muslim-school-accusing-it-of-promoting-Islamism.html.

[166] Amaury Brelet, "Génération Identitaire Accuse Un Imam

(also known as the Battle of Poitiers), where Charles Martel, ruler of the Franks, stopped the advancing Muslim army of Abdul al-Rahman in the year 732. Qatar also financed the Assalam mosque[167] in Nantes and the Grand Mosque of Paris[168] are other examples.

Qatar is not alone in building mosques in France. The Brookings Institution wrote in 2019: "According to the [French] Ministry of Interior, 151 imams have been sent by Turkey, which has undertaken a spate of religious outreach to Muslims across Europe over the past decade." Turkey controls 400 mosques out of 2,500 in France.[169]

Qatar financed the European Institute of Human Sciences[170] - an Islamic facility close to the French branch

---

D'avoir Donné Le Nom Arabe De La Bataille De Poitiers à Sa Mosquée" (Valeurs Actuelles, July 5, 2018), https://www.valeursactuelles.com/societe/generation-identitaire-accuse-un-imam-davoir-donne-le-nom-arabe-de-la-bataille-de-poitiers-a-sa-mosquee/.

[167] Maria Magassa-Konaté, "Nantes : Assalam, Une Mosquée Ouverte Aidee Par Un Qatari," SaphirNews.com | Quotidien d'actualité sur le fait musulman en France, November 19, 2012, https://www.saphirnews.com/Nantes-Assalam-une-mosquee-ouverte-aidee-par-un-Qatari_a15716.html.

[168] Editors, "Le Qatar Envisage D'investir 10 Milliards D'EUROS Dans Des Groupes Français," nouvelobs.com, November 7, 2012, https://www.nouvelobs.com/societe/20121106.AFP4166/le-qatar-envisage-d-investir-10-milliards-d-euros-dans-des-groupes-francais.html.

[169] Giulio Meotti, "Erdoganistan: The New Islamic Superpower?" Gatestone Institute, March 28, 2021, https://www.gatestoneinstitute.org/17202/erdogan-turkey-islamic-superpower.

of the Muslim Brotherhood -- that offers courses in Islamic theology.

This plan to spread Islam is brilliant: embedding its philosophy, ideology religious beliefs into every corner of western democracy; particularly targeting education and public relations; propaganda.

It has not taken long for the establishment of the #IslamophobiaIndustry; a conglomerate of governments, global organizations, and individuals; professors, politicians and pundits, who promote the idea that Islam is benign. That Islam as practiced in the more than 50 Muslim countries and in the West is compatible with Western civilization. To say otherwise one is to be considered an Islamophobe.

At what point do enough people wake up from their insular slumber and realize that their society has been hijacked? What does it take? It seems a great deal. Despite what we know about the evolution of Jew hatred to the point that it led to the Holocaust, we are once again allowing ourselves to be taken hostage by apathy and allowing freedom of thought and freedom of speech to be subverted, slowly but surely by the #IslamophobiaIndustry. We are giving in to fear of being disliked, or even shunned, for exercising our God-given right, and dare I say obligation, to criticize all theories, philosophies and ideologies; including Islam, an ideology

---

[170] Bernadette Sauvaget and Willy Le Devin, "Le Qatar Verserait 35,000 Euros Chaque Mois à Tariq Ramadan," Libération, April 5, 2019, https://www.liberation.fr/france/2019/04/05/le-qatar-verserait-35-000-euros-chaque-mois-a-tariq-ramadan_1719428/.

that is diametrically opposed to the values espoused in Western Culture.

During the reign of Hitler and the Third Reich there was a certain *ignorantia affectata*, a willful blindness, toward the machinations of the Nazis. Today, there is an active attempt to disbelieve what is right before our eyes. A refusal to name evil for what it is.

From my book, *Back to the Ethic: Reclaiming Western Values: The Age of the Enlightenment (the Age of Reason)* in eighteenth-century Europe changed the way of thinking of the newly educated elite. For centuries, people had lived on the land at the mercy of nature; but Western Europe was modernizing. The culture was moving beyond the constraints of nature, from a pastoral culture to industrial. And with this shift came a change in the understanding of God. Just as we were no longer so strongly bound to the earth and the perfidies of nature, now, it was thought, we no longer needed an immutable and divine God.[171]

Those were heady times: progress was the new idol, and reason, science, and art were undermining religion. Rationalist philosophers pursued an "objective" reality of God. Hume, Descartes, Voltaire, Locke, Diderot, Mendelssohn, and Kant questioned the traditional beliefs and prejudices of the time, especially those of religion, and emphasized the primacy of reason and the strict scientific method. Voltaire proclaimed that the decline in religion would reduce hatred, fanaticism, and savagery. "With the decline in the strength of religious

---

[171] Karen Armstrong, in *A History of God: The 4000-Year Quest of Judaism, Christianity, and Islam* (New York, NY: Alfred A. Knopf, 1993), p. 295.

creeds . . . there would follow a concomitant decline in human hatreds, in the urge to destroy another man" because of his religious beliefs. Over time, people would become indifferent to religion and this indifference would lead to tolerance.[172]

But the indifference has led to the acquiescence to, and the appeasement of, the intolerable. A headlong dive into suicide by democracy.

Journalist Giulio Meotti wrote:

> "...radical Islam has been able to horrify the West into submission. We have paralysed ourselves. We censor the cartoons, the graphic photos of the terrorists' victims and even the faces and names of the jihadists.[173] The Islamic terrorists, on the other hand, are not publicity-seekers; they are soldiers ready to die and kill in the name of what they care about.

> "The Western establishment censors images of our enemies' crimes while giving prominence to our "guilt". The French government censored the "gruesome torture" of the victims at the Bataclan Theater, who were castrated, disemboweled and had their eyes gouged out by the Islamist terrorists.[174] It was a mistake: it was

---

[172] George Steiner, in *In Bluebeard's Castle: Some Notes towards the Redefinition of Culture* (New Haven, CT: Yale University Press, 1971), p. 47.

[173] Julian Borger, ed., "French Media to Stop Publishing Photos and Names of Terrorists," The Guardian (Guardian News and Media, July 27, 2016), https://www.theguardian.com/media/2016/jul/27/french-media-to-stop-publishing-photos-and-names-of-terrorists.

in the public interest to know exactly what enemy we are facing. [175]

I suggest that the rise of Islamophobia is the result of the banality of evil in the west. The slow drip, drip, drip of losing or giving up critical thinking in the name of groupthink that has been spread by government and media.

The "banality of evil" is a term created by the controversial Hannah Arendt following the Eichmann trial. She was trying to answer the question "Why did Nazis behave this way?" Were they inherently evil? She used the term "thoughtlessness," when describing Eichmann. He didn't think. He didn't have to think. He had been fed hate for Jews. His hate was condoned by most of German society. Perhaps they stopped thinking for themselves, as well. Perhaps they had been overcome with groupthink.[176]

---

[174] Victoria Finan, "Bataclan Victims Castrated by ISIS Killers and Had Their Eyes Gouged Out," Daily Mail Online (Associated Newspapers Ltd., July 16, 2016), https://www.dailymail.co.uk/news/article-3692359/French-government-suppressed-gruesome-torture-Bataclan-victims-official-inquiry-told-castrated-eyes-gouged-ISIS-killers.html

[175] Giulio Meotti, "Is Radical Islam Horrifying the West into Paralysis?" Gatestone Institute, July 5, 2017, https://www.gatestoneinstitute.org/10603/radical-islam-west.

[176] Michal Aharony, "Why Does Hannah Arendt's 'Banality of Evil' Still Anger Israelis?" Haaretz.com, the online English edition of Haaretz Newspaper in Israel (Haaretz Daily Newspaper Ltd., May 11, 2019), https://www.haaretz.com/israel-news/.premium.magazine-why-does-hannah-arendt-s-banality-of-evil-still-anger-israelis-1.7213979.

And that to me is the meaning of the banality of evil; Groupthink that prevents one from standing up and saying "No." Often it is fear of being ostracized, labeled, bullied. And that fear is understandable. Here is one example. Dániel Tóth-Nagy, a candidate for the Liberal Democrats in the UK, was suspended from the party for comments he made, such as "There is no such thing as Islamophobia."[177]

Arendt also wrote, "that there were no voices from the outside to arouse his (Eichmann) conscience." Had Germans been prepared for the hate? Were they afraid of reprisal? Of being ostracized? Had the government silenced their sense of right and wrong?

What is truly worrisome is that Germany is again allowing itself to be taken over; again, by a belief system that silences free speech.[178]

A new survey[179] on self-censorship in Germany, GERMANY! has shown that Germans censor their own speech to an astounding degree. Asked whether it is

---

[177] Jen Mills, "Lib Dem Candidate Suspended over Comments about Muslims," Metro.co.uk, April 18, 2019, https://metro.co.uk/2019/04/18/lib-dem-candidate-suspended-comments-muslims-9243430/.

[178] Judith Bergman, "Germany: A Shocking Degree of Self-Censorship," Gatestone Institute, July 4, 2019, https://www.gatestoneinstitute.org/14362/germany-self-censorship.

[179] Renate Kocher, "Allensbach-Umfrage: Immer Mehr Tabuthemen," Faz.net (Frankfurter Allgemeine Zeitung GmbH, May 22, 2019), https://www.faz.net/aktuell/politik/inland/allensbach-umfrage-ueber-meinungsfreiheit-und-kritische-themen-16200724.html.

"possible to express oneself freely in public" a mere 18% answered yes. By contrast, 59% of Germans said that in their circle of friends and acquaintances they express themselves freely.

"Nearly two-thirds of citizens are convinced that 'today one has to be very careful on which topics one expresses oneself', because there are many unwritten laws about what opinions are acceptable and admissible" according to the survey[180], conducted by Institut für Demoskopie Allensbach for the newspaper *Frankfurter Allgemeine Zeitung* (FAZ).

> *"The refugee issue is one of the most sensitive topics for the vast majority of respondents, followed by statements of opinion on Muslims and Islam,"* it stated. By contrast, *"The situation is different when it comes to topics such as climate protection, equal rights, unemployment or child rearing, about which one can express oneself frankly, according to the overwhelming majority"*

Fifty-seven percent of Germans say that it is getting on their nerves that they are "increasingly being told what to say and how to behave". Germans from the formerly Communist GDR complain more about this than the average German, as they have "fresh historical memories of regulation and constriction" according to the survey, which ends on the following note:

> *"It makes a big difference whether a society generally accepts and submits to meaningful*

---

[180] Renate Kocher, "Allensbach-Umfrage: Immer Mehr Tabuthemen," Faz.net (Frankfurter Allgemeine Zeitung GmbH, May 22, 2019)

norms, or whether citizens feel that they are increasingly being watched and evaluated... Many citizens miss being respected in the sense that they want their concerns and positions to be taken seriously, [and] that important developments are openly discussed..."

Gotz Aly in his book, "Why the Germans Why the Jews," wrote:

"At no point were Germans predestined to follow a path that ended in the abyss of inhumanity, but ultimately that was the path they went down."

I suggest, today, that we are facing another crisis and that we are falling once again into the banality of evil, of actions that come from ordinary people who take on groupthink. They do not question. This behaviour is often exhibited in totalitarian states, but we are witnessing this groupthink in the West. We have been indoctrinated with the idea that criticizing Islam as a religion or political ideology is hateful. It is Islamophobia. It is an irrational fear of Islam. Period. And citizens around the world have internalized a fear of being labeled Islamophobic.

Silencing free speech, freedom of thought does not happen in a vacuum. It doesn't spontaneously erupt. It is aided and abetted by great public relations with a dollop of guilt, and money. Lots of money.

CHAPTER 9: HOW DOES DAWAH PROMOTE ISLAM AND ISLAMIC RENEWAL?

"Conquest through dawah, that is what we hope for...We will conquer Europe, we will conquer America, not through the sword but through dawah."

~ Youssef Qaradawi, Egyptian Qatar-based intellectual and spiritual leader of the

Muslim Brotherhood[181]

The #IslamophobiaIndustry has but one goal: promoting the Caliphate. Make no mistake: this is a clash of cultures; two opposing cultures which cannot live in the same space. This is accomplished by silencing criticism of Islam; the religion and ideology, whether it comes from people, like Tommy Robinson,[182] Robert Spencer, Pamela Gellar, or Lauren Southern,[183] or media outlets

---

[181] Editors, "Yusuf Al-Qaradawi [- Profile]," Counter Extremism Project, 2021, https://www.counterextremism.com/extremists/yusuf-al-qaradawi.

[182] "Tommy Robinson's Facebook, Instagram Pages Removed FOR 'Organised Hate'," The Irish Times, February 26, 2019, https://www.irishtimes.com/news/world/uk/tommy-robinson-s-facebook-instagram-pages-removed-for-organised-hate-1.3807426.

[183] Diane Weber Bederman, "I Stand by Canadian Lauren Southern Because SILENCE IS COLLUSION," The Bederman Blog (Diane Weber Bederman, March 23, 2018), https://dianebederman.com/i-stand-by-canadian-lauren-

and governments; to promoting Islam as a way of life through dawah -- Islamic renewal and outreach.

Youssef Qaradawi, intellectual and spiritual leader of the Muslim Brotherhood, said victory will come by:

> *"Conquest through dawah, that is what we hope for...We will conquer Europe, we will conquer America, not through the sword but through dawah."*[184]

The Muslim Brotherhood[185] would promote *dawah* in the West through Islamic groups. This was shared in a 1995 speech to an Islamic conference in Ohio, USA and can be traced to Mohamed Akram's vision. He wrote about the need for Islamic centres in towns and cities. This would become "The House of Dawa."

> *"...the 'center's' role should be the same as the 'mosque's role during the time of God's prophet, God's prayers and peace be upon him, when he marched to "settle' the Dawa' in its first generation in Medina (Mohammed ethnically cleansed two Jewish tribes in Medina and*

---

southern-because-silence-is-collusion/.

[184] John Mintz and Douglas Farah, "In Search of Friends Among The Foes," The Washington Post (The Washington Post Company, September 11, 2004), http://www.washingtonpost.com/wp-dyn/articles/A12823-2004Sep10.html.

[185] "Muslim Brotherhood (MB)," DiscoverTheNetwork.org - A Guide to the Political Left (Internet Archive Wayback Machine, April 23, 2020), https://web.archive.org/web/20200423074744/http://www.discoverthenetworks.com/groupProfile.asp?grpid=6386.

murdered the third). From the mosque he drew the Islamic life and provided to the world the most magnificent and fabulous civilization humanity knew.

"This mandates that, eventually, the region, the branch and the Usra turn into 'operations rooms' for planning, direction, monitoring and leadership for the Islamic center in order to be a role model to follow."

ICNA (Islamic Circle of North America) Canada is an Islamic nation-wide organization striving "to build an Exemplary Canadian Muslim Community" by "total submission to Him [Allah] and through the propagation of true and universal message of Islam."[186]

They promote "the propagation of true and universal message of Islam is only possible in Canada when whole Canadian Muslim Community transformed into a Dawah community by practicing and propagating the true Islamic Way of Life. With the vision of building an exemplary Canadian Muslim community it is very important to spread the word of Islam..."

ICNA (Islamic Circle of North America) Canada shares this on their on-line syllabus:

"[Hadith] 1820. Abu Hurairah (May Allah be pleased with him) said: The Messenger of Allah (PBUH) said, "The Last Hour will not come until the Muslims fight against the Jews, until a Jew will hide himself behind a stone or a tree, and the stone or the tree will say: `O Muslim, there is

---

[186] Editors, "About ICNA," icnacanada.net (Islamic Circle of North America, 2020), https://icnacanada.net/about-2/.

a Jew behind me. Come and kill him,' but Al-Gharqad tree will not say so, for it is the tree of the Jews." [Al-Bukhari and Muslim]."

"Commentary: Gharqad is a thorny plant which is well-known in the area of Palestine. Allah can bestow the power of speech to whatever thing He likes. When Allah wills, He will give mastery to the Muslims. He will help them even by means of plants and stones which will assist the Muslims against the Jews by informing them about the whereabouts of the Jews."

"The Jews have predominance over the Muslims in spite of the fact that they are a minority. But according to this true narration, the situation will definitely change before the Day of Resurrection, and the Muslims will dominate the Jews. Allah is the Master and Rubb of everything."

What better way to spread the word than through Islamic centres.

I have witnessed the rise of Islamic centres. Many, of course, in major cities, but I came to fully understand the stealth of this growth when I discovered an Islamic center in the heart of a small town in rural Ontario whose roots go back to Ireland. The town is small but on the few streets in the main core there were four or five churches. Now one church is gone and the Islamic Centre is there. There are no Muslims in the area. Neither are there many Jews or people of colour. It was small town Christian Ontario.

Islam has had a remarkable ability to spread its value system through propaganda.

Propaganda: information, especially of a biased or misleading nature, used to promote or publicize a particular political cause or point of view.

"At its most basic, propaganda is biased or misleading information circulated through some form of mass media with the intent of promoting a political agenda or viewpoint. Propaganda is deliberately not objective and is usually part of a larger psychological campaign to influence people toward a specific opinion. It may include outright lies or more subtle misinformation and censorship."[187]

Propaganda is the foundation upon which the #IslamophobiaIndustry sits. The marketing of the term Islamophobia has been so successful that governments, media outlets, institutions of education, from kindergarten to universities, have become accomplices in silencing criticism of Islam: as a religion and a political system. At present, no other religion or political system, from communism to fascism has been treated with similar kid gloves.

---

[187] Guy Bergstrom, "Understanding the Mechanisms of Propaganda," The Balance Small Business (Dotdash publishing family, August 29, 2019), https://www.thebalancesmb.com/what-is-propaganda-and-how-does-it-work-2295248.

CHAPTER 10: IS THERE AN ISLAMIC TROJAN HORSE INFECTING EDUCATION?

"Whoever learns something in the name of Allah, seeking that which is with Him, he will win. And whoever learns something for other than Allah, he will not reach the goal, nor will his acquired knowledge bring him closer to Allah."

~ Hasan Al-Basri Rahimahullah

There is the new "tolerance" being taught in our edifices of higher learning. It is acceptable to belittle and demean Christianity and Judaism but not a negative word about Islam. Shortly after the beheading May 22, 2013 of a British soldier in London a debate took place at Oxford Union. The statement for debate:

"This house believes that Islam is a religion of peace."

And the vote was: Yes, 286; No, 168. [188]

Democracy thrives where education promotes the ideals of western culture. In the name of tolerance, we have opened our doors to others whose cultural norms are antithetical to Western values. Teaching children about different cultures, different forms of government, and different religions is not the same as having curriculum

---

[188] Scott Johnson, "Is Islam a Religion of Peace?," Power Line (Power Line, August 25, 2013), https://www.powerlineblog.com/archives/2013/08/is-islam-a-religion-of-peace.php.

content determined by foreign governments proselytizing our students. In the West, questions are being raised about the influence of China's values in our school systems. I wrote about that in an earlier chapter. Yet, we seem hesitant to investigate, let alone criticize, the influence of Muslim countries on our education system. Let's take a look at the influence Islam is having on our children's education.

Muslim organizations, as well as countries, have been funding universities around the world in order to promote Islam in the same way that China has promoted their ideology through institutes of learning in the West.[189]

The director of the University of Oxford's Research Center for Islamic Legislation and Ethics (CILE)[190] (CILE) is Tariq Ramadan, grandson of Muslim Brotherhood founder, Hassan al-Banna.

- Since 2012, Pakistan has contributed $4,895,309 to five separate American universities.

- Turkey has contributed $37,724,394 to 15 separate American universities.

- The Iraqi government has donated $44,006,913 to four universities in America since 2012.

---

[189] Ryan Mauro and Alex Van Ness, "Clarion Exclusive Report: Foreign Influence Ops on US Universities [Incl. John Esposito]," Campus Watch (Clarion Project, September 6, 2019), https://www.meforum.org/campus-watch/59321/clarion-exclusive-report-foreign-influence-ops-on.
[190] "The Research Center for Islamic Legislation and Ethics (CILE)," CSIA-Oxford.org (University of Oxford, 2015), https://www.csia-oxford.org/research-center-islamic-legislation-and-ethics-cile.html.

- Since 2012, Kuwait has contributed to 17 separate American universities totaling $65,782,667.

- Since 2017, the Palestinian Authority has provided two monetary gifts to Harvard University totaling $1,050,000.

- Since 2012, the UAE has given 32 American Universities a total of $230,945,101.

The International Institute of Islamic Thought (IITT)[191] is a privately held non-profit organization. It was founded in 1981 in Pennsylvania, and is headquartered in Herndon, Virginia, in the suburbs of Washington, DC.

"The International Institute of Islamic Thought (IIIT) is a center of excellence in educational research and Islamic thought whose main interest is on carrying out evidence-based research in advancing education in Muslim Societies and the dissemination of this research through publication and translation, teaching, policy recommendations, and strategic engagements.

IIIT's 2012 documentary says it stands for "reviving the Islamic legacy and addressing the crisis of the Muslim Ummah [worldwide Muslim community]." Further, it wants to "define Islamic values in ways easily understood and integrated into American political values and global democratic values."[192]

---

[191] "International Institute of Islamic Thought (IITT)," iiit.org (International Institute of Islamic Thought (IITT), 2018), https://iiit.org/en/home/.
[192] "International Institute of Islamic Thought (IIIT)," Clarion Project, June 29, 2020, https://clarionproject.org/international-institute-islamic-thought/.

Advancing education in Muslim societies? In America? In the West?

Think about the information that young people are receiving from the Institute. The ideology it spreads. An ideology based on an ethic; Sharia Law that is diametrically opposed to western values. We know this to be true because of information shared widely by Islamic organizations in the West.

ICNA (Islamic Circle of North America) Canada[193] shares the book *Riyad-us-Saliheen*[194] with its members, followers and supporters where it says:

> *"The political system of Islam is totally incompatible with western democracy.*[195] *The concept of government party and the opposition is alien to Islam. All belong to one Ummah with only one goal and pursue the same aims and objects of Islamic guidelines."*

How did we get to a place where The International Institute of Islamic Thought (IITT) has agreements with many universities?[196]

---

[193] Editors, "Islamic Circle of North America (ICNA) Canada," ICNACanada.net, 2020, https://icnacanada.net/.

[194] "Riyad-Us-Saliheen (2 Vol. Set)" (Dar-us-Salam Publications, 2020), https://dar-us-salam.com/english/hadith-sunnah/h04-riyad-us-saliheen-2-vol-set.html.

[195] Editors, "Canadian Islamic Organization REFUTES Trudeau's Claim That Islam Is Compatible with Democracy," Centre for Investigative Research Canada, June 22, 2018, https://circanada.com/2018/06/21/canadian-islamic-organization-refutes-trudeaus-claim-that-islam-is-compatible-with-democracy/.

[196] Ryan Mauro and Alex Van Ness, "Clarion Exclusive Report: Foreign Influence Ops on US Universities [Incl. John Esposito],"

George Mason University, just outside Fairfax, Virginia, signed an agreement at IIIT headquarters on September 18, 2008. The IIIT representative was its Vice President, Jamal Barzinji. A 1988 FBI file[197] states that Barzinji was "characterized as" a Muslim Brotherhood leader. In 2003, his home was raided because, in the words of U.S. Customs Service Special Agent David Kane, Barzinji "is not only closely associated with Palestinian Islamic Jihad (PIJ) but also with Hamas."[198] In 2011, it was reported[199] that the Justice Department stopped a planned indictment of Barzinji.

A few months later, George Mason University announced that IIIT had donated $1.5 million to establish an endowed Chair in Islamic Studies at its College of Humanities and Social Sciences.[200] The University's

---

Campus Watch (Clarion Project, September 6, 2019)

[197] "Second Annual ISNA Conference on Economic Development Sponsored by the Islamic Society of North America (ISNA), Kansas City, Missouri, May 28-30, 1988." Washington: Investigative Project on Terrorism (IPT), 1988. Extract from declassified FBI investigative records on the North American Islamic Trust (NAIT).

[198] Mintz, Jason. "USA v. SAFA Group EDVA 02-MG-114 20 March Main Affidavit REDACTED Released Oct 31 2017." Washington: Investigative Project on Terrorism (IPT), October 2003.

[199] Patrick Poole, "(PJM Exclusive) Holder's DOJ Scuttled More Terror-Related Prosecutions," pjmedia.com (PJ Media, April 28, 2011), https://pjmedia.com/blog/patrick-poole/2011/04/28/pjm-exclusive-holders-doj-scuttled-more-terror-related-prosecutions-n11527.

[200] James Greif, "George Mason University Receives $1.5 Million Gift from IIIT for an Endowed Chair in Islamic Studies," Media and Public Relations (George Mason University, November 3, 2008),

2008 press release boasts that it has been named as the #1 university in the nation to watch by *U.S. News and World Report.*

Nazareth College's Center for Interfaith Studies and Dialogue, located in Rochester NY, signed a "Memorandum of Understanding" with IIIT[201] in January 2006. On December 7, 2011, IIIT endowed an academic Chair in Interfaith Studies and Dialogue.[202] I have attended many interfaith groups as a chaplain. I learned one very important thing. There is no interfaith unless all those sitting at the table respect the other. If one of the participants believes that their religion is superior to others, and teaches that, how does one promote interfaith?

The Dean of the College of Arts and Sciences, of Shenandoah University, in Winchester, Virginia, Dr. Calvin Allen Jr., signed a "Memorandum of

---

https://web.archive.org/web/20081224224717/http://eagle.g mu.edu/newsroom/722/.

[201] Silva, Dennis, and Iqbal J. Unus. "MOU between Center for Interfaith Studies and Dialogue (CISD) at Nazareth College, Rochester NY and The Fairfax Institute (TFI) at International Institute of Islamic Thought (IIIT) Herndon VA." Agreements. International Institute of Islamic Thought (IIIT), January 13, 2006.
https://web.archive.org/web/20080414181652/http://www.iii t.org/Portals/0/agreements/CISD.pdf.

[202] "IIIT Chair Inaugurated at Nazareth College," IIIT chair inaugurated at Nazareth College > IIIT > NEWS (International Institute of Islamic Thought (IIIT), January 10, 2012),
https://web.archive.org/web/20120210070538/http://iiit.org/ NewsEvents/News/tabid/62/articleType/ArticleView/articleId/ 244/IIIT-Chair-Inaugurated-at-Nazareth-College.aspx.

Agreement" with IIIT, again represented by Jamal Barzinji.[203] The website states, "IIIT's instructional division, The Fairfax Institute, will designate an instructor to co-teach with Dr. Allen a course on Islamic civilization." Dr. Calvin Allen spoke at a IIIT fundraiser on August 26, 2011.[204]

On March 17, 2013, Hartford Seminary, the Connecticut theological college, announced that it had received the necessary funding for an endowed chair in Islamic Chaplaincy.[205] The largest donor was IIIT who had given the college $1 million.

The President of Hartford Seminary, Professor Heidi Hadsell, said it has "established a productive, creative and effective relationship" with IIIT. On July 25, 2012, Hadsell spoke at an IIIT fundraiser.[206] She talked about

---

[203] "IIIT Enters into Agreement with Shenandoah University," Shenandoah University (International Institute of Islamic Thought (IIIT), April 14, 2008), https://web.archive.org/web/20080414181150/http://iiit.org/AboutUs/Agreements/Shenandoah/tabid/111/Default.aspx.

[204] "IIIT Hosts Friends of IIIT Iftar/Dinner," IIIT.org (International Institute of Islamic Thought (IIIT), August 26, 2011), https://web.archive.org/web/20111015143123/http://www.iiit.org/NewsEvents/News/tabid/62/articleType/ArticleView/articleId/228/IIIT-Hosts-Friends-of-IIIT-IftarDinner.aspx.

[205] Hartford Seminary Offers First Program to Educate Muslim Community Leaders. Hartford Seminary, October 11, 2011. Hartford Seminary. https://web.archive.org/web/20111217082144/http://www.hartsem.edu/pages/news-events/2011-Press-Release-Imam-Community-Program.aspx.

[206] "Prof Heidi Hadsell Delivers Al Faruqi Memorial Lecture at Friends of IIIT Iftar," Prof Heidi Hadsell Delivers Al Faruqi

"the continued support that the seminary receives from IIIT, particularly in the area of imam training and education, and the study of Christian-Muslim relations in general."

The press release about the endowed chair says the Islamic Chaplaincy program began in 2003 "to prepare Muslims for chaplaincy positions in hospitals, prisons, universities and the military. It remains the only such accredited program in the United States, and graduates have been named to positions in many such institutions across the United States, most notably at Yale University, Williams College, and Princeton University."

What do these Chaplains teach? Are they well-versed on the faiths of others? Do they respect the faiths of others? They pray the Al Fatiha every day. I share this prayer with you in a later chapter.

The Al-Aqsa Islamic Society has been involved in many interfaith activities. It has hosted Philadelphia's Interfaith Peacewalk since 2003, and has a full-time private Islamic school called Al-Aqsa Islamic Academy.

Imam Abdelmohsen Abouhatab, who is of Egyptian origin, delivered several antisemitic sermons at the Al-Aqsa Islamic Society in Philadelphia, PA, reports the Middle East Media Research Institute (MEMRI).

He said the Jews are the vilest people[207] in terms of their nature and moral values and that the "nefarious" Jewish

Memorial Lecture at Friends of IIIT Iftar (International Institute of Islamic Thought (IIIT), August 8, 2012), https://web.archive.org/web/20120926205213/http://iiit.org/NewsEvents/News/tabid/62/articleType/ArticleView/articleId/268/Default.aspx.

media causes people to see Muslims as "oppressive and predatory lions." He said that the "enemies of Allah" are ordering heads of state to come to the Knesset, where they sit and "plot against their people, according to what the others want."

The result of this infiltration of Islam into our universities has led to hateful teachings, particular against the Jews and Israel, in America. Rep. Lee Zeldin (R-N.Y.) called for the firing of City University of New York (CUNY) of Professional Studies professor Mohammad Abbasi, after a video of him preaching to a congregation in New Jersey showed him making anti-Semitic statements.[208]

"With the help of Allah, [the Muslims] will erase this filth called Israel," Abbasi concluded during his address to the Islamic Center of Union City, based on a video posted on YouTube on June 25. Abbasi, an imam, claimed that the Quran predicted that Jews will have an advantage over Muslims in the future, and that Jews bring corruption, mischief and tumult throughout the world according to the Quran.

Oberlin professor "Professor of Peace," Mohammad Jafar Mahallati, Iranian regime's ambassador to the UN in 1988, stated: "The establishment of the Zionist entity

---

[207] Mordechai Sones, "Philadelphia Imam: 'The Jews Are the Vilest People'," Israel National News (Arutz Sheva, March 7, 2019), https://www.israelnationalnews.com/News/News.aspx/26005 4.

[208] Dean Blake, "Zeldin Calls for Firing of City University of New York Professor after Anti-Semitic Sermon," JNS.org (Jewish News Syndicate, July 30, 2021), https://www.jns.org/zeldin-calls-for-firing-of-city-university-of-new-york-professor-after-anti-semitic-sermon.

was itself in violation of provisions of the United Nations Charter.[209] Mahallati frequently designated the entire state of Israel as Palestinian territory.

> *"Palestine is an Islamic territory, an Islamic heritage, and it remains an Islamic point of identity. The land of Palestine is the platform of the Ascension of the Prophet Mohammad; its significance is that it contains the first kiblah direction–towards which Muslims prayed. Its occupation by Zionist usurpers is a transgression against all Muslims of the world and its liberation is therefore a great religious obligation and commitment."*

Canada is not immune to the Islamic influence. In December 2010, Huron University College, London, Ontario, began a "cooperative venture" with IIIT to add an Islamic Studies program to its college.[210] It states, "IIIT has agreed to match funds raised by the Muslim Association of Canada and the London Muslim Mosque, both based in London, Ontario, Canada."

---

[209] Benjamin Weinthal, "Oberlin College's 'Professor of Peace' Urged Elimination of Jewish State," JPost.com (The Jerusalem Post, February 27, 2021), https://www.jpost.com/diaspora/antisemitism/oberlin-colleges-professor-of-peace-urged-elimination-of-jewish-state-660298.

[210] "Western Canadian University Introduces Islamic Studies," IIIT News (International Institute of Islamic Thought (IIIT), December 20, 2010), https://web.archive.org/web/20140530025135/http://iiit.org/NewsEvents/News/tabid/62/ArticleType/ArticleView/ArticleID/202/PageID/192/Default.aspx.

Ingrid Mattson, former ISNA (Islamic Society of North America) President and a member of IIIT's Advisory Council, became the London and Windsor Community Chair in Islamic Studies[211] on July 1, 2012. According to the press release, Huron University College is affiliated with the University of Western Ontario and is an affiliate member of the Toronto School of Theology.

The Saudis have been spending *billions* of dollars funding Middle East Centers at American universities, hundreds of madrassas for children in the country, and as many as 80 percent of all mosques[212] in the United States.

Since 1979, Saudi Arabia via its vast oil wealth enabled by the immense rise in oil prices, has financed the building of thousands of mosques, Islamic schools (madrassas), as well as other Islamic centers and institutions that espouse an ultraconservative brand of Islam, often termed "extremist" or "radical," that follows the Wahhabi or Salafi doctrines of Islam. A *New York Times* article calculated the Saudi investment from 1964 to 2004 in non-Muslim-majority countries alone at an astonishing 1,359 mosques, 210 Islamic centers, 202 colleges, and 2,000 schools.

---

[211] "IIIT Advisory Council Member Dr. Ingrid Mattson Joins Huron University College," IIIT News (International Institute of Islamic Thought (IIIT), June 28, 2012), https://web.archive.org/web/20140715220711/http://iiit.org/NewsEvents/News/tabid/62/articleType/ArticleView/articleId/262/Default.aspx.

[212] Ralph Peters, "How Saudi Arabia Dangerously Undermines the United States," New York Post (NYP Holdings, Inc., April 16, 2016), https://nypost.com/2016/04/16/how-saudi-arabia-undermines-the-united-states/.

This Saudi campaign to influence American universities seems to date back to a 1976 million-dollar grant to the University of Southern California. By 1979, the Saudis were giving Duke University $200,000 for a program in Islamic and Arabian Development studies.

Italian journalist, Giulio Meotti wrote: "In 1979, Saudi Aramco World magazine published a list of Middle Eastern gifts, including $200,000 from the Saudis to Duke University for a program in Islamic and Arabian development studies; $750,000 from the Libyan government for a chair of Arab culture at Georgetown University; and $250,000 from the United Arab Emirates for a visiting professorship of Arab history, also at Georgetown.

Until that time, Riyadh spent one hundred billion dollars to spread Wahhabism, the most anti-Semitic and extremist version of Islam.

Leading the list of beneficiaries is Harvard University, with about 30 million dollars. The jewel of the Ivy League received 20 million in 2005 alone.

"20 million dollars were donated to the Middle East Studies Center at the University of Arkansas; 5 million dollars to the Center for Middle East Studies at Berkeley, in California; 11 million to Cornell University in Ithaca, New York and a half million dollars to Texas University (the seventh university, in order of size, in the United States); 1 million to Princeton; 5 million dollars to Rutgers University.

A 2018 report[213] found that "elite U.S. universities took more than half a billion dollars" from Saudi Arabia in

---

[213] Prof. Arnon Gutfeld, "The Saudi Specter over the American

gifts and donations between 2011 and 2017; as far back as 2005, Georgetown and Harvard each received $20 million "to support Islamic studies on their respective campuses."

A Department of Education report released on October 20, 2020 stated that more than one-third of the nearly $20 billion in foreign donations and contracts made to American universities between just 2014 and 2020 were never disclosed as required by federal law, according to "Institutional Compliance with Section 117 of the Higher Education Act of 1965."[214]

Among those "gifts" were more than $3 billion from the Muslim Brotherhood's number one state backer, Qatar; more than $1.1 billion from the chief disseminator of "radical" Islamic ideology, Saudi Arabia; and nearly $1.5 billion from China.[215]

The Arab donations are spreading in Europe as well. In April, a scandal involved St. Andrews University, the third most important in the British academy and a cradle of royal nobility. Hundreds of thousands of pounds were discovered to have been sent from Damascus to fund a center for "Syrian studies" there.

Education System," Jerusalem Center for Public Affairs, May 23, 2019, https://jcpa.org/article/saudi-specter-over-american-education-system/.

[214] "Institutional Compliance with Section 117 of the Higher Education Act of 1965." Washington: United States Department of Education Office of the General Counsel, October 27, 2020.

[215] Raymond Ibrahim, "Bribed: Subverting American Universities," Gatestone Institute, November 25, 2020, https://www.gatestoneinstitute.org/16786/subverting-american-universities.

In March, there was the scandal involving the London School of Economics, one of the best-known universities in the world, that conferred a doctorate to Saif al Islam Gaddafi, the son of the Libyan dictator. Shortly after receiving his doctorate, Saif al Islam "dropped" a donation to the university of a half million pounds, donated by the Gaddafi Foundation named after his father.

Oxford has a research center funded by the Iranian regime, while at Cambridge the funds come from Saudi Arabia, Oman and Iran.

Scholarships and degree programs are the favorite and easiest weapons of the Islamist regimes to influence the Western academies and their freedoms. Eight universities, including Oxford and Cambridge, have accepted more than 233.5 million pounds sterling from Saudi and Muslim sources since 1995. The total sum, revealed by Anthony Glees, the director of Brunel University's Centre for Intelligence and Security Studies, amounts to the largest source of external funding to UK universities.

Universities that have accepted donations from Saudi royals and other Arab sources include Oxford, Cambridge, Durham, University College London, the London School of Economics, Exeter, Dundee and City.

The consequences of the funding have been very clear: "70 per cent of political science lectures at the Middle Eastern Centre at St Antony's College, Oxford, were "implacably hostile" to the West and Israel.

At Georgetown, the money was funneled toward its Center for Muslim-Christian Understanding, which was quickly renamed the Prince Alwaleed bin Talal Center for

Muslim-Christian Understanding. The center, part of the Edmund A. Walsh School of Foreign Service, trains many of America's diplomats and it spreads anti-Semitic and anti-western ideas.

There are 17 federally funded centers on American college campuses devoted solely to Middle Eastern studies centers and most of them support pro-Islamist ideas. The Soviet Union during the Cold War invested much less for its propaganda operations in the West.

But there is another big difference. The Western intelligentsia fought the Communist efforts to subvert the West. Their post-modern heirs are offering appeasement to the Islamist agenda. The glorious Western academy is becoming a madrassa.

In 2019, the U.S Department of Education threatened to pull funding from a Middle East studies course jointly run by Duke University and the University of North Carolina at Chapel Hill because of its pro-Islam bias and that it did not present enough "positive" imagery of Judaism and Christianity in the region.

The Education Department warned the Duke-UNC Consortium for Middle East Studies that it's about to lose federal grant money if the program isn't revised to meet department standards.[216,217] Robert King, the

---

[216] Erica L. Green, "U.S. Orders Duke and U.N.C. to Recast Tone in Mideast Studies," The New York Times (The New York Times Company, September 19, 2019), https://www.nytimes.com/2019/09/19/us/politics/anti-israel-bias-higher-education.html.
[217] World Israel News Staff, "Trump Administration Targets Duke, UNC-Chapel Hill for Biased, Pro-Islamic Middle East Studies Program," worldisraelnews.com (World Israel News

assistant secretary for post-secondary education, mapped out the violations that the program was committing in a letter sent to university officials at the end of August.

"There is a considerable emphasis placed on understanding the positive aspects of Islam," the letter states. While very few courses addressed "the historic discrimination faced by, and current circumstances of, religious minorities in the Middle East, including Christians, Jews, Baha'is, Yazidis, Kurds, Druze and others."

In 2005, a member of the Saudi royal family, Prince Alwaleed bin Talal Alsaud, donated $40 million — $20 million to Harvard and another $20 million to Georgetown University — to advance "Islamic studies," Saudi-style.[218] The money funded four new senior staff professorships and an endowed chair at Harvard, and three new faculty chairs and certain targeted scholarships at Georgetown.

The October 2020 US Department of Education Office of General Counsel reported on Georgetown University's Prince Alwaleed Bin Talal Center for Muslim-Christian Understanding:[219]

(WIN), September 22, 2019), https://worldisraelnews.com/trump-administration-targets-duke-unc-chapel-hill-for-biased-pro-islamic-middle-east-studies-program/.

[218] Gitika Ahuja, "Saudi Prince Donates $40 Million to Harvard, Georgetown Universities," ABC news (ABC News Network, December 13, 2005), https://abcnews.go.com/International/story?id=1402008.

[219] "Institutional Compliance with Section 117 of the Higher Education Act of 1965." Washington: United States

"The Center also received criticism for deceptively labeling itself as pluralistic; according to critics, the 'Christian' studies portion of the Center was a 'misnomer' as there was no Christian representation. Additional worries spawned from Saudi Arabian infiltration of an institution commonly known to siphon graduates into government employment. Such concerns were salient because the Saudi Arabians had communicated that their money would 'follow' the Center's first Director. This strategy of funding a particular director [John Esposito] is concerning, as it would allow a foreign government unduly to guide the Center's content.

"This donation empowered the Saudi Arabian government to advance a particular narrative about Islamic society to the West via a legitimate Western institution like Georgetown University...

"The Saudi Arabian government had successfully impacted American foreign policy thinking through money alone. The Saudi Arabian government invested significantly into the dissemination of its favored ideological views at Georgetown University and several other U.S. academic institutions."

One main source of Saudi funding goes directly to U.S. universities and colleges through Middle Eastern Studies (MES) programs and centers.[220,221] A second major

---

Department of Education Office of the General Counsel, October 27, 2020.

[220] Stanley Kurtz, "Following the Foreign Money," National

source of funding is financial assistance to organizations associated with universities such as student organizations and those that they have helped establish. There is concern that the Saudis are purposefully attempting to influence the opinions and social impressions of future American policymakers by financing MES programs and centers located at what many consider "feeder-schools" to U.S. government agencies such as the State Department. Using Sarah Stern's editorial efforts in the release of *Saudi Arabia and the Global Terrorist Network* in 2011, records from the U.S. Department of Education are used to show the extent of Saudi gifts; they totaled a staggering $329 million in funding from 1995 to 2008. These donations have become critical to the operations of these universities and in many cases have rejuvenated their MES programs.

The Middle East Studies center at the University of Arkansas was given $20 million. The University of California at Berkeley was given $5 million for its Middle East Studies Center. Cornell was given $11 million. Texas got half a million. Rutgers University of New Jersey got $5 million, and Princeton got $1 million.

The influx of Saudi millions into American universities has generated the expected surge in Saudi

---

Review, March 26, 2008, https://www.nationalreview.com/2008/03/following-foreign-money-stanley-kurtz/.

[221] Stanley Kurtz, "All Foreign Gifts Report: U.S. Department of Education," nationalreview.com (The National Review, March 31, 2008), https://web.archive.org/web/20080501093827/http://www.nationalreview.com:80/kurtz/allforeigngiftsreport.html.

students now enrolled at such American schools. In 2005, there were 3,000 Saudi students in American universities. That number had grown to nearly 60,000 by 2014-15.[222] Several high-caliber American universities like University of Texas at Austin, Stanford, and UC Berkeley reciprocated in recent years by establishing satellite schools in Saudi Arabia.[223]

The significant rise of Saudi students in the United States led to new organizations such as the Muslim Student Association (MSA) in college campuses across the country. Per capita there are more than 10 times as many Saudi students than those from China enrolled in U.S. universities.

MSA was one of the first Saudi-funded Islamic organizations in North America that declared its main goal to be furthering the global "Islamic Movement." Larry Poston, in his book *Islamic Da'wah in the West*, used MSA's own publications in 1975 to illustrate that their main purpose was to spread Islam to non-Muslims in North America and that the best place to do so was the university campuses, which the MSA deemed the "most curious, the most inquisitive and the most open-minded audience for Islam."

MSA and its students helped with the development of several other organizations such as the Islamic Society of

---

[222] Denis MacEoin, "Foreign Muslim Funding of Western Universities," Middle East Forum (Gatestone Institute, August 19, 2016), https://www.meforum.org/6205/foreign-muslim-funding-western-universities.
[223] Tamar Lewin, "American Universities Create Partnerships in Saudi Arabia," The Tech (Massachusetts Institute of Technology, March 7, 2008), https://thetech.com/2008/03/07/saudi-v128-n10.

North America (ISNA), the North American Islamic Trust (NAIT), founded by University of Indiana MSA and later designated as an unindicted co-conspirator in the Holy Land Foundation trial, as money was transferred to Hamas through its accounts, is a financing arm that holds title to hundreds of U.S. mosques and manages bank accounts for Muslim groups using Islamic principles, Saudi donations, combined with other Gulf-state oil contributions to U.S. universities in the millions, had arguably shifted the campus demographics into a pro-Palestinian, anti-Israeli disposition across many American universities.[224] Perhaps this shift and its influence were best represented by the rapid escalation in campus anti-Israeli events, such as Israel Apartheid Week, along with an increase of pro-Palestinian events throughout U.S. campuses.

These university gifts and contracts have been sent by multiple Qatari entities either owned by the government or closely connected to the Qatar royal family. They include, for example, RasGas Company Limited; Qatar Petroleum; Qatar National Research Fund (QNRF) which is member of the Qatar Foundation.

The regime-controlled Qatar Foundation, itself, hands tens of millions of dollars to schools, colleges and other educational institutions across Europe and North America. Indeed, Qatar is now the largest foreign donor to American universities. Since 2012, the Department of Education (DOE) reports that Qatar has given close to

[224] John Mintz and Douglas Farah, "In Search of Friends Among The Foes," The Washington Post (The Washington Post Company, September 11, 2004), http://www.washingtonpost.com/wp-dyn/articles/A12823-2004Sep10.html.

$1.5 billion ($1,478,676,069 to be exact) to U.S. universities in the form of monetary gifts and contracts.[225] Its funds pay for the teaching of Arabic and lessons on Middle Eastern culture and their ideological bent is front and center as in the lesson plan in American schools titled. "Express Your Loyalty to Qatar."[226]

The Qatari regime already has been financing an extensive influence operation in Europe, funding think tanks, activist organizations, football clubs, news agencies, mosques, and now Italian schools, colleges and education programs. The influence operation has also engaged in political activities that benefit Qatar while inculcating virulent anti-Semitism that continues to spread in Italian society.[227]

About 600 thousand euros, exactly 196.165 euros per year for three years, is the sum that the Qatar government will pay to Italy according to a cooperation agreement on education, universities and scientific research. The agreement provides for the promotion of exchanges and visits of experts in all fields of education, as well as student delegations and sports school groups; encourages the holding of educational, scientific and

---

[225] "Qatar Has given $1.5 Billion to U.S. Universities in the Form of Monetary Gifts and Contracts," Qatarileaks.com, June 13, 2019, https://qatarileaks.com/en/leak/qatar-has-given-15-billion-to-us-universities-in-the-form-of-monetary-gifts-and-contracts.

[226] Daniel Pipes, "Examining Qatar's Influence," DanielPipes.org, January 29, 2019, http://www.danielpipes.org/18699/qatar-influence.

[227] Staff Writer, "Italy Sold Its Education System to Qatar," TheArabPosts.com (The Arab Posts, May 28, 2020), https://thearabposts.com/italy-sold-its-education-system-to-qatar/.

technical exhibitions at local schools and the exchange of documents and curricula drawn up by the respective school authorities. It also provides that the Parties will encourage participation in joint training courses for teachers, which will have to be agreed with the appropriate exchanges of information. The interference of Qatar in the Italian school system will have an open field from the early years of childhood education, from kindergarten to technical and professional training.

Professors whose salaries, fellowships, or think tanks are funded in part by Qatar are already hesitant to criticize the Muslim Brothers. Many say a sort of taboo has developed against needlessly antagonizing the political Islam by criticizing policy positions that the Italian government considers red lines, for fear of upsetting the generous donor.

Soeren Kern reports that in recent years, Algeria, Kuwait, Libya, Morocco, Saudi Arabia, Turkey, Qatar and the United Arab Emirates, among others, have distributed hundreds of millions of euros to finance the spread of Islam in Europe through the mosques.

Professor Abdul Hadi Palazzi of Rome's University of Vellectri stated, "Over 80 percent of European mosques are controlled by extremists who belong to radical pseudo-Islamic movements that have absorbed anti-Semitic motifs." to denounce and actively discourage the spread of anti-Semitism."[228]

---

[228] Andrew Harrod, "Abe Foxman Discovers Islamic Anti-Semitism," Jihad Watch, March 9, 2021, https://www.jihadwatch.org/2021/03/abe-foxman-discovers-islamic-anti-semitism.

In April 2016, Turkey's PM, Recep Tayyip Erdoğan, inaugurated one of the largest mosques in the United States. Funded by the Turkish government, the Diyanet Center of America (DCA) is a massive complex that sits on nearly 17 acres in Lanham, Maryland; not far from Washington D.C.[229] Construction began in 2012, and the center was opened in 2016. The DCA is the head of 28 other Diyanet branches across the United States. The DCA is among the wealthiest Islamic organizations across America, with its registered 501(c) reporting more than $93 million of assets in its most recently filed tax return.

In the US, the DCA's research arm, the Diyanet Islamic Research Institute, openly partners with organizations such as the International Institute of Islamic Thought (IIIT), one of the most prominent Muslim Brotherhood institutions in the world.

The Danish Parliament has approved a new law that bans foreign governments from financing mosques in Denmark.[230] The measure is aimed at preventing Muslim countries, particularly Qatar, Saudi Arabia and Turkey, from promoting Islamic extremism in Danish mosques and prayer facilities.

Muslim immigrants to Denmark have not integrated well. Jensen said that the Muslim community is plagued with "low education levels, low participation in ... [the]

---

[229] Adam Smith, "Erdoğan's American Mosque Spreads Islamism," Middle East Forum, July 29, 2021, https://www.meforum.org/62539/turkish-regime-mosque-near-dc-spreads-islamism.

[230] Soeren Kern, "Denmark Bans Foreign Funding of Mosques," Gatestone Institute, March 15, 2021, https://www.gatestoneinstitute.org/17167/denmark-mosques-foreign-funds.

labor [market], and high crime rates."[231] A large percentage of these immigrants "do not want to assimilate," preferring instead to "build up parallel societies" in their new host country. Jensen attributes this to the "rigid" precepts in the Islamic religion. These precepts, which include ingrained prejudice against women, Jews, and homosexuals, clash sharply with Denmark as a "modern country where equality ... is taken for granted." The "clan mentality" and distrust of state institutions prevalent in the Arab world also contrast sharply with Danish values.

The Ministry of Foreign Affairs and Integration in Denmark passed legislation March 15, 2021 regarding the financing of mosques. This legislation came about as a result of information regarding a donation from Saudi Arabia of 4.9 million Danish kroner (€660,000; $780,000) to fund the Taiba Mosque, located in the "multicultural" Nørrebro district, also known as "little Arabia." The donation was made by means of the Embassy of Saudi Arabia in Denmark. The Taiba Mosque, one of the most conservative in Denmark, has been the base for a number of Islamists convicted of terrorism offenses.

Foreign Minister Mattias Tesfaye said:

> *"Today there are extreme forces abroad that are trying to turn our Muslim citizens against Denmark and thus divide our society. Several times in recent years, the media have reported on Danish mosques receiving millions from the*

---

[231] Marilyn Stern, "Morten Uhrskov Jensen on Denmark's Cap on Non-Western Immigration," Middle East Forum, August 5, 2021, https://www.meforum.org/62551/jensen-denmarks-cap-on-non-western-immigration.

Middle East, among others. The government will oppose this. This bill is an important step towards fighting attempts by Islamic extremists to gain ground in Denmark. With this, we can take a targeted approach to the donations that undermine the values on which Danish society is based. The bill will not solve all the problems that extreme Islamists and anti-democratic forces can give rise to. But it is a good step on the road, and it will be a benefit to society every time we can stop an anti-democratic donation in Denmark."

Denmark's first purpose-built mosque — the Grand Mosque of Copenhagen, officially known as the Hamad Bin Khalifa Civilization Center — opened in June 2014 after receiving a donation of 227 million Danish kroner (€30 million; $36 million) from Hamad bin Khalifa al Thani, the former emir of Qatar.

Critics of the mega-mosque, which has a capacity to host 3,000 worshippers indoors and another 1,500 in an inner courtyard, said that the organization behind the facility, the Danish Islamic Council (Dansk Islamisk Råd, DIR), was promoting a highly conservative interpretation of Islam.

In September 2013, when the mosque was still under construction, the Copenhagen Post reported that the facility was planning to rebroadcast Al-Aqsa TV, a television broadcaster controlled by the Palestinian terrorist group Hamas.

In 2021, Prime Minister Mette Frederiksen wrote: "Sharia does not belong in Denmark."

Meanwhile, Turkey has bankrolled the construction of 27 mosques in Denmark, including in the cities of Aarhus,

Ringsted and Roskilde and in the towns of Fredericia, Hedehusene and Holbæk.

Denmark joins a growing list of European countries — including Austria, Belgium, France, Germany, Italy, the Netherlands and Switzerland — which have taken varying degrees of action to prevent foreign governments from financing the construction and upkeep of mosques on their territories.

CHAPTER 11: HOW DOES ISLAM REACH OUT TO YOUNG STUDENTS?

"Democracy cannot succeed unless those who express their choice are prepared to choose wisely. The real safeguard of democracy, therefore, is education."

~ *Franklin D. Roosevelt*

Has Islam infiltrated our public schools from K-12?

Democracy thrives where education promotes the ideals of western culture. In the name of tolerance, we have opened our doors to others whose cultural norms are antithetical to Western values. Teaching children about different cultures, different forms of government, and different religions is not the same as having curriculum content determined by foreign governments proselytizing our students. In the West, questions are being raised about the influence of China's values in our school systems. I wrote about that in an earlier chapter. Yet, we seem hesitant to investigate, let alone criticize, the influence of Muslim countries on our education system. Let's take a look at the influence Islam is having on our children's education.

How did it come about that young Muslim children in Philadelphia sang songs with lyrics like 'chopping off heads 'and 'liberate Al-Aqsa Mosque' while 'defending Palestine with our bodies' and about martyrdom?[232]

---

[232] Ariel Zilber, "Disturbing Video Shows Young Muslim

Now this took place in a Muslim school, but are religious schools exempt from rules about teaching hate?

The clip, which was first uploaded to Facebook by the Muslim American Society Islamic Center in Philadelphia, shows a group of children wearing Islamic headdress adorned with Palestinian symbols and colors. A translation of the video was provided by the Middle East Media Research Institute.

The Muslim American Society issued a statement following the airing in Facebook vowing to investigate the 'unintended mistake and an oversight.'

Unintended oversight? How, then, was it possible that the teachers felt quite comfortable teaching these songs, let alone filming them and sharing them?

How did we in the West arrive here?

Following the terrorist attacks of 9/11, amid concerns about the potential for rising anti-Islam sentiment, some school boards provided professional development for their teachers. But did these attempts at inclusion actually promote a pro-Islam agenda?

The Massachusetts Department of Education, for example, organized special seminars in Islamic history for K-12 teachers. [233] These educational materials are

---

Children at a Philadelphia Islamic Center Singing about 'Chopping off Heads', Martyrdom and 'Defending Palestine with Our Bodies'," Daily Mail Online (Associated Newspapers Ltd, May 6, 2019), https://www.dailymail.co.uk/news/article-6994509/Muslim-children-Philadelphia-school-sing-chopping-heads-army-Allah.html.

[233] Stanley Kurtz, "Saudi in the Classroom," NationalReview.com (The National Review, July 29, 2020),

Saudi funded. In 2004, Sandra Stotsky, a former director of a professional development institute for teachers at Harvard and a former senior associate commissioner of the Massachusetts Department of Education wrote in her book *The Stealth Curriculum* "Most of these materials have been prepared and/or funded by Islamic sources here and abroad, and are distributed or sold directly to schools or individual teachers, thereby bypassing public scrutiny." The Massachusetts department accepted a proposal with participation from federally approved Harvard's Center for Middle Eastern Studies. Harvard's outreach program delivered seminars that promoted Islam as a religion, while sharply criticizing alleged American prejudice against the Muslim world. Harvard's outreach training prompted K-12 teachers to design celebratory treatments of the life and teachings of Mohammad and the "revelation" and spread of Islam, with exercises calling on students to "appoint imams," memorize Islamic principles, and act out prayer at a Mosque, girls told to wear hijabs during Islam Appreciation Week demonstrated the influence of Saudi funding of MES centers across the United States.

These events were not limited to the years following 9/11, however. In 2017 Tony Pagliuso, whose daughter went to Newton South High School, was taken aback by an article from the "Arab World Studies Notebook" his daughter was given to read about the Middle East. The article claimed that Israeli soldiers had raped and murdered hundreds of Palestinian women.[234]

---

https://www.nationalreview.com/2007/07/saudi-classroom-stanley-kurtz/.
[234] Andy Levin, "CAMERA Focuses on Newton Schools' Arab-Israeli Conflict Curriculum," Newton TAB (Garrett Co.,

136

What is the "Arab World Studies Notebook"? Title VI of the Higher Education Act, a federal program enacted in 1958, in part to train international experts to meet the nation's security needs, gives credibility to these materials. The "Arab World Studies Notebook" is produced by Arab World and Islamic Resources, (AWAIR www.awaironline.org) a Berkeley, Calif.-based publisher of supplementary instructional materials. The 540-page book was first published in 1990 and last revised in 1998.

AWAIR received funding from organizations that include Saudi Aramco, a Saudi government-owned oil company. The second organization involved in the manual is the Middle East Policy Council of Washington, which helps print and disseminate the 500-page manual of essays, lesson plans and primary sources. The council lists the manual as the primary resource material for its teacher-training program. According to the group's Web site (www.mepc.org), more than 16,000 educators have attended its workshops in 175 cities in 43 states. The manual itself claims to have reached 25 million students. The council's board of directors includes executives from companies with huge financial stakes in Saudi Arabia, including Boeing, ExxonMobil Saudi Arabia, the Carlyle Group and the Saudi Bin Ladin Group.

AWAIR's (Arab World and Islamic Resources) mission is to counter the "rampant negative stereotypes of Arabs and Muslims held by most Americans." Recognizing that no work is of greater importance than the preparation of our young people for their roles as thoughtful and informed citizens of the twenty-first century and

---

November 21, 2017), https://newton.wickedlocal.com/news/20171121/camera-focuses-on-newton-schools-arab-israeli-conflict-curriculum.

recognizing too that U.S. involvement with the Arab World and with the wider world of Islam is certain to remain close for many years, AWAIR's goal is to increase awareness and understanding of this world region and this world faith through educational outreach at the pre-collegiate level.

The Notebook's editor, Audrey Shabbas, acknowledges that its purpose is to provide "the Arab point of view." The "Notebook" claims that Muslims actually beat Columbus to the New World, supposedly sailing across the Atlantic in 889. One analysis of the book stated "Arab World Studies Notebook" is designed to "induce teachers to embrace Islamic religious beliefs" and to "support political views" favored by the Middle East Policy Council (formerly the Arab American Affairs Council). [235,236,237]

The Council has been described as a moderate Washington-based organization that works to promote discussion and understanding of U.S. policies in the Middle East.

---

[235] Kathleen Kennedy Manzo, "Supplementary Text on Arab World Elicits Criticism," edweek.org (Editorial Products in Education Inc., March 1, 2005), https://www.edweek.org/teaching-learning/supplementary-text-on-arab-world-elicits-criticism/2005/03.

[236] JTA Staff, "Tainted Teachings, What Your Kids Are Learning about Israel, America, and Islam, Parts 1 through 4," Campus Watch (Middle East Forum, October 27, 2005), https://www.meforum.org/campus-watch/9987/tainted-teachings-what-your-kids-are-learning.

[237] Melanie Phillips, "From Congress to Classrooms: Reframing the Israel Narrative," JNS.org (Jewish News Syndicate, October 17, 2019), https://www.jns.org/opinion/from-congress-to-classrooms-reframing-the-israel-narrative.

How do these materials enter the education system?

A study from 2015 stated Saudi influence enters the classrooms in three different ways. The first is through teacher-training seminars that provide teachers with graduate or continuing-education credits. The second is through the dissemination of supplementary teaching materials designed and distributed with Saudi support. Such materials flood the educational system and are available online. The third is through school textbooks paid for by taxpayers, some of them vetted by activists with Saudi ties, who advise and influence major textbook companies about the books' Islamic, Arab, Palestinian, Israeli and Middle Eastern content.

The fingers of Islam reach more than printed materials, though. In Massachusetts, a class took a field trip to a mosque where students were encouraged to pray to Allah.[238] When did participating in another's prayers become part of one's education? Why would any school allow leaders in a Mosque to invite young people to pray? It is wonderful to be present at ceremonies from other religions; what a great way to earn about the other. But to have others pray? What has taken place amongst public school leadership that they would even contemplate such a practice?

In areas in Canada, rooms have been set aside for Muslim students attending public school so they can come together and pray despite the fact that all prayer

---

[238] Todd Starnes, "School Apologizes after Students Pray to Allah on Field Trip to Mosque," Fox News (FOX News Network, LLC, November 3, 2015), https://www.foxnews.com/us/school-apologizes-after-students-pray-to-allah-on-field-trip-to-mosque.

was removed from public schools long ago. These prayers denigrate and disrespect others as I write about in the chapter on the Al Fatiha prayer.

Equally interesting, and surprising, was the absence of claims by The American Civil Liberties Union (ACLU) and other organizations, which pursue any alleged Christian teachings or affiliations in public schools, that this violated the U.S. Constitution.

But there is more.

The state of Qatar is also involved in K-12 education around the world through the Qatar Foundation International (QFI). In the U.S. alone, the Qatar Foundation has given $30.6 million over the past eight years to public schools, ostensibly for teaching Arabic and promoting cultural exchange.

From the website:

> *"QFI is committed to providing K-12 students in Qatar and the Americas the skills that will enable them to be engaged global citizens. A core part of QFI is its Arabic Language and Culture Program. QFI grants to K-12 public and public charter schools implement in-school ARABIC programs. So far, the organization has supported:*
>
> * *22 schools in North America and 8 in Brazil, reaching over 2100 students;*
>
> * *29 Jurisdictions supported: Rio de Janeiro; Vancouver, B.C.; the District of Columbia; and 26 U.S. states (Arizona, California, Colorado, Connecticut, Florida, Georgia, Hawaii, Illinois, Iowa, Louisiana, Maryland, Massachusetts,*

Michigan, Minnesota, Montana, New Hampshire, New Jersey, New York, Ohio, Oregon, Pennsylvania, Utah, Tennessee, Texas, Virginia, and Washington).

Additionally, with support from QFI, the New York City Department of Education (DOE) launched a dual-language Arabic program at PS/IS 30 in September, 2013. The program, funded by a grant from QFI, began in PS/IS 30's kindergarten and provides a rich curriculum for English-speakers learning Arabic and Arabic-speakers learning English. It was the first of its kind in New York City."[239]

Could pro-Islam sentiment be entering curriculum in more subtle ways? Pearson Education, a "global learning services company," best known for its ownership of the Financial Times and its international textbook business, published the book, The Middle East: Conflict, Crisis and Change 1917-2012, in 2016 for students taking Edexcel exam board's re-vamped international General Certificate of Secondary Education (GCSE) in History. It is noteworthy that Pearson also owns the exam board. The book targets 16-year-olds in the UK about the Arab-Israeli conflict.

According to an analysis jointly commissioned by the Zionist Federation and UK Lawyers for Israel, the volume contains "unforgivable bias" suggesting it "whitewashes

---

[239] "Qatar Foundation International," The Center for Citizen Diplomacy (PYXERA Global, 2019),
https://www.centerforcitizendiplomacy.org/network/qatar-foundation-international/.

anti-Jewish violence" and contains "hard-core anti-Zionist revisionist material."

A spokesperson for Pearson stated the company would "immediately launch an independent and impartial review, and will take action if necessary."[240,241]

However, the company maintained that it always "aimed to present impartial, objective content."

It aimed. But seems to have failed.

An interesting note: In May of 2014, Pearson PLC won a major contract from Common Core testing consortium.[242] Pearson would conduct the testing of students in states that use Common Core testing for their public schools throughout the United States at $24 per student.

The Obama administration's Department of Education was giving grants to pay for the testing in the states that implemented them, within their $4.35 billion "Race to

---

[240] Mathilde Frot, "Pearson to Review GCSE Textbook on Israel and Palestine after 'Bias' Claim," www.jewishnews.co.uk (Jewish News - Britian's Biggest Jewish Newspaper, October 21, 2019), https://jewishnews.timesofisrael.com/pearson-to-review-gcse-textbook-on-israel-palestine-conflict-after-bias-claim/.

[241] Camilla Turner, "Pearson Launches Urgent Review of GCSE Textbook after Complaints That It 'Whitewashed' Jewish History," The Telegraph (Telegraph Media Group, October 26, 2019), https://www.telegraph.co.uk/news/2019/10/26/pearson-launches-urgent-review-gcse-textbook-complaints-whitewashed.

[242] "Preparing America's Students for Success.," Home (Common Core State Standards Initiative, 2021), http://www.corestandards.org/.

142

The Top" grant program.[243] It amounted to a $350 million deal for Pearson PLC.

Pearson PLC-owned Random Penguin House advanced a combined $65 million to President Obama and his wife Michelle for their memoirs.[244]

Finally, there is the influence of CAIR, the Council on American–Islamic Relations, a Muslim civil rights and advocacy group. It is headquartered on Capitol Hill in Washington, D.C., with regional offices nationwide. CAIR's library program was launched in 2015 with the aim of providing up to sixteen thousand public and school libraries across the country with books and writings that it had selected on Islam and the Middle East. CAIR founder Omar Ahmad had stated how CAIR could eventually gain influence in Congress: "This can be achieved by infiltrating the American media outlets, universities and research centers," going on to suggest how this would give them an entry point that would allow them to pressure U.S. policymakers. Why is a Muslim advocacy group choosing the materials that will shape our children's views of the world?

How can our children choose wisely when they receive unchecked, unbalanced Islamic propaganda from their teachers?

---

[243] "Fact Sheet - Race to the Top," Home (U.S. Department of Education, December 29, 2009), https://www2.ed.gov/programs/racetothetop/factsheet.html
[244] Ken Pittman, "Obama 'Quid pro Quo' Revenge via Impeachment? [Opinion]," 1420 WBSM, January 23, 2020, https://wbsm.com/obama-quid-pro-quo-revenge-via-impeachment-opinion/.

CHAPTER 12: WHAT IS THE SHARIA-COMPLIANT ECONOMY AND WHY DOES IT MATTER?

"A universal Islamic banking system is a jihad worth pursuing."

~ Malaysian Prime Minister Mohamed Mahathir

In all probability, you have not heard about the Sharia Compliant economy, or that you can purchase stocks in this economy at many of your local banking institutions. The Sharia compliant economy is part of the Muslim Brotherhood plan. Remember it was Mohamed Akram who gave voice to the modern implementation of Islam in the west which included banking and finance.[245] I wrote about this in the chapter about spreading Islam.

As you read this chapter, ask yourself what would happen if China decided to run a parallel economy in the west.

Malaysian Prime Minister Mohamed Mahathir told a banking conference in Kuala Lumpur in November 2002 that "a universal Islamic banking system is a jihad worth pursuing."[246,247,248]

---

[245] "Muslim Brotherhood (MB)," DiscoverTheNetwork.org - A Guide to the Political Left (Internet Archive Wayback Machine, April 23, 2020), https://web.archive.org/web/20200423074744/http://www.discoverthenetworks.com/groupProfile.asp?grpid=6386.

[246] Dr. Rachel Ehrenfeld and Alyssa A. Lappen, "Financial Jihad," ACDemocracy (American Center for Democracy,

Today, Muslims are re-engaging their traditional values for modern times. Both in Muslim and non-Muslim majority societies, traditional values like modesty, the concept of halal, Islamic principles regulating finance are being negotiated for the modern context.[249]

Tarek Fatah, a Canadian Muslim writer, broadcaster and political activist, wrote:

> "Sharia banking[250,251] traces its roots to the 1920s but didn't take hold until the late 1970s. Two men in particular understood the role international financial institutions could play in carrying out Islamic political objectives. Abul Ala Maududi[252] of the Jamaat-e-Islami in Pakistan,

---

September 22, 2005), https://acdemocracy.org/financial-jihad-2/.

[247] Dr. Rachel Ehrenfeld and Alyssa A. Lappen, "Tithing for Terrorists," American Center for Democracy, October 12, 2007, https://acdemocracy.org/tithing-for-terrorists/.

[248] "Establishment - Background," Islamic Financial Services Board (IFSB), June 2021, https://www.ifsb.org/background.php.

[249] Salaam Gateway Editors, "State of the Global Islamic Economy 2020/2021 Report," Salaam Gateway - Global Islamic Economy Gateway, 2020, https://www.salaamgateway.com/specialcoverage/SGIE20-21.

[250] Mark Polege, "Sharia-Compliant Finance and How We Are Funding Jihad in the Heartland," Breitbart News, September 25, 2011, https://www.breitbart.com/national-security/2011/09/25/Sharia-Compliant-Finance-And-How-We-Are-Funding-Jihad-in-the-Heartland/.

[251] "About Shariah Finance," Shariah Finance Watch (Center for Security Policy), accessed August 22, 2021, https://shariahfinancewatch.org/about-shariah-finance/.

[252] Editors, "Sayyid Abul A'la Maududi," Islam Times, May 16,

who had concentrated his efforts on establishing a truly Islamic state and society, and in the 1940s had already recognized "the cultural and political Westernizations of Islam as a loss of religious and national identity to the Muslim World." The other was Hassan al-Banna, founder of the Muslim Brotherhood in Egypt."[253]

Al-Banna and later Syed Qutb[254], who succeeded him, laid down principles of Islamic finance. Al-Banna viewed finance as a critical weapon to undermine the infidels — and "work towards establishing an Islamic rule on earth." He understood that Muslims must create an independent Islamic financial system[255] to parallel and later supersede the Western economy.

The Islamic Development Bank (IDB) was established in 1973 "in accordance with the principles of the Shariah," as prescribed by the Muslim Brotherhood, and launching the fast-growing petrodollar-based Islamic financing

---

2009, https://www.islamtimes.org/en/article/4995/sayyid-abul-a-la-maududi.

[253] Tarek Fatah, "Huffpost Exclusive: Sharia Banking Goes Bankrupt," HuffPost Canada (HuffPost Canada, December 17, 2011), https://www.huffingtonpost.ca/tarek-fatah/sharia-banking_b_1011704.html.

[254] Steven G. Zenishek, "Sayyid Qutb's 'Milestones' and Its Impact on the Arab Spring," ed. CDR Youssef Aboul-Enein, Sayyid Qutb's "Milestones" and Its Impact on the Arab Spring (Small Wars Journal, May 9, 2013), https://smallwarsjournal.com/jrnl/art/sayyid-qutb%E2%80%99s-%E2%80%9Cmilestones%E2%80%9D-and-its-impact-on-the-arab-spring.

[255] Dr. Rachel Ehrenfeld and Alyssa A. Lappen, "Tithing For Terrorists," American Center for Democracy, October 12, 2007, https://acdemocracy.org/tithing-for-terrorists/.

market. The IDB, more a development than commercial bank, was established largely "to promote Islamic banking worldwide."

[A]n Islamic organization must serve God..." and ultimately sustain "the growth and advancement of the Islamic way of life," writes Nasser M. Suleiman in Corporate Governance in Islamic Banking.

It is important to learn about this economy because of Zakat; a type of tax that all people who buy these funds must pay. That Zakat goes to Muslim charities.

According to the Qu'ran (9:60):

> "...recipients of zakat include the poor, the needy, those who serve the needy, and to free the slaves, but recipients also include 'those who fight in the way of Allah' and 'people engaged in Islamic military operations for whom no salary has been allotted in the army, or volunteers for jihad without remuneration.'"

> ~ Reliance of the Traveler, The Classic Manual of Islamic Sacred Law

Which charities? What do they do?

For many years the Holy Land Foundation, which was eventually investigated and declared a terrorist organization under President George W. Bush, had used the guise of charity to raise and funnel $12.4 million dollars to the infrastructure of the Hamas terror organization.[256],[257]

---

[256] Editors, "Holy Land Foundation Convictions," Federal Bureau of Investigation, November 25, 2008, https://archives.fbi.gov/archives/news/stories/2008/november/hlf112508.

Money raised was sent to "zakat committees," which would launder the cash to Hamas' arsenals and the families of suicide bombers.

Think about this: The USA has shut down the three largest Sharia-compliant charities in the U.S. – the Holy Land Foundation, Benevolence International Foundation, and the Global Relief Foundation – after proving they funded terrorist organizations.[258]

According to HSBC, a British multinational investment bank and financial services holding company, the Islamic finance industry showed an annual growth rate of 28% during the years 2006-2009 (despite the Global Financial Crisis in 2007-08). Thomson Reuters reports an average growth rate of 10% per year, with the total assets under management around at USD 2 trillion in 2015 and USD 3.25 trillion by 2020.

Thomson Reuters' Islamic Finance Development Report for 2018[259] saw potential for the industry to grow to US$

---

[257] Todd Bensman, "When Terrorists Learned 'Lawfare' Works: The Holy Land Foundation Trial's 10-Year Anniversary," pjmedia.com (PJ Media, May 19, 2020), https://pjmedia.com/homeland-security/todd-bensman/2018/12/03/when-terrorists-learned-lawfare-works-the-holy-land-foundation-trials-10-year-anniversary.

[258] Ilana Diamond Rovner, "FindLaw's United States Seventh Circuit Case and Opinions," Global Relief Foundation Incorporated v. New York Times Company (FindLaw, December 1, 2004), https://caselaw.findlaw.com/us-7th-circuit/1308560.html.

[259] Mohamed, Shereen, Abdulaziz Goni, and Shaima Hasan. "Islamic Finance Development Report 2018." Thomson Reuters, 2018.

3.8 trillion in assets by 2023 – an average projected growth of 10% per year.

With a growing Muslim population, stable economy and openness to the world, Canada is poised to become the North American hub for Islamic finance,[260] local experts have predicted.

A recent report (2019) by the Toronto Financial Services Alliance (TFSA), a public-private entity that seeks to build Toronto as a global financial centre, and Thomson Reuters predicted that Canada could be home to almost $18bn in sharia-compliant mortgages, while international Islamic bonds (sukuk) could generate $130bn in national infrastructure investments.

The global Islamic finance market is growing moderately, because of the strong investments in the Halal Sectors, infrastructure, and Sukuk (bonds), especially through electronic modes in all products and services. The factors driving the growth of the market are directing investment toward the tremendous growth opportunities in the promising Islamic sectors. The industry's total worth, according to key industry stakeholder organizations, across its three main sectors (banking, capital markets, and TAKĀFUL), was estimated to be USD 2.05 trillion in 2017. Islamic banking is the largest sector in the Islamic finance industry, contributing to 71%, or USD 1.72 trillion, of the industry's assets.[261]

---

[260] Jillian Kestler-D'Amours, "Canada: The next Hub of Islamic Finance?" Middle East Eye, April 27, 2016, https://www.middleeasteye.net/news/canada-next-hub-islamic-finance.

[261] Editors, "Global Islamic Finance Market - Growth, Trends, and Forecast (2018 - 2024)," Research and Markets - Market

Takaful is a type of Islamic insurance where members contribute money into a pool system to guarantee each other against loss or damage.

It is projected that the Muslim world will be doing 50% of their banking needs with Islamic institutions by 2020.

A UK-based company aims to boost international opportunities of Sharia finance even further. "...beyond Africa, the UK presents a huge prospect for the Islamic finance market. The country became the first western nation to issue a sovereign sukuk in 2014, and now it is the biggest centre for Sharia-compliant finance in the West. There are five licensed, fully Sharia-compliant banks in the UK, and more than 20 additional banks offer some form of Islamic banking." Frank Gaffney, founder of the Center for Security Policy, warns succinctly that it is "green-lighting a seditious system that supports jihad."

Under the US Constitution, it is a little more difficult for Sharia finance to proliferate at the same rate as it is growing in the UK and Canada, because "the biggest challenge in introducing takaful, sukuk and Islamic finance in the US is the First Amendment of the US Constitution, which prohibits the making of any law respecting an establishment of religion or impeding the free exercise of religion as well as the Establishment Clause."[262]

Research Reports, 2021, https://www.researchandmarkets.com/research/bq7pb4/glob al_islamic.

[262] Camille Paldi, "Challenges for Islamic Finance in the USA," InternationalFinance.com (International Finance Publications Ltd., March 14, 2017), https://internationalfinance.com/challenges-for-islamic-finance-in-the-usa/.

The International Monetary Fund (IMF) has played a key role in the expansion of Sharia finance and in the establishment of the Islamic Financial Services Board.

Sharia Compliant funds mean they are in accord with Sharia Law.[263] The concept of screening companies before making investments in them is derived from the Shari'ah principle that Muslims should not participate in an activity that does not comply with the teachings of Islam (Mian, 2008).

I think it is important to note that Sharia Compliant funds discriminate against Jews and Israel.[264] No company associated with a Jew or Israel can be on the exchange. Questions are being raised about Azzad Asset Management in America working with CAIR Philadelphia.

The Council on American-Islamic Relations (CAIR) is considered a terrorist organization by the United Arab Emirates. Azzad Asset Management is an Islamic finance company that advises its clients to pursue "faith-based, socially responsible investment" strategies. Azzad is a halal investment firm located in Falls Church, Va. Azzad was founded by its CEO Bashar Qasem.

American shareholders have complained that Azzad proposes expensive and burdensome regulations on companies doing business in Israel. Other critics have

[263] "About Shariah Finance," Shariah Finance Watch (Center for Security Policy), accessed August 22, 2021, https://shariahfinancewatch.org/about-shariah-finance/.
[264] Leonard Getz, "Sharia Finances Are Being Used to Bolster American Islamist Organizations," JNS.org (Jewish News Syndicate, June 26, 2020), https://www.jns.org/opinion/sharia-finances-are-used-to-bolster-american-islamist-organizations/.

called it a "gateway drug to full BDS," the radical BDS campaign aimed at isolating Israel through economic warfare. [265,266] To ensure that its investments comply with halal Islamic principles, Azzad maintains a Shariah Council of three experts—the most prominent being Dr. Mohamed Adam El-Sheikh, a Sudanese activist from the Muslim Brotherhood, a transnational Sunni Islamist movement with ties to violent jihadist groups. El-Sheikh is one of the founders of the movement's American branch, the Muslim American Society, which was responsible for the video of Muslim schoolchildren at a North Philadelphia Mosque singing about beheading Jews. I wrote about this earlier.

These funds are available in the West where we say we do not tolerate discrimination based on race, colour, creed, religion or sexual orientation. Would the West tolerate discrimination against black people, or gay people? Here are some other organizations that sell these funds. HSBC,[267]Franklin Templeton, [268] RBC, [269]

---

[265] Leonard Getz, "Shariah Finance Used to Fund American Islamist Organizations," Leonard Getz | The Blogs (The Times of Israel, July 1, 2020), https://blogs.timesofisrael.com/shariah-finance-used-to-fund-american-islamist-organizations/.

[266] Islam Religion Guardian, "Sharia Finances Are Used to Bolster American Islamist Organizations," Islamreligionguardian.com, June 26, 2020, https://www.islamreligionguardian.com/sharia-finances-are-used-to-bolster-american-islamist-organizations/.

[267] "HSBC Islamic Global Equity Index Fund," Global Asset Management from HSBC in the UK (HSBC Asset Management, 2021), https://www.assetmanagement.hsbc.co.uk/en/institutional-investor/investment-expertise/equities/islamic-global-eq-

and S&P Dow Jones Indices[270] has created many Shariah-compliant indexes for Muslim investors.

The Canadian banking sector reportedly has about $18 billion worth of Sharia-compliant mortgages in 2020. Sharia financing is rapidly expanding into the insurance sector as well.[271]

There are already a number of Islamic finance players, with the most established being United Muslim Financial; Habib Canadian Bank; Al-Ittihad Investment; Al Yusr; Manzil Bank; Ijara Community Development Corp.; Islamic Co-Operative Housing Corp.; Ansar Co-operative Housing Corp.; Qurtuba Housing Co-op; An-Nur Housing Cooperative; Amana Auto Finance Canada; Assiniboine Credit Union; newer players such as Iana Financial; WealthSimple Halal; ShariaPortfolio Canada; Global Iman Fund, as well as a number of other medium-sized and smaller player and mortgage cooperatives. Besides, there are a growing number of conventional banks and

---

index-fund.

[268] "Franklin Templeton Shariah Funds - Understanding Shariah Equity Investing, April 2017." Dubai: Franklin Templeton Investments, April 2017.

[269] "Socially Responsible Investing," RBC Wealth Management (RBC Dominion Securities Inc., 2021), https://ca.rbcwealthmanagement.com/web/abbas.fazal/sri.

[270] "Iman Fund - Shariah Mutual Fund and Investing," Shariah Investing | Mutual Fund | Iman Fund (Quasar Distributors, LLC, 2021), https://www.investaaa.com/.

[271] Christine Douglass-Williams, "Canada: Sharia Financing Rapidly Expanding with Increasing Sharia-Adherent Population," JihadWatch, February 15, 2020, https://www.jihadwatch.org/2020/02/canada-sharia-financing-rapidly-expanding-with-increasing-sharia-adherent-population.

financial institutions opening Islamic windows or planning to do so, among them Canadian Imperial Bank of Commerce or the Canada Mortgage and Housing Corp.

Dr. Zuhdi Jasser, President of American Islamic Forum for Democracy[272] states:

> *"Sharia-compliant finance only empowers Muslim Sharia Law leaders whose real long-term vision is to impose Sharia Law on the world and recreate an Islamic Empire. These leaders want to overpower capital free markets and create their version of an Islamic economy. Bankers and business leaders are being duped."*

> *"The largest single source of funds for Islamic terrorism[273] is zakat which typically goes through the Islamic banking system. Using the system of zakat 'al-Qaeda was able to receive between $300m and $500m' over a decade 'from wealthy businessmen and bankers representing 20% of Saudi GNP, through a web of charities and companies acting as fronts, with the notable use of Islamic banking institutions.'"*

---

[272] "American Islamic Forum for Democracy," American Islamic Forum for Democracy | At Home with American Liberty and Freedom, 2016, https://aifdemocracy.org/.

[273] Editors, "What's Wrong with Sharia Compliant Finance?," What's Wrong with Sharia Compliant Finance? (Sharia Watch UK Ltd., 2017), https://web.archive.org/web/20171025134711/http://www.shariawatch.org.uk/?q=content%2Fwhat-s-wrong-sharia-compliant-finance-0.

Timur Kuran, Turkish American economist, Professor of Economics and Political Science, and Gorter Family Professor in Islamic Studies at Duke University warns: "The real purpose of Islamic economics has not been economic improvement but cultivation of a distinct Islamic identity to resist cultural globalization."[274] It has served the cause of global Islamism, known also as "Islamic fundamentalism," by fueling the illusion that Muslim societies have lived, or can live, by distinct economic rules.

A board of Muslim scholars decide which funds are acceptable.[275] This same board also decides on the charities receiving the Zakat collected from those buying the funds. Criteria used in screening out non-compliant vehicles include those outlined by the Shariah Supervisory Boards of the Dow Jones Islamic Market Index (DJIM) and S&P Shariah Indices. There is also an annual Shariah audit and purifying certain prohibited types of income, such as interest, by donating them to a charity.

Shariah boards are constituted of Islamic scholars whose fees can run into millions of dollars per year, adding to the overall cost of managing the fund. The scholars have varying interpretations of Islamic law, making it difficult and time-consuming for them to arrive at a consensus

---

[274] Timur Kuran, Islam and Mammon: The Economic Predicaments of Islamism (Princeton, NJ: Princeton University Press, 2006).
[275] James Chen, "Shariah-Compliant Funds Definition," ed. Gordon Scott, Investopedia, May 30, 2021, https://www.investopedia.com/terms/s/shariah-compliant-funds.asp.

for analysis and implementation regarding a particular course of action.

An independent, six-member Shari'ah board of Islamic scholars contributed to the original design of the DJIM (Dow Jones Islamic Market Index)[276]and continues to provide periodic input. Shaykh Nizam Yaquby,[277] Bahrain, was trained in the Islamic sciences in Bahrain and Makkah before going on to study at McGill University. He continues to sit on a plethora of Sharia advisory boards including Morgan Stanley, Arab Banking Corporation, Citigroup Inc, Abu Dhabi Islamic Bank, Barclays, BNP Paribas, Credit Agricole CIB, Dow Jones Islamic Index, Lloyds TSB, and HSBC Amanah.

Shaykh Dr. Mohd Daud Bakar,[278] Malaysia, Founder and Executive Chairman of Amanie Group is a Shariah board member of various financial institutions, including the National Bank of Oman (Oman), Noor Islamic Bank (Dubai), Amundi Asset Management (France), Morgan Stanley (Dubai), Bank of London and Middle East (London), BNP Paribas (Bahrain), Dow Jones Islamic Market Index (New York), First Gulf Bank (UAE), amongst many others.

---

[276] "Dow Jones Islamic Market Indexes." Dow Jones, February 16, 2007.

[277] Editors, "Nizam Yaquby," The Muslim 500 (Royal Islamic Strategic Studies Centre (MABDA المركز الملكي للبحوث الإسلامية والدراسات), 2021),
https://themuslim500.com/profiles/nizam-yaquby/.

[278] Editors, "Dr. Mohd Daud Bakar – 16th Kuala Lumpur Islamic Finance Forum," 16th Kuala Lumpur Islamic Finance Forum (KLIFF2021) (CERT Centre for Research and Training, 2021),
https://kliff.com.my/sp-datuk-dr-mohd-daud-bakar/.

Shaykh Justice Muhammad Taqi Usmani,[279] Pakistan, a traditional Sunni is a leading scholar of Hadith, Islamic jurisprudence and Islamic finance. He is considered to be the intellectual head of the Deobandi School of Islamic learning, as well as an authority outside of the Deobandi School. He served as Judge of the Shari'at Appellate Bench of the Supreme Court of Pakistan from 1982 to May 2002. He specialises in Hadith, Islamic jurisprudence and financial matters.

Shaykh Dr. Mohamed A. Elgari,[280] Saudi Arabia, is a graduate from the University of California. He holds a PhD in Economics. He is an Associate Professor of Shari'a Compliant Economics and the former Director of the Centre for Research in Islamic Economics at King Abdul Aziz University in the Kingdom of Saudi Arabia.Dr. Mohammed serves as a member of the Islamic Fiqh Academy as well as the Islamic Accounting and Auditing Organization for Islamic Financial Institution (AAOIFI). He is an Advisor on the Shari'a board of the Dow Jones Islamic index in addition to several Islamic financial institutions across the world.

Shaykh Abdul Sattar Abu Ghuddah,[281] Syria, internationally respected Sharia'a scholar and advisor

---

[279] Editors, "Muhammad Taqi Usmani," The Muslim 500 (Royal Islamic Strategic Studies Centre (MABDA المركز الملكي للبحوث الإسلامية والدراسات,) 2021), accessed August 22, 2021, https://themuslim500.com/profiles/muhammad-taqi-usmani/.
[280] "Sheikh Dr. Mohammed Ali Elgari," Islamic Finance House, 2021, https://www.ifh.ae/sharia-supervisory/sheikh-dr-mohammed-ali-elgari/.
[281] "Islamic Finance Industry Mourns the Passing of Internationally Respected Shariah Scholar and Advisory Sheikh Dr. Abdul Sattar Abu Ghuddah," DDCAP Group, December 30,

was a member until recently when he passed away aged 80 in October 2020 in Canada. Sheikh Dr Abdul Sattar Abu Ghuddah was one of the world's leading legal scholars in the field of Islamic finance. He received his education and training in Sharia'a and Fiqh (Jurisprudence) at two of the premier institutions in Islamic studies in the world – Al Azhar University and Damascus University.

Muslim scholars have put together the following benchmarks clarifying what is not acceptable as an investment under Shariah.

- Alcohol – Brewers or distillers of alcohol or any firm exclusively involved in the production or sale of alcohol;

- Banks – and other banking Institutions involved in interest; (Insurance companies are usually included in this section too)

- Gambling – Casino and gambling outlets;

- Pornography Manufacturers, retailers and distributors of pornographic material as well as firms involved in pornographic activity;

- tobacco – Manufacturers of tobacco and tobacco related products;

- Ancillary Activity – Any business though not directly engaged in the above, derives greater than 5% of its income from the above, or

---

2020, https://www.ddcap.com/islamic-finance-industry-mourns-the-passing-of-internationally-respected-shariah-scholar-and-advisory-sheikh-dr-abdus-sattar-abu-ghuddah/.

- Any other forms whose activities the Shariah Board feels are prejudicial to the interests of Islam or Muslims.

The COVID-19 global pandemic has caused an economic recession world-wide. Dr. Zamir Iqbal, Vice President, Finance (Chief Financial Officer) of the Islamic Development Bank in Saudi Arabia, has stressed the ways that Islamic finance can contribute to post-pandemic recoveries both economically and socially.[282] "Non-conventional measures need to be adopted to get debt under control," he said. "Islamic finance is much more relevant now because it has always argued that financing should always be based on underlying real economic activity."

Dr. Iqbal believes that Islamic finance is uniquely placed to contribute to the overall recovery. "Islamic finance advocates risk-sharing solutions to put the economy back on track, while Islamic social finance provides for developing very strong social safety nets," he added.

Much of the reason for this, he argues, comes from integration of finance with Islamic morals and ethics — and their appeal to human compassion and cooperation — which may better equip the sector to help alleviate poverty and kickstart poorer segments of society. However, he cautioned that "results don't come through wishful thinking, but by formalizing and creating strong institutions around market, non-market and moral

---

[282] "Does Shariah-Compliant Finance Have the Power to Change the World? | Bloomberg Professional Services," Bloomberg.com, November 3, 2020, https://www.bloomberg.com/professional/blog/does-shariah-compliant-finance-have-the-power-to-change-the-world/.

dimensions." Out of 43 respondents more than two-thirds felt Shariah-compliance in investing was more important than maximizing returns.

Dr. Hurriyah El Islamy, Executive Board Member, Foreign Investment and International Relations Badan Pengelola Keuangan Haji, concurred. While she conceded that money markets and capital markets have their place in the investment universe of her sovereign wealth fund, she believes Islamic finance has the greatest amount to contribute to society. "We should be ready to venture into the real economy to create something with the funds that we have; be socially responsible, have good governance," she said. "It means working together with society, with the central government, and with governments from rural areas, to create something that will benefit people in their real lives."

Bloomberg is committed to connecting the Islamic finance network globally and building data and technology tools to help advance this burgeoning sector.[283]

---

[283] "Does Shariah-Compliant Finance Have the Power to Change the World? | Bloomberg Professional Services," Bloomberg.com, November 3, 2020

CHAPTER 13: WHY DOES ISLAM SAY NO TO LIBERALISM? SHIRK

"And they set up rivals to Allah, to mislead (men) from His path! Say: 'Enjoy (your brief life)! But certainly, your destination is the (Hell) Fire!'"

~ Ibraaheem 14:30

Islam teaches that one can worship only one God. The Ten Commandments teaches this. It is the first commandment. "I am the Lord Your God. You shall have no other gods before me." That's idol worship.

According to several Muslim scholars, liberalism (democracy), is a religion and is in conflict with the teachings of Islam. This belief goes against all the statements that Islam is compatible with the West. Yet, rarely, if ever, do we hear politicians or journalists talk about this. Why is that? Why are people in positions of power afraid to state facts about Islam? Facts shared by Islam, itself?

In Saskatchewan, Canada, Muhammad Mustafa Mustaan preaches:

"Democracy is nothing else but something which gives you the right to choose anything. The biggest shirk [Arabic term for idolatrous and heretical polytheism] is when you give your own self the right to choose whatever you want. So, democracy, in no terms, is compatible with Islam."[284]

---

[284] Rebel Editors, "Muhammad Mustafa Mustaan," The Rebel (The Rebel Media, September 6, 2015),

He spoke in Saskatoon public schools, including Walter Murray Collegiate Institute, a high school of 1,300 students.

Here is the explanation; it is called shirk.[285]

In Islam, shirk (Arabic: شرك širk) is the sin of practicing idolatry or polytheism, i.e. the deification or worship of anyone or anything besides the singular God, i.e. Allah. Literally, it means ascribing or the establishment of "partners" placed beside God. Shirk is one of the greatest possible offenses in the eyes of Allah. It means, roughly, "polytheism", and is the opposite of tawhid, which is "monotheism", the assertion of the absolute oneness of Allah.

Those who practice shirk are termed mushrikun: a polytheist, one who falsely associates (something) with God.

How do followers of Islam who are in government in the West avoid shirk? Being a mushrikin?

American Muslim scholar Daniel Haqiqatjou from Houston, Texas has written a scholarly article about the dangers of liberalism.[286] He attended Harvard

---

https://web.archive.org/web/20150906183217/http://www.therebel.media/muhammad_mustafa_mustaan.

[285] Editors of Encyclopaedia Britannica, Thinley Kalsang Bhutia, and Adam Zeidan, "Shirk," Encyclopædia Britannica (Encyclopædia Britannica, Inc., April 23, 2020), https://www.britannica.com/topic/shirk.

[286] Rachel Ehrenfeld, "American Muslim Scholar Says Liberalism Is a Dangerous Religion, 'Distinct from Islam,'" The American Center for Democracy, April 18, 2018, https://news.acdemocracy.org/american-muslim-scholar-says-liberalism-is-a-dangerous-religion-distinct-from-islam/.

University where he majored in Physics and minored in Philosophy.

According to his Facebook page, Haqiqatjou completed a Master's degree in Philosophy at Tufts University. Haqiqatjou also studies traditional Islamic sciences part-time. He writes and lectures on contemporary issues surrounding Muslims and Modernity. He is also a contributor to the Muslim Debate Initiative.

Here are some excerpts from the article. Haqiqatjou says:

> "Liberalism is a dangerous religion, 'distinct from Islam' For the past month or so I've been lecturing at a couple of different venues on the topic of liberalism and I've been sharing my thoughts on liberalism trying to educate the Muslim community on liberalism, and really the dangers of liberalism and how we can critique it.

> "...I justify this in terms of the Quran is that as Allah says that he hasn't made any man with two hearts within him, meaning that you can't be faithful to two separate faiths, two religions at the same time.

> "I do consider liberalism as a 'deen', as a complete religion and faith even though it's not considered to be such but we can we can understand it in that way."

If this is true; if liberalism and Islam are two distinct religions, and following two religions is considered shirk, one of the greatest offenses in the eyes of Allah, how do Muslims in the Western governments manage to remain Muslim when it appears they are polytheists?

Daniel Haqiqatjou continues "...what's the God of liberalism? If liberalism is a religion, what would be considered the God of that? I think that really the God of liberalism is the human self.... you're the one who decides what is acceptable or not as opposed to God or something else.

> "So, the Golden Rule is something that's found in different forms throughout liberal philosophy classically and even in the present day. What is the golden rule is treat others as you wish to be treated. So, if you think about it this treat others as you wish to be treated, so your own moral orientation, your own interests, and what you view as right and wrong and beneficial, you yourself, then that is the criterion for what is in fact proper or correct action. So again, it's very self centered. it's very self-oriented."

We in the West are taught the Golden Rule is one of the most important pillars of a liberal democracy. Rabbi Hillel said: "That which is hateful to you, do not do to your fellow. That is the whole Torah." Jesus said: "Do unto to others what you would have them do to you, for this sums up the Law and the Prophets.

Haqiqatjou adds:

> "I think that we need to be able to critique liberalism. We need to be able to speak intelligently and about it and be able to not only say that liberalism is something distinct from Islam... Dr. Sherman Jackson, has (written) a few essays on this topic of Islam and liberalism... The point that he makes is that yes Islam and

liberalism are separate intellectual traditions and there are definitely conflicts.

"...well where does Islam and liberalism conflict and how big are those conflicts? Are they really dangerous? I argue that they are dangerous and they are problematic and we should be able to critique that and there are different ways to do that."

So, we have a Muslim scholar saying that it is incumbent upon Muslims to critique liberals/democracy. I assume he believes that non-Muslims should be able to critique Islam.

He also said:

"I can concede and agree with secularists that the ideal form of governance is one that maximizes freedom, happiness, etc., as the atheists contend here. But by that definition combined with the Islamic position on what happiness, harm, etc., entail, that ideal form of governance is one that is determined by God's law, which is the Sharia. In other words, if you anchor happiness and harm in reality, which we know through revelation not the blind musings of random atheistic philosophers, the secular ideal can be used to champion the application of Sharia."

From *Democracy: The Religion of the Infidels*[287]

---

[287] Jonathan D. Halevi, "Al-Qaeda's Intellectual Legacy: New Radical Islamic Thinking Justifying the Genocide of Infidels," Jerusalem Viewpoints (Jerusalem Center for Public Affairs, December 1, 2003), https://www.jcpa.org/jl/vp508.htm.

Abu Muhammad al-Maqdisi, leader of the Bayat al-Imam extremist group whose operatives were arrested in Jordan in 1995 wrote democracy is a prohibited innovation that contradicts Islamic values and embodies a new heretical religion. Its followers are "infidels" and "polytheists," even if they consider themselves as Jews or Christians by religion. Al-Maqdisi based his claim on the following arguments:

> *"Democracy gives legitimacy to the legislation of the masses or to the despotic regime. It is not [the expression of] the rule of Allah... Allah ordered his Prophet to execute the commands given to him and forbade him to follow the emotions of the nation, the masses, and the people."*

We are welcoming people into Western culture who are adamantly opposed to our way of life.

Why?

CHAPTER 14: WHAT IS THE EFFECT OF IMAMS ON INTOLERANCE?

"Can you imagine the outcry if clerics of other faiths preached sermons calling for the death of any other group?"

~ Zionist Organization of America (ZOA)

If we have learned nothing else these past few decades, we should have learned that messages from the pulpit carry great weight and that religious leader carry great power. We have witnessed the damage done by Catholic priests to children; the most vulnerable in any society.

Clergy represent God to their parishioners, if not overtly then certainly covertly. I learned this as a Chaplain in Canada's largest hospital in the most diverse city of the world. When I was called to a room I knew that I represented that patient's views on God and religion. What I said would have great influence because I was a symbol of their idea of God.

Innate, endemic, systemic Jew hatred developed over the millennia in the Catholic Church and later in the Protestant Church because of the teachings of the clergy; statements that Jews killed Christ or that Jews kill Christian children for their blood at Passover to make Matza. No priest, no reverend is allowed to make these statements, today. But the damage done over the millennia has been catastrophic. The Holocaust is a direct result of these teachings. In 2019, the Church of England shared its report[288] titled *"God's Unfailing Word:*

---

[288] The Faith and Order Commission. "God's Unfailing Word -

Theological and Practical Perspectives on Christian-Jewish Relations." The 121-page report said attitudes towards Judaism over centuries had provided a "fertile seed-bed for murderous anti-Semitism," and that Anglicans and other Christians must repent for the "sins of the past," as well as actively challenge anti-Semitic attitudes or stereotypes.

Today, Imams all over the world are sharing prayers and sermons that reflect badly on Jews and Christians, too often calling for death to the other. Why is this allowed? What happened?

Young imams are being trained in a network of Islamic schools across the UK that have been accused of promoting intolerance and misogyny, a secret Government report has warned.[289]

The report claims preachers emerging from some of the dozens of Darul Uloom madrasas scattered across Britain have views as extreme as those held by radical clerics who move to the UK from Islamic countries – and may spread them to worshippers.

Forty-eight Darul Ulooms; which can be translated as House of Knowledge, and follow a strict syllabus called Dars-E-Nizami, have been identified.

Theological and Practical Perspectives on Christian – Jewish Relations." London: Church of England by Church House Publishing, November 13, 2019.

[289] Abul Taher, "Disturbing Secret Government Report Exposes Extremist Alert in 48 British Islamic Schools," Daily Mail Online (Associated Newspapers, May 4, 2019), https://www.dailymail.co.uk/news/article-6993333/Disturbing-secret-Government-report-exposes-extremist-alert-48-British-Islamic-schools.html.

It espouses the literal following of the Koran and is used by the hardline Islamic movement Deobandism, whose training schools produced the Taliban in Pakistan and Afghanistan.

At least four Darul Ulooms have previously been criticized by the education regulator Ofsted. Ofsted is the Office for Standards in Education, Children's Services and Skills. They inspect services providing education and skills for learners of all ages. They also inspect and regulate services that care for children and young people. Inspectors found students being taught that music and dancing comes from the devil and that women do not have the right to refuse sex to their husbands.

The ban on music is similar to the one imposed by Islamic State, which carry out public floggings on those who break the rule.

The madrasas operate in many cities, including London, Manchester, Glasgow and Leicester, but the report cites the Darul Uloom High School in Birmingham as an example of an 'extremist madrasa'. It was investigated by Ofsted after leaflets stating that music and dancing were 'acts of the devil' were found on its premises. The school, which has around 175 pupils, was also exposed by a Channel 4 investigation in 2011 that found pupils being taught to hate Jews, Christians and Hindus.

Al-Azhar University[290] (Jamiat al-Azhar in Arabic) describes itself as the most important religious university in the Muslim world with as many as 90,000 students

---

[290] Editorial Team, "Al-Azhar University," MuslimHeritage.com (Foundation for Science, Technology and Civilisation, UK (FSTCUK), April 10, 2001), https://muslimheritage.com/al-azhar-university/.

studying there at any one time. It is one of the chief centres of Islamic learning and the greatest and the most influential in the Sunni Islamic world. (One might say it is the Islamic equivalent to the Vatican). For more than a thousand years, Al-Azhar has produced thousands of eminent scholars, distinguished educationalists, preserving Islamic heritage and strengthening Islamic identity.

The University trains Imams who fan out all over the world. A highly influential 766-page treatise by Al-Azhar's former Grand Imam Tantawi, cites Koranic sources to justify Muslim Jew-hatred and violence, and advises that "gentle persuasion can do no good with [Jews], so use force with them and treat them in the way you see as effective in ridding them of their evil." The current Grand Imam of Al-Azhar, Ahmed Al-Tayeb, justifies antisemitism, absurdly saying: "Since the inception of Islam 1,400 years ago, we have been suffering from Jewish and Zionist interference in Muslim affairs.

Imams in mosques in North Carolina, New Jersey, California, Texas, and Pennsylvania were videotaped preaching anti-Jewish sermons including the same genocidal "come and kill the Jew hiding behind the tree" hadith. Sermons in U.S. mosques also accused Jews of killing the prophets; called for cleansing the Temple Mount of "the filth of the Jews"; prayed to "turn Jerusalem and Palestine into a graveyard for the Jews" and annihilate Jews one by one; accused Zionists of treating Palestinians the way Nazis treated the Europeans; charged that some Jews literally turned into monkeys and pigs; and claimed that Jews are running everything; and that the pro-Israeli lobby has been using the United States as a cash cow.

On Friday December 8, 2017, at the Tajweed Institute Islamic Center in Houston, Texas, Imam Raed Saleh Al-Rousan, preached and posted on Youtube and Facebook the full hadith in Arabic calling for the murder of Jews: "The Muslims will kill the Jews, and the Jews will hide behind the stones and the trees, and the stones and the trees will say: Oh Muslim, oh servant of Allah, there is a Jew hiding behind me, come and kill him, except for the Gharqad tree, which is one of their trees."[291]

On December 8, 2017, Syrian American Imam Abdullah Khadra preached the same thing from his mosque in Raleigh NC.

On Friday December 8, 2017, Imam Aymen Elkasaby gave a sermon at the Islamic Center of Jersey City, New Jersey, calling for genocide against the Jewish people saying: "Count them one by one, and kill them down to the very last one. Do not leave a single one on the face of the Earth." Imam Elkasaby also called Jews "apes and pigs," "the most cowardly of nations," "the weakest of all peoples," and "plundering oppressors."

And then there is Omar Suleiman[292], the founder and president of the Dallas-based Yaqeen Institute for Islamic Research[293], who delivered the daily prayer at the House

[291] "Zionist Organization of America (ZOA)," Zionist Organization of America (ZOA), January 15, 2018, https://zoa.org/2018/01/10377423-zoa-fire-four-imams-calling-for-murdering-jews/.
[292] Editors, "Dr. Omar Suleiman, Founder & President (CEO)," Yaqeen Institute for Islamic Research, 2021, https://yaqeeninstitute.ca/team/omar-suleiman.

of Representatives in America in September 2019. Why would the House of Representatives ask such a man to say a prayer for peace? Suleiman has a history of anti-Israel statements. During the 2014 Gaza war, Suleiman wrote on his Facebook page, "God willing on this blessed night as the 3rd Intifada begins, the beginning of the end of Zionism is here. May Allah help us overcome this monster, protect the innocent of the world, and accept the murdered as martyrs."

He has also reportedly claimed that Israel was the "51st state," and wrote on Facebook in 2015, ""Want to know what its [sic] like to live under Nazis? Look no further than how the Palestinians are treated daily by apartheid Israel."

Suleiman is also a supporter of the boycott, divestment and sanctions movement against Israel.

And then there is Canadian Imam Younus Kathrada of the Muslim Youth of Victoria Islamic Center, British Columbia, Canada. Here are his words following the fall of Afghanistan and its takeover by the Taliban, August 20, 2021:[294]

---

[293] Editors. Yaqeen Institute for Islamic Research, 2021. https://yaqeeninstitute.ca/. URL https://yaqeeninstitute.org for Dallas TX -based parent institute connects to the Canadian branch's website.

[294] MEMRI TV Editors, "Canadian Imam Younus Kathrada Calls for Support of the 'Mujahideen' In Afghanistan, Adds: The Jews and the Christians Are Our Enemies," MEMRI.org (Middle East Media Research Institute, August 24, 2021), https://www.memri.org/tv/canadian-imam-younus-kathrada-support-mujahideen-afghanistan-jews-christians-enemies.

Kathrada emphasized that the Jews and Christians are the enemies of the Muslims. He prayed to Allah to grant victory to the mujahideen who wage Jihad in Afghanistan and success to the "brothers" in establishing shari'a.

"The [Jews and Christians] are willing to spend mountains of gold in order to take us away from Islam. So, they will spend it, but don't fear, at the end of the day, they are not going to win. Allah tells us that they will spend it, and that it will be for them a source of regret. Hmmm... A source of regret... Twenty years in Afghanistan, I don't need to say any more... A source of regret. Then they will be overcome. Does this sound familiar to you? Have you been listening to the news? Let's say: Allah Akbar..."

"They will attack what is most sacred to us. But all of that [which] they do is only a small portion of what is really in their hearts, of the hatred that they have towards us in their hearts..."

"Do not think that the Jews and Christians are our friends – they are our enemies..."

"I incite you to show support for your brothers in Afghanistan, who want to establish the shari'a in their land..."

"We see that the West wants to talk about the rights of women. The rights of women... Ah, yes, her right to be a prostitute. Her right to sleep around with whomever she wishes. I want you to understand what those rights are, by the way. Her rights to be abused. Her right to show her

body off to men, who get off on watching her in porn and other than that..."

"Allah grant victory to the mujahideen [fighting] for Your sake everywhere. Allah grant success to our brothers in Afghanistan, so that they establish your shari'a on this land."

These are just a few examples of hate coming from the clergy.

Why is this permitted?

In April 2019 the Zionist Organization of America (ZOA) National President Morton A. Klein forwarded his testimony on Hate Crime and the Rise of White Nationalism to the U.S. House of Representatives Committee on the Judiciary.[295] And asked: "Can you imagine the outcry if clerics of other faiths preached sermons calling for the death of any other group? "

Can you?

Ignorance often leads to fear of the other. We must educate ourselves by reading the statements made by Imams, the religious leaders and teachers of Islam, the ideology. I have always believed that statements made by religious leaders and experts carry far more weight than comments made by lay people. When a religious leader speaks, we need to listen; to pay attention.

---

[295] Klein, Morton A. "Written Testimony of Zionist Organization of America (ZOA) National President Morton A. Klein, Hearing Title: Hate Crimes and the Rise of White Nationalism, before the U.S. House of Representatives Committee on the Judiciary, 116th Congress." New York: Zionist Organization of America (ZOA), April 9, 2019.

CHAPTER 15: WHAT IS THE AL FATIHA?

"Those who have evoked the Wrath of Allah [SWT] are the Jews [or Israelites] who knew the full truth through Prophet Mousa [Alyhi Al Salam: AAS] but deviated from this truth with selfishness, pride and prejudice. They thus deserved the Wrath of Allah [SWT]. The astray, on the other hand, are the Christians who deviated from the Message of Prophet Isa [AAS] out of ignorance and ill-knowledge..."

~ Muhammad ash-Shawkani

Let's take a look at the most important prayer in each of the three Abrahamic religions. These are the prayers that encapsulate the deepest teachings of that religion. They are the "soul" of the religion.

This is the most important prayer in Christendom, the prayer which Jesus Christ taught to His disciples:[296]

Our Father, Who art in heaven

Hallowed be Thy Name;

Thy kingdom come,

Thy will be done,

on earth as it is in heaven.

---

[296] Diane Weber Bederman, "What Do Judaism Christianity and Islam Have in Common? Part 3," Diane Bederman - Your Passionate Voice of Reason, November 12, 2017, https://dianebederman.com/what-do-judaism-christianity-and-islam-have-in-common-part-3/.

Give us this day our daily bread,

and forgive us our trespasses,

as we forgive those who trespass against us;

and lead us not into temptation,

but deliver us from evil. Amen.

This is a prayer of petition in which a Christian asks God to remove the temptations from one's own lives. The Lord's Prayer, or the Perfect Prayer as it is also called, is the most important prayer of all other prayers and it is used and accepted by all Christians throughout the land.

For the Jews the most important prayer is the "Shema."

Shema Yisrael (*"Hear, O Israel"*) are the first two words of a section of the Torah that is the centerpiece of the morning and evening prayer services, encapsulating the monotheistic essence of Judaism:

"Hear, O Israel: God is our Lord, God is one."

The Shema is a daily affirmation of allegiance to God and to the covenant obligations that allegiance entails. The Jewish people have a legal contract with God.

It is the oldest fixed daily prayer in Judaism, recited morning and night since ancient times. It consists of three biblical passages, two of which specifically say to speak of these things "when you lie down and when you rise up." In its entirety, the Shema consists of three paragraphs: Deuteronomy 6:4–9, Deuteronomy 11:13–21 and Numbers 15:37–41.

"You shall love the Lord your God with all your heart, with all your soul, and with all your might. And these words which I command you today

shall be upon your heart. You shall teach them
thoroughly to your children, and you shall speak
of them when you sit in your house and when
you walk on the road, when you lie down and
when you rise. You shall bind them as a sign
upon your hand, and they shall be for a reminder
between your eyes. And you shall write them
upon the doorposts of your house and upon your
gates."

In Islam, the *Al-Fātiha* is the most important prayer. It is the first sūrah (chapter) of the Qur'ān, and was one of the earliest portions of the Qur'ān revealed to the prophet Muhammad by the angel Gabriel. The entire Qur'ān was revealed in the years from 610 to 632 AD.

The *Al-Fātiha*, recited at least seventeen times daily by Muslims in the canonical prayers, reminds one of the praise and gratitude due to God for His Attributes of Infinite Goodness and All-Mercifulness, not merely for His Goodness and Mercy to us in this life but ultimately, on the Day of Judgement when those who die while not believing that "There is no true god but God, and Muhammad is the Messenger (Prophet) of God" or are not Muslim will lose Paradise forever and will be sent to Hellfire as God said:

> *"And whoever seeks a religion other than Islam,*
> *it will not be accepted from him and he will be*
> *one of the losers in the Hereafter." Quran 3:85*

In this Surah, the Fatihah *Allah* has taught His servants how to supplicate and speak to Him, simply and without a mediator.

In fact, besides referring to the Resurrection, this Surah presents facts concerning the Unity of the Divine

Essence, Unity of Attributes, Unity of Divine Acts, and Unity of Worship. It is the essence of the whole meaning of the Qur'an.

The recitation of this Surah, because of its extreme importance, is frequently emphasized in Islamic traditions and narrations.

As for its virtue, it is narrated from the holy Prophet (S) that:

> "The reward of any Muslim who recites the Surah 'Opening', is like that of a person who has recited two thirds of the Qur'an, and so much reward would he receive as if he has given every believing Muslim, man or woman, a free will offering "

> "In the name of God, the infinitely Compassionate and Merciful.

> Praise be to God, Lord of all the worlds. The Compassionate, the Merciful.

> Ruler on the Day of Reckoning. You alone do we worship, and You alone do we ask for help.

> Guide us on the straight path, the path of those who have received your grace; not the path of those who have brought down wrath, nor of those who wander astray.

> Amen."

Verse 7A, 'Those who wander astray' refers to the misguided Christians; and / maqdubi 'alayhim / and Verse 7b, 'those who have brought down Wrath' refers to the misguided Jews.

This prayer has been said at multi-faith gatherings and following Islamic terrorist attacks. After the Manchester bombing, a Muslim leader was given the honour of saying the opening prayer at the meeting of the Oldham city council. He shared the Al Fatiha, in Arabic, that demeans, denigrates and dehumanizes non-Muslims.[297] Think about that.

Osman Haji Madad, Sahaba Masjid, in Edmonton, Alberta:

> *"Who are those who earned the wrath of Allah? They are the Jews...[298] Those who were cursed by Allah. Allah was angry at them and turned them into monkeys and pigs."*

Founder and President of Al-Maghrib Institute (Born and raised in Canada):

> *"Adiyy ibn Hatim [one of the companions of Muhammad], May Allah, exalted be He, be please with him, asked the Prophet, blessings and peace of Allah be upon him, he said: "Who are the "Al-Maghdoubi Alaihim"? Who are those that evoked Allah's anger, that made Allah angry at them?"*

And the Prophet, blessings and peace of Allah be upon him, said "Houm Al-Yahood" [Arabic], they are the Jews. And so, every time you're reciting Surah [chapter] Al-

---

[297] Diane Weber Bederman, "What Do Judaism Christianity and Islam Have in Common? Part 3," Diane Bederman - Your Passionate Voice of Reason, November 12, 2017, https://dianebederman.com/what-do-judaism-christianity-and-islam-have-in-common-part-3/.
[298] Christians, Jews and Kuffar, YouTube.com (TIFRIBvideos, 2016), https://www.youtube.com/watch?v=42cSYW-P1iU.

Fatiha [first chapter of the Quran], and in fact in some Muslim countries they want to take out the verses because they want to have good relationships with Israel... they said let's not teach in our curriculum the verses that deal of and speak about the Jews and praise be to Allah, the scholars said:

> "What are [they] going to do with "Ghairi Al-Maghdoubi Alaihim" [not those who have incurred [Your] wrath]? Are they going to take Surah [chapter] Al-Fatiha from the curriculum? They cannot take it out..."

And so, because the Muslim youth aren't growing up on the "Aqida" [Islamic faith] and most beloved people to them are becoming actors and actresses, Jewish actresses, Christian actresses, when they hear a speech about how Allah, Exalted and Glorified be He, condemned the Jews, they say: What's wrong with Seinfeld? Every Wednesday at 8 pm, prime time television, they're watching Seinfeld and he's funny. [They say:] Are you telling me Seinfeld is going to hellfire? And that's in their mind. Because they have laughed and spent very joyous moments with the sitcom and now they cannot understand what Allah, Exalted and Glorified be He, is telling them in the Quran... If the Jews evoked Allah's anger then they did it for a reason and Allah page after page in the Quran shows us the reason why the Jews evoked Allah's, Exalted and Glorified be He, anger."

Omar Subedar, Imam at Makki Masjid in Brampton, Ontario and Vice President of Mathabah Institute:

> "First, I'm going to recite the verse. I seek refuge in Allah from Satan the accursed. In the name of Allah, the Beneficent the Merciful. Not the path

180

of those who have incurred Your anger or the path of those who have deviated, who have fallen astray. Now, who are these people? Whom are these categories Allah (swt) is referring to? The first group, the prophet (pbuh) has identified as the Jews, and the second group 'those who have deviated', the prophet, peace and blessing be upon him, has identified them as the Christians."[299]

Musleh Khan, Toronto Police Muslim Chaplain:

"Al-Timidhi reports in an authentic Hadith the Prophet (PBUH) was asked by a companion: those who have earned your anger, the Prophet (PBUH) says this refers to the Yahoudi [Jews] and then companion continue to ask the Prophet responds and says this refers to the Nasara [Christians] and those who have gone astray..."

Younus Kathrada, Vancouver, British Columbia:

"Pointing specifically at different groups here. As we said, although the Ayat (verses) include all non-Muslims whether they'd be Christians or Jews or other than them. But we speak about those who earned the wrath and the anger of Allah, Exalted and Glorified be He, specifically here the scholars speak of the Jews Al-Yahoud. Why? Well, if you look in the Quran, it's because they are the ones who are the most argumentative. They're the ones who knew, they have knowledge of things and yet they rejected

---

[299] Ramadan Tafseer in Five | Surah Fatihah - V.7 Part A - "The Path of Favour", YouTube.com (Mathabah, 2015), https://www.youtube.com/watch?v=CP_9fZC1KjI&t=9s.

it. So of course, they earned the wrath and the anger of Allah, Exalted and Glorified be He… We find that even in the Sunnah [narrations attributed to Muhammad statement or deeds] the Prophet [Mohammad], peace be upon him, they, because they know and yet they reject. Those who went astray, you know, because they don't base things on knowledge. It's all about emotion. And Glorified be Allah, the more we think about it, look at today even, you know, if you look at many of the Christians today, they like to talk about, everything is love, it's not based on knowledge. Nothing is knowledge-based. Everything is emotions, ok, and so they've gone astray because they refused to seek that knowledge and they refuse to act upon this knowledge that is present"

Sheikh Mashhoor Hasan explained in a lecture[300] in a Toronto mosque the meaning this chapter. The following are excerpts from his lecture translated by Abu Umar Abdulaziz: "Not those whom you have become angry on, not those who have deviated. The prophet [Mohammad], peace be upon him, said in Jami` at-Tirmidhi [collection of hadiths, narrations attributed to Mohammad], after he recited this verse, he said:

Those whom Allah is angry on [are] the Jews, and those who deviated they are the Christians. Why were the Jews called the ones whom Allah is angry on? And why the Christians called the ones went astray? It is very easy, but most of the Muslims they resemble themselves with these

---

[300] Tafsir Suratul Fatiha 04, YouTube.com (ibndaqeeq, 2012), https://www.youtube.com/watch?v=Q8U4UUrca9Y.

ones [Jews] or with these ones [Christians]... The Jews have been called the ones whom Allah is angry on because they had knowledge. They have knowledge but they don't act on this knowledge. And those who are astray [the Christians] are called astray because they do actions and they do acts of worship but they do have knowledge. "

According to Osman Haji, Imam of the Sahaba Masjid mosque in Edmonton Alberta, the Jews, who angered Allah, were cursed by Allah who "turned them into monkeys and pigs,"[301] Muhammad ash-Shawkani:

"In this 7th and last Ayah [verse] of [Surah – chapter] Al Fatiha, Allah [SWT] mentions the Muslims who practice Islam, the Jews and Christians... Those who have evoked the Wrath of Allah [SWT] are the Jews [or Israelites] who knew the full truth through Prophet Mousa [Alyhi Al Salam: AAS] but deviated from this truth with selfishness, pride and prejudice. They thus deserved the Wrath of Allah [SWT]. The astray, on the other hand, are the Christians who deviated from the Message of Prophet Isa [AAS] out of ignorance and ill-knowledge..."

"In his book *Commentary on The Holy Quran (Volume 1, SURAH AL-FATIHA)*, Mirzā Ghulām Ahmad, the leader and the founder of the Ahmadiyya Movement in Islam,

---

[301] Rachel Ehrenfeld, "What Are Praying Muslims Repeating 17 Times Daily?" ACDemocracy (American Center for Democracy, January 30, 2018), https://acdemocracy.org/what-are-praying-muslims-repeating-17-times-daily/.

explained verse no.7 of Al-Fatiha. The following are excerpts from the book (p. 338-340):

> *"All commentators are agreed that those who incurred Divine wrath and those who went astray are the Jews and Christians respectively. A prayer to be safeguarded against these mischiefs, not to be included among those who went astray, nor among those who incurred Divine wrath, has been taught. This must be repeatedly offered in the five daily Prayer services. It is thus clear that this is the biggest and most serious mischief which must be safeguarded against. It should be called the mother of mischiefs... Those who incurred Divine displeasure are the Jews and those who went astray are the Christians..."*

The following are the recommended daily prayers for Muslims in which the disbelievers are mentioned:

> *"Du'a [supplication] to overcome enemies... Our Lord! Forgive us our sins and our transgressions, establish our feet firmly, and give us victory over the disbelieving people." (3:147) The Witr (The Last Night prayer) ...we also abandon and reject anyone who disobeys you... Your punishment surely overtakes the disbelievers... The most comprehensive Supplication... You are our protector and give us victory over the disbelieving people."*

In Canada, public school boards are offering Muslim prayer rooms. These rooms have raised concerns by others. What is being taught?

In the 1990s, just a few years after The Lord's Prayer was removed from Canadian public schools, Muslim families requested the right for their children to pray in school; particularly on Friday, their Holy Day. Schools in Peel Region, just outside Toronto, Ontario, have been providing Muslim students a space for Friday prayers for 20 years.[302] The school board stresses that it is not promoting or teaching any religion.[303]

Since fall, 2016, Muslim students in the Peel Region have been sharing their dismay regarding their religious rights in public schools.

The Muslim students want the right to pray not only on Fridays, but every day of the week, if it is convenient for them. They also want the right to write their own sermons rather than rely on a series of six sermons provided by local Imams.

Campaign leader Shahmir Durrani, a University of Toronto at Mississauga student and activist for the Canadian Muslim Youth Federation, said:

> *"Eliminate the prohibition of allowing students to pray together outside of Jummah [Friday] prayers if it is convenient. [to the students] The board should not be policing religion."*

---

[302] Diane Weber Bederman, "Muslim Prayer in Public Schools," The Bederman Blog (Diane Weber Bederman, February 5, 2018), https://dianebederman.com/muslim-prayer-in-public-schools/.

[303] Editors, "Religious Accommodation," Religious Accommodation (Pell District School Board, 2021), https://www.peelschools.org/about/inclusion/religious-accommodation/Pages/default.aspx.

He added that the policy is unjust because it specifically targets Islam.

Maleeha Baig, a student at the same university and coordinator for the High School Muslim Student Associations, a subsidiary of the youth federation said:

> "Policing this one group [Muslims] based on prejudice and control... could have serious psychological impacts."

Imam Ibrahim Hindy also said:

> "The restriction risks evoking memories of dictatorial regimes where freedom of speech is tightly restricted, especially among newcomers to Canada. Regardless of whether that is the intent, that is the memory it triggers."

Most recently Hamza Aziz, 19, said he and other Muslim students felt insulted at the inference that their sermons could degenerate into hate speech.

> "It's as though you're looking at students through a lens of guilt, and making them feel like suspects as opposed to Canadians with rights and values," the student at Mississauga's John Fraser Secondary School said. "It's as though you're looked down upon."

I think the most important comment was made by Shahmir Durrani:

> "'The board should not be policing religion' and that the policy is unjust because it specifically targets Islam."

Let's take a moment and think about these concerns. Muslim students who are given the freedom to pray in public, non-sectarian schools where the Lords' Prayer is no longer shared, feel put upon, insulted that an adult would want to supervise their prayers.[304] Not just any adult; a Muslim. It is an attack on free speech. It is policing Muslims. Except it is not policing Muslims. It is adult supervision over a group of people who demanded the right to say this prayer on public school property. As students, they need to be supervised especially regarding sermons as they are still students of Islam. Yet Muslim leaders turned it into an attack on Islam. An attack on human rights.

In the past few years, parents of non-Muslim students have lodged complaints.

Ram Subrahmanian, a Hindu member of the group *Keep Religion Out Of Our Public Schools (KROOPS)*, whose youngest child is in the last year of high school in Peel, says he is against all religious practice at schools.

> *"You cannot expect the public system to meet the requirements of your religion. As Canadians, we are secular, we are accepting and we are tolerant but that doesn't mean that we will allow others to impose themselves on us."[305]*

---

[304] Diane Weber Bederman, "Muslim Students Insulted at Public Schools," The Bederman Blog (Diane Weber Bederman, January 8, 2017), https://dianebederman.com/muslim-students-insulted-at-public-schools/.

[305] Kristina Jovanovski, "Canadian Groups Are Lashing out about Muslim Prayer in Schools," The World (PRX and WGBH Boston, May 24, 2017), https://www.pri.org/stories/2017-05-24/canadian-groups-are-lashing-out-about-muslim-prayer-schools.

He says his religious group is sensitive to issues involving Muslims. Since 1947, India and Pakistan have fought three wars with each other. Since then, violence between Hindus and Sikhs and Muslims in India itself have also been bitter and violent. Does he have an irrational fear of Islam?

Ron Banerjee, of Canadian Hindu Advocacy, said he received complaints from Hindu parents who were concerned about the potential for inflammatory preaching against their faith.[306] Do they have an irrational fear of Islam?

According to Amira Elghawaby, the communications director for the National Council of Canadian Muslims (formerly known as CAIR-CAN) this issue is:

> *"...simply Islamophobia. It's anti-Muslim sentiment ... couched in a concern about religion in schools. It would be disheartening if indeed people are bringing any sort of baggage from their own maybe experiences in another country to this debate. That would be unfortunate."*

Yet, Muslims are bringing their own baggage.

It is the threat of being labeled an Islamophobe that makes criticizing these actions difficult, if not impossible. Yet Canada, like many western countries, prides itself on its multiculturalism, its respect for diversity. What about the concerns of Hindu families, Jews and Christians?

---

[306] Charles Lewis, "Muslim Prayers during Class Time Draws Fire at Toronto School," nationalpost.com (Postmedia Network Inc., July 5, 2011), https://nationalpost.com/holy-post/muslim-prayers-during-class-time-draws-fire-at-toronto-school.

Considering the ruling to remove Christian prayer from the schools, should we be opening our schools to prayer from different religious groups? Does allowing different groups to break off into their own prayer spaces promote diversity and inclusiveness?

Do the prayers being shared in our public schools promote tolerance, inclusion and accommodation? Do they promote our common shared values of caring for the other and acknowledging that all people are born with equal intrinsic value, and that all life is sacred? If not, and the Al Fatiha appears to attack all non-Muslims, Jews and Christians in particular, why do we allow them to be said in public schools? [307]

---

[307] Diane Weber Bederman, "Hate Incidents All Start with Words," The Bederman Blog (Diane Weber Bederman, April 3, 2019), https://dianebederman.com/hate-incidents-all-start-with-words/.

CHAPTER 16: WHY ARE GOVERNMENTS AND MEDIA PROMOTING ISLAMOPHOBIA?

"The most successful tyranny is not one that uses force to assure uniformity but the one that removes awareness of other possibilities...that makes it seem inconceivable that other ways are viable, that removes the sense that there is an outside."

~ Alan Bloom

The #IslamophobiaIndustry has managed to convince us that saying anything negative about Islam is racist, even though Islam is not a race. That Islam attacks Jews, Christians, Hindus, and all other non-Muslims is irrelevant.

The #IslamophobiaIndustry is expert in silencing free speech, freedom of thought and public relations. They have cornered the market on guilt. We are often told following a terror attack by a Muslim that we must protect the Muslim communities from backlash as if they were the victims. In the wake of the Ottawa, Canada shootings, the police chiefs of Toronto and Ottawa wrote to local Muslim leaders[308], assuring them of their good

---

[308] Robert Spencer, "In Wake of Ottawa Shootings, Police Chiefs Send Letters to Muslim Leaders Inviting Muslims to Contact Them If They Fear 'Backlash,'" Jihad Watch, October 22, 2014, https://www.jihadwatch.org/2014/10/in-wake-of-ottawa-shootings-police-chiefs-send-letters-to-muslim-leaders-inviting-muslims-to-contact-them-if-they-fear-

will and urging Muslims to contact them in case of a "backlash."[309]

Canadian Prime Minister Justin Trudeau said:

> *"Democracy only works in a country like Canada if people are free to express their fears, their concerns, their opinions, and we get an opportunity to respond to them."*

But what of the fears expressed about Islam?

Sadly, freedom of speech is under attack from accusations of Islamophobia. And these attacks are aided and abetted by governments and media outlets around the world. While you read this chapter, keep in mind that China tried to silence Americans with economic coercion after a pro-Hong Kong tweet.[310] America was not silenced.

> *"When the public's right to know is threatened, and when the rights of free speech and free press are at risk, all of the other liberties we hold dear are endangered."*
>
> ~ Christopher Dodd

---

backlash.

[309] Robert Spencer, "Canada's Jihad Denial," FrontPageMag Archive (Frontpagemag.com, October 23, 2014), https://archives.frontpagemag.com/fpm/canadas-jihad-denial-robert-spencer/.

[310] David Mulroney, "Opinion: The NBA'S China Crisis Is Proof That Economic Diplomacy Is No Slam Dunk," TheGlobeandMail.com (The Globe and Mail Inc., October 15, 2019), https://www.theglobeandmail.com/opinion/article-the-nbas-china-crisis-is-proof-that-economic-diplomacy-is-no-slam/.

Let's start with Muslim media outlets which have the same purpose as the Chinese media outlets that are available in the west.

Al Jazeera media network, a colossus that reaches more than 300 million people and is funded by the government of Qatar is one of the world's largest and best-known broadcasters. Daniel Pipes writes "Its English-language stations produce slick propaganda against Qatar's enemies, dressed up in Western liberal rhetoric."[311]

Al Jazeera opened in 1996 in Arabic and in English in 2006. It is considered a "soft power tool on the international stage."

I believe the word that best fits that description is propaganda.

Egypt has accused Qatar[312] for its support for Islamist groups, including Hamas, a militant Palestinian Brotherhood affiliate whose political leadership has enjoyed a safe haven in Doha.

Yet, in 2011, then Secretary of State Hillary Clinton congratulated Al Jazeera TV news network for its work in covering uprisings throughout the Middle East.[313]

---

[311] Daniel Pipes, "Examining Qatar's Influence," DanielPipes.org (Daniel Pipes, January 29, 2019), http://www.danielpipes.org/18699/qatar-influence.

[312] Daniel Marans, "Al Jazeera Employees Fear Consequences of Qatar Crisis for Network," HuffPost Canada (BuzzFeed, Inc., June 9, 2017), https://www.huffingtonpost.ca/entry/al-jazeera-employees-fear-qatar-crisis-consequences_n_593a9ffee4b0c5a35c9ea755.

[313] David Folkenflik, "Clinton Lauds Virtues of Al Jazeera: 'It's Real News'," NPR.org (National Public Radio, March 3, 2011),

"You've got a global — a set of global networks — that Al Jazeera has been the leader in, that are literally changing people's minds and attitudes," Clinton told members of the U.S. Senate Foreign Relations Committee.

"Viewership of Al Jazeera is going up in the United States because it's real news," Clinton said.

"You may not agree with it, but you feel like you're getting real news around the clock instead of a million commercials and, you know, arguments between talking heads, and the kind of stuff that we do on our news," Clinton said. "Which, you know, is not particularly informative to us, let alone foreigners."

It was announced in 2019 that Al Jazeera Media Network would partner with Bloomberg Media Distribution as part of a content license agreement to expand its global business news coverage.[314] Select Bloomberg content like digital video and charts will run on Al Jazeera's English-language digital properties, the company said. Al Jazeera's content will also be available to Bloomberg terminal subscribers.

Al Jazeera also has a social media channel AJ+ and is aimed at young American Progressives. Documentaries focus on Israel as an evil empire as well as Saudi Arabia (also a Sunni Muslim country).

AJ+ also produced an anti-Semitic Holocaust-denial video. The video denied that exterminations took place

---

https://www.npr.org/sections/thetwo-way/2011/03/03/134243115/clinton-lauds-virtues-of-al-jazeera-its-real-news.

[314] "Al Jazeera Partners with Bloomberg to Expand Business Coverage," Reuters (Thomson Reuters, February 11, 2019), https://mobile.reuters.com/article/amp/idUSKCN1Q00K3.

at Nazi concentration camps and claimed that the Zionist movement was the biggest beneficiary from the Holocaust.

Another outlet, also funded by Qatar, is the New Arab or Al-Araby Al-Jadeed.[315] It is a pan-Arab media outlet headquartered and registered in London, England.[316] It was first launched in March 2014 as an online news website by Qatari company Fadaat Media with the objective: "To set up and operate television and broadcasting stations and services, publishing and printing newspapers and magazines." And as a counter to Al Jazeera as it was felt that Al Jazeera was too close to the Muslim Brotherhood.

The station is led by the Emir of Qatar, Sheikh Tamim bin Hamad Al Thani. The driving force behind the station is Azmi Bishara, the Palestinian director of the Doha-based Arab Centre for Research and Policy Studies, and a close confidant of the emir.

Now Pakistan, Turkey and Malaysia are launching a BBC style English television channel to highlight the issues of Muslims and fight Islamophobia in the West. Under the joint venture, web series and films will be produced to spread knowledge on Islamic history to educate and inform Muslims and the world giving Muslims a dedicated media presence.[317]

---

[315] Justin Vela, "Qatar to Launch Al Jazeera Counterweight," The National (The National, June 17, 2021), https://www.thenationalnews.com/world/qatar-to-launch-al-jazeera-counterweight-1.244186.
[316] "Home Page | The New Arab," The New Arab (Fadaat Media Ltd., 2021), https://english.alaraby.co.uk/.
[317] "Malaysia, Turkey and Pakistan to Jointly Launch Channel to Counter Islamophobia - Times of India," The Times of India

While Muslim countries are promoting their ideology through their media outlets, western governments and journalists are failing us.

The European Commission against Racism and Intolerance (ECRI) has delivered an 83-page report. [318],[319]

> *"ECRI considers that, in light of the fact that Muslims are increasingly under the spotlight as a result of recent ISIS-related terrorist acts around the world, fueling prejudice against Muslims shows a reckless disregard, not only for the dignity of the great majority of Muslims in the United Kingdom, but also for their safety.*
>
> *In this context, it draws attention to a recent study by Teeside University suggesting that where the media stress the Muslim background of perpetrators of terrorist acts, and devote significant coverage to it, the violent backlash*

(Bennett, Coleman & Co. Ltd., September 30, 2019), https://timesofindia.indiatimes.com/world/rest-of-world/malaysia-turkey-and-pakistan-to-jointly-launch-channel-to-counter-islamophobia/articleshow/71377023.cms.

[318] Matt Dathan, "European Human Rights Chiefs Order the British Press NOT to Reveal When Terrorists Are Muslims in Crackdown on Freedom of Speech," Daily Mail Online (Associated Newspapers Ltd, October 5, 2016), https://www.dailymail.co.uk/news/article-3823706/European-human-rights-chiefs-orders-British-press-NOT-reveal-terrorists-Muslims.html.

[319] CBN News, "EU: British Press Should Not Report When Terrorists Are Muslim," CBN News (Christian Broadcasting Network, Inc., October 6, 2016), https://www1.cbn.com/cbnnews/world/2016/october/eu-british-press-should-not-report-when-terrorists-are-muslim.

against Muslims is likely to be greater than in cases where the perpetrators' motivation is downplayed or rejected in favour of alternative explanations."

The report "strongly recommends that the authorities find a way to establish an independent press regulator according to the recommendations set out in the Leveson Report. It recommends more rigorous training for journalists to ensure better compliance with ethical standards."

Chair Christian Ahlund, said: 'It is no coincidence that racist violence is on the rise in the UK at the same time as we see worrying examples of intolerance and hate speech in the newspapers, online and even among politicians.'

In other words, reporting facts cannot be tolerated as those facts may upset certain people and cause a backlash against them. Better to put one's head in the sand and pretend it doesn't exist. And if it does not exist there is no need to investigate any of it.

It also claims Islamophobia rises when media reports when terrorists are Muslim. As a result, European human rights chiefs have told the British press it must not report when terrorists are Muslim. The report recommends ministers 'give more rigorous training' to journalists. "[W]here the media stress the Muslim background of perpetrators of terrorist acts, and devote significant coverage to it, the violent backlash against Muslims is likely to be greater than in cases where the perpetrators' motivation is downplayed or rejected in favour of alternative explanations.

Do these changes in reporting explain the delay in reporting the 2016 Cologne New Year's Eve gang rapes which were held back for three days? Twelve hundred females were sexually abused in German cities during New Year's Eve celebrations.[320] The police document stated detectives believe 2,000 men were involved across various cities.

Between 1997 and 2013 at least 1,400 children were subjected to appalling sexual exploitation in Rotherham, England. Children as young as 11 were raped by multiple perpetrators, abducted, trafficked to other cities in England, beaten and intimidated. That's 16 years. All but one of the perpetrators was Muslim of Pakistani heritage.

Allison Pearson, an award-winning columnist and the chief interviewer of the Daily Telegraph, reported in August 2014:

> *"Men of Pakistani heritage treated white girls like toilet paper. They picked children up from schools and care homes and trafficked them across northern cities for other men to join in the fun. They doused a 15-year-old in petrol and threatened to set her alight should she dare to report them. They menaced entire families and made young girls watch as they raped other children."* [321,322]

---

[320] Yermi Brenner and Katrin Ohlendorf, "Time for the Facts. What Do We Know about Cologne Four Months Later?" The Correspondent, May 2, 2016, https://thecorrespondent.com/4401/time-for-the-facts-what-do-we-know-about-cologne-four-months-later/1073698080444-e20ada1b.

[321] Allison Pearson, "Rotherham: In the Face of Such Evil, Who

Rotherham has the third-most-segregated Muslim population in England: The majority of the Pakistani community, 82 percent, lives in just three of the town's council electoral wards. Rotherham's abusers found that their ethnicity protected them because they belonged to a community few wished to challenge. Professor Alexis Jay, appointed to the Panel of the Independent Inquiry into Child Sexual Abuse in 2015 and appointed as Chair of the Inquiry by the Home Secretary in August 2016, wrote the report on this abuse of girls. She observed that the South Yorkshire Police "regarded many child victims with contempt."

The Professor noted that Rotherham is not an isolated case. Similar abuses have taken place in towns and cities across England. The abusers are not pedophiles, but groups of men who enjoy having sex with young girls, and have no problem with violence.

> "Denis MacShane, MP for Rotherham from 1994 to 2012, actually admitted to the BBC's World at One that: "there was a culture of not wanting to rock the multicultural community boat, if I may put it like that. Perhaps, yes, as a true Guardian reader and liberal Leftie, I suppose I didn't want to raise that too hard."

Is the Racist Now?" The Telegraph (Telegraph Media Group, August 27, 2014), https://www.telegraph.co.uk/news/uknews/crime/11059138/Rotherham-In-the-face-of-such-evil-who-is-the-racist-now.html.
[322] Diane Weber Bederman, "#Rotherham: Where Are the #Metoo Feminists?" The Bederman Blog, January 11, 2018, https://dianebederman.com/rotherham-where-are-the-metoo-feminists/.

"Equally horrifying is the suggestion that certain Pakistani councillors asked social workers to reveal the addresses of the shelters where some of the abused girls were hiding. The former deputy leader of the council, Jahangir Akhtar, is accused of "ignoring a politically inconvenient truth" by insisting there was not a deep-rooted problem of Pakistani-heritage perpetrators targeting young white girls. The inquiry was told that influential Pakistani councillors acted as "barriers to communication" on grooming issues."

"Far from discouraging racism, the Labour policy of withholding the ethnic identity of men who preyed on white girls backfired spectacularly.

"Criminally, it endangered hundreds of children who might otherwise have been spared. A recent poll showed that 44 per cent of young Britons believe that Muslims do not share the same values as the rest of the population, while 28 per cent said they felt Britain would be "better off" with fewer Muslims.

"Thanks to Prof. Jay, it has been stated publicly for the first time that the fear of appearing racist was more pressing in official minds than enforcing the law of the land or rescuing terrified children. It is one of the great scandals of our lifetime."

One would think that this would be the only attack on white girls by Muslims from Pakistan. But no. There was a scandal in 2010.

A report detailing how gangs of Asian men in Birmingham were grooming schoolgirls with alcohol and drugs was not made public after senior officers warned that such information could inflame racial tensions ahead of the 2010 General Election.

West Midlands Police were warned that more than 100 predominantly white school children - some as young as 13 - were at serious risk of child exploitation, with abusers approaching pupils at the school gates.

Police said they had identified 75 suspects, most boasting a history of sexual violence and most of whom came from the Pakistani community in Birmingham.

The report, which was released under the Freedom of Information Act, but was redacted, identified one school where teachers had brought the problem to the police's attention.

It said officers had identified almost 140 potential victims some as young as 13, who were being plied with drugs and alcohol and then sexually abused and raped.

But the police report, which was shared with social services and other agencies at the time, stated:

"The predominant offender profile of Pakistani Muslim males... combined with the predominant victim profile of white females has the potential to cause significant community tensions. There is a potential for a backlash against the vast majority of law-abiding citizens from Asian/Pakistani communities from other members of the community believing their children have been exploited."

This is the result of the spread of Islam as a race and Islamophobia as racist by government and its institutions. All of it done by the #IslamophobiaIndustry.

"Freedom of the Press, if it means anything at all, means the freedom to criticize and oppose."

~ George Orwell

Controlling free speech has taken the form of 'cooperating' with the internet giants -- Facebook, Google, Twitter and YouTube -- on voluntary initiatives such as the EU "Code of Conduct on countering illegal online hate speech online"[323], which requires social media giants to act as censors on behalf of the European Union and to remove within 24 hours content that is regarded as "illegal hate speech"[324].

In 2015, German Chancellor Angela Merkel was overheard confronting Facebook CEO Mark Zuckerberg over incendiary posts on the social network that might "offend Muslims."[325]

---

[323] "The EU Code of Conduct on Countering Illegal Hate Speech Online," European Commission, June 25, 2021, https://ec.europa.eu/info/policies/justice-and-fundamental-rights/combatting-discrimination/racism-and-xenophobia/eu-code-conduct-countering-illegal-hate-speech-online_en.

[324] Judith Bergman, "Facebook: More Government Censorship," Gatestone Institute, July 16, 2019, https://www.gatestoneinstitute.org/14293/facebook-government-censorship.

[325] Javier E. David, "Angela Merkel Caught on Hot Mic Griping to Facebook CEO over Anti-Immigrant Posts," CNBC (CNBC LLC, September 27, 2015),

This began a new censorship programme on social media. Unknown people decide what is and is not Islamophobic. Whatever that means.

This control of free speech has also brought about national legislation, such as Germany's censorship law,[326] in 2018. This law requires social media platforms to delete or block any alleged online "criminal offenses", such as libel, slander, defamation or incitement, within 24 hours of receipt of a user complaint. If the platforms fail to do so, the German government can fine them up to 50 million euros for failing to comply with the law.

In Denmark, an outspoken critic of Islam, Jaleh Tavakoli, a Danish-Iranian blogger and author of the book, *Public Secrets of Islam*, shared an online video of the rape and murder of two Scandinavian young women in Morocco by Islamic State terrorists.[327] Tavakoli was not only charged for sharing the video but was threatened that the state would take away her foster daughter. Tavakoli explained[328] that she shared the video because

---

https://www.cnbc.com/2015/09/27/angela-merkel-caught-on-hot-mic-pressing-facebook-ceo-over-anti-immigrant-posts.html.

[326] Judith Bergman, "Germany: Full Censorship Now Official," Gatestone Institute, October 21, 2017, https://www.gatestoneinstitute.org/11205/germany-official-censorship.

[327] "Fifteen Men Charged over Beheadings of Female Hikers in Morocco," Sky News (Sky UK, December 31, 2018), https://news.sky.com/story/fifteen-men-charged-over-beheadings-of-female-hikers-in-morocco-11595382.

[328] Sebastian Goos and Maja Kærhus Jørgensen, "[Translated] Shared Murder Video Online - Now Authorities Want to Remove Danish Debater's Foster Child," nyheder.tv2.dk (TV 2 DANMARK, March 14, 2019), https://nyheder.tv2.dk/2019-03-

the international media was reporting that the Danish woman had been beheaded -- while no such information was to be found in the Danish media. How are citizens supposed to be able to even talk about Islamic terrorism -- or any terrorism -- if governments criminalize people who post information about the atrocities committed by such terrorists?

French judges condemned the journalist Éric Zemmour -- who is under heavy police protection for his criticism of Islam -- for "religious hate." Zemmour, apparently, was found "guilty" by a French court of saying that Muslims should be given "the choice between Islam and France" and that "in innumerable French suburbs there is a struggle to Islamize territory."[329] Perhaps this choice would be impossible for Muslims in France to make if they believe in shirk. I wrote about shirk in CHAPTER SHIRK: Why does Islam say no to liberalism? Freedom of expression and the freedom to criticism of Islam are under threat in France.

The French parliament passed another law, severely punishing anyone who says or writes something that might contain "hate speech".[330,331] The law is so vague

---

14-delte-drabsvideo-paa-nettet-nu-vil-myndigheder-fjerne-dansk-debattoers-plejebarn.

[329] Franceinfo with AFP and France Televisions, "[Translated] Eric Zemmour Definitively Condemned for Anti-Muslim Remarks," Franceinfo, September 19, 2019, https://www.francetvinfo.fr/societe/justice/eric-zemmour-definitivement-condamne-pour-des-propos-anti-musulmans_3623557.html.

[330] Le Figaro with AFP and Reuters , "[Translated] Online Hate: the Assembly Votes on the Avia Bill at First Reading," Le Figaro, July 9, 2019, https://web.archive.org/web/20190709145543/http://www.l

that an American legal scholar, Jonathan Turley, felt compelled to react. "France has now become one of the biggest international threats to freedom of speech," he wrote.[332]

There is no free speech in Islam. In terms of Islamic law, the public utterance of hurtful speech and blasphemy constitute violations of the right to freedom of expression. Freedom must be limited when it reaches the bounds of hate speech and blasphemy and when it infringes the human dignity of Muslims worldwide.[333]

The fear of appearing Islamophobic has infected governments all over the world. Why is there a fear? Why should a government fear criticizing an ideology? This reminds me of the fear of Nazism which almost destroyed western civilization. Too many governments feared them and appeased them and were taken down. Why should any western government fear critiquing Islam?

---

efigaro.fr/politique/haine-en-ligne-l-assemblee-vote-la-proposition-de-loi-avia-en-premiere-lecture-20190709.

[331] Judith Bergman, "Facebook: More Government Censorship," Gatestone Institute, July 16, 2019

[332] Jonathan Turley, "France Has Turned into One of the Worldwide Threats to Free Speech," TheHill.com (Nexstar Media Inc., July 7, 2019), https://thehill.com/opinion/civil-rights/451813-france-has-turned-into-one-of-the-worldwide-threats-to-free-speech.

[333] Nazeem MI Goolam, "The Cartoon Controversy: a Note on Freedom of Expression, Hate Speech and Blasphemy," The Comparative and International Law Journal of Southern Africa 39, no. 2 (July 2006): pp. 333-350, https://www.jstor.org/stable/23252640.

Federica Maria Mogherin, an Italian politician who has served as High Representative of the Union for Foreign Affairs and Security Policy and Vice-President of the European Commission since November 2014, shared her concerns, and one assumes the views of the Commission, on Islamophobia:

> *"One issue on which I believe it is crucial that Arabs and Europeans work together very closely: we need to preserve diversity in our societies. We need to prevent the rise of hate, starting with preventing Islamophobia in our societies. We need to work together to make sure that in all our countries, no one excluded in Europe as in the Arab world, everyone is accepted, protected and respected as a human being, whatever his or her background is, whatever religious belief, gender, age, identity. We value diversity and we believe that everyone needs to find his and her place in our societies. So, we have a joint interest and a joint responsibility to nourish and preserve diversity and together with that the dignity of every single human being".*[334]

Do we reduce Islamophobia by removing references to Islamic terrorism? This was attempted in America. Philip Haney, a former Department of Homeland Security agent wrote about this phenomenon in the Obama administration.[335]

---

[334] Judith Bergman, "The EU Courts the Arab League," Gatestone Institute, May 7, 2019, https://www.gatestoneinstitute.org/14188/eu-courts-arab-league.

[335] Philip Haney, "DHS Ordered Me to Scrub Records of Muslims with Terror Ties," TheHill.com (Nexstar Media Inc.,

As the number of successful and attempted Islamic terrorist attacks on America increased, the type of information that Obama administration ordered removed from travel and national security databases was the kind of information that, if properly assessed, could have prevented subsequent domestic Islamist attacks like the ones committed by Faisal Shahzad[336] (Ma y 2010), Detroit "honor killing" perpetrator Rahim A. Alfetlawi[337] (2011); Amine El Khalifi, who plotted to blow up the U.S. Capitol[338] (2012); Dzhokhar or Tamerlan Tsarnaev, who conducted the Boston Marathon bombing[339] (2013); Oklahoma beheading suspect Alton Nolen[340] (201

February 5, 2016), https://thehill.com/blogs/congress-blog/homeland-security/268282-dhs-ordered-me-to-scrub-records-of-muslims-with-terror.

[336] Jim Lehrer and Ailsa Chang, "Shahzad 'Extremely Defiant' at Sentencing for Failed NYC Bombing," PBS.org (Public Broadcasting Service, October 5, 2010), https://www.pbs.org/newshour/show/shahzad-extremely-defiant-at-sentencing-for-failed-nyc-bombing.

[337] "Cops: Killer Felt Stepdaughter Ignored Faith," https://www.inquirer.com (The Philadelphia Inquirer, May 4, 2011), https://www.inquirer.com/philly/news/nation_world/201105 04_Cops__Killer_felt_daughter_ignored_faith.html.

[338] U.S. Attorney's Office, Eastern District of Virginia, "Virginia Man Sentenced to 30 Years in Prison for Plot to Carry out Suicide Bomb Attack on U.S. Capitol," archives.fbi.org (Federal Bureau of Investigation, September 14, 2012), https://archives.fbi.gov/archives/washingtondc/press-releases/2012/virginia-man-sentenced-to-30-years-in-prison-for-plot-to-carry-out-suicide-bomb-attack-on-u.s.-capitol.

[339] "Boston Marathon Bombing of 2013," Encyclopædia Britannica (Encyclopædia Britannica, Inc., 2021), https://www.britannica.com/event/Boston-Marathon-bombing-of-2013.

4); or Muhammed Yusuf Abdulazeez,[341] who opened fire on two military installations in Chattanooga, Tennessee (2015).

Canada has been busy changing its references to Islamists, as well.[342] In the 2018 Public Report on the Terrorism Threat to Canada, [343] Canada decided to remove the phrase "inspired by violent Sunni Islamist ideology and terrorist groups" from its list of banned terrorist organizations. Public Safety Minister Ralph Goodale explained he wanted the terrorist threat report to use language that "did not impugn or condemn an entire religion."

---

[340] Erik Ortiz et al., "Man Beheaded Co-Worker in Moore, Oklahoma, Workplace Attack: Police," NBCNews.com (NBC Universal News Group, June 11, 2015), https://www.nbcnews.com/news/crime-courts/man-beheaded-co-worker-moore-oklahoma-workplace-attack-police-n212396.

[341] Kyle Shideler, "Another Jihad Attack, Another MB Mosque - Will There Be an Investigation?," Center for Security Policy, July 17, 2015, https://centerforsecuritypolicy.org/another-jihad-attack-another-mb-mosque-will-there-be-an-investigation/.

[342] Rob Breakenridge, "Commentary: Properly Describing the Terror Threat Means Acknowledging Religious Extremism Exists," Global News (Global News, a division of Corus Entertainment Inc., April 19, 2021), https://globalnews.ca/news/5238890/terror-threat-canada-shia-sunni/.

[343] "2018 Public Report on the Terrorism Threat to Canada," 2018 Public Report on the Terrorism Threat to Canada § (2019), https://www.publicsafety.gc.ca/cnt/rsrcs/pblctns/pblc-rprt-trrrsm-thrt-cnd-2018/index-en.aspx.

"The idea, the objective here is to get language which is precise, which focuses on the issue that is being reported on in a clear and accurate way that does not impugn an entire community or an entire religion that is not responsible for the terrorist behavior."

Does that mean removing references to Islam or Muslims? Have we erased references to the Mafia for fear of impugning the entire Italian community?

The European Union drafted the European Convention on Human Rights in 1950. Each of the numbered "articles" protects a basic human right. Taken together, they allow people to lead free and dignified lives.[344]

Article 10 of the European Convention on Human Rights states that Europeans are free "to hold opinions and to receive and impart information and ideas without interference by public authority and regardless of frontiers." These rights come with responsibilities which can impede some freedoms for the good of the citizenry. Freedom to hold opinions can be affected by the need to protect public safety including "the prevention of disorder or crime, for the protection of health or morals, for the protection of the reputation or rights of others." The proverbial admonition against calling out fire in a movie theatre when there is no fire. A limit on free speech. Article 10 also protects "the right of others to have their religious

---

[344] "European Convention on Human Rights," European Convention on Human Rights - Official texts, Convention and Protocols (European Court of Human Rights, 2021), https://www.echr.coe.int/Pages/home.aspx?p=basictexts&c.

feelings protected," as well as "the legitimate aim of preserving religious peace."

Sounds good, except that Islamic leaders took Elisabeth Sabaditsch-Wolff to court in 2009 for two seminars about Mohammed and his wife Aisha.

Ms. Sabaditsch-Wolff was criminally convicted under Austria's "defamation of religion" law for "publicly denigrating" the Islamic prophet Muhammad "in a way likely to arouse justified indignation." Her crime? Asking in a private seminar *"A 56-year-old and a six-year-old? What do we call it, if it is not pedophilia?"* She was referring to Islamic texts[345] stating that Muhammad married Aisha when she was six years old, and consummated their marriage when she was nine. It is an accurate account of authoritative Islamic scripture.

The discussion seemed to suggest that the prophet was a pedophile and in Islam one cannot say anything negative about the Prophet. Except this was in Europe where one used to have the freedom to compare and contrast and criticize all ideologies, theologies and theories. She was fined for disparaging religion.[346]

---

[345] "Sahih Bukhari : Book Of 'Merits of Al-Ansaar,'" Sahih Bukhari : Book Of "Merits of Al-Ansaar", accessed September 6, 2021, https://www.sahih-bukhari.com/Pages/Bukhari_5_58.php.

[346] Andrew C. McCarthy, "In Europe, Free Speech Bows to Sharia," National Review (National Review Institute, October 27, 2018), https://www.nationalreview.com/2018/10/free-speech-sharia-european-court-of-human-rights-ruling/?fbclid=IwAR2U0X9Mk8rUkm3sEdeIk7BCHjJEfkqF7o2fh95ZQ8s6UweO0A44iyUB9oA.

Elisabeth Sabaditsch-Wolff's appeal to the Grand Chamber of the European Court of Human Rights (ECHR) was rejected in 2019.

The ECHR is saying that quoting the Koran could be seen as racist! That reliance on scripture could be classified as "an abusive attack on the Prophet of Islam, which could stir up prejudice and put at risk religious peace." Have they ruled on quoting the Bible?

Sadly, governments around the world are aiding and abetting the #IslamophobiaIndustry with new laws that silence criticism of Islam by journalists.

> "Freedom of the press, or, to be more precise, the benefit of freedom of the press, belongs to everyone – to the citizen as well as the publisher... The crux is not the publisher's 'freedom to print'; it is, rather, the citizen's 'right to know.' "

~ Arthur Hays Sulzberge

The EU is openly working at influencing the "free press" with its own political agendas.

The European Federation of Journalists (EJF), the largest organization of journalists in Europe, representing more than 320,000 journalists in 71 journalists' organizations across 43 countries is leading a Europe-wide campaign called "Media against Hate."[347]

Their mission is countering hate speech and discrimination in the media, both on and offline, by

---

[347] "About 'Media Against Hate,'" #MediaAgainstHate (European Federation of Journalists (EFJ), 2016), http://europeanjournalists.org/mediaagainsthate/about/.

promoting ethical standards, while maintaining respect for freedom of expression. They believe that the rights to equality and freedom of expression are mutually reinforcing and essential to human dignity.

Their concern is "As hate speech and stereotypes targeting migrants proliferate across Europe, balanced and fair media reporting is needed more than ever. Despite some good journalism practices, additional training and resources for media professionals and media organisations will help promote dialogue and democratic processes."

Involving partners from across Europe, including Article 19, Media Diversity Institute (MDI), Croatian Journalists' Association (CJA), Cooperazione per lo Sviluppo dei Paesi Emergenti (COSPE), Community Media Institute (COMMIT), Community Media Forum Europe (CMFE) and the EFJ, the #MediaAgainstHate campaign aims to: improve media coverage related to migration, refugees, religion and marginalized groups in general and improve the capacity of journalists, media, Civil Society Organizations (CSO) and community media to counter hate speech, intolerance, racism and discrimination.

In 2017 the Swedish government began to introduce three major changes to the Basic Laws of the Realm. The first proposition "Revised Fundamental Laws for the Media" (2017/18:49)[348] has already been sent to the

---

[348] Margot Wallström and Morgan Johansson, "Ändrade Mediegrundlagar Proposition 2017/18:49," Sveriges Riksdag, November 30, 2017, https://www.riksdagen.se/sv/dokument-lagar/dokument/proposition/andrade-mediegrundlagar_H50349/html.

Riksdag (parliament) for preparation by the Committee on the Constitution.

The proposal has been criticized, for example, by Judge Katarina Rikte of the Court of Appeal for Skåne and Blekinge:

> *"What they do with these rules is to open up a giant black hole in the constitution. It's not the case that you can't publish or express anything in a media outlet covered by constitutional protection. You may publish anything, but you can be punished afterwards for certain publications."*

> *"Within just a few years, the journalists who do not agree with the government's narrative, or who suffer from the poor judgement to embark on investigative reporting, may be in serious trouble."*

Then there was the 91-year-old Swedish pensioner fined for hate speech after posting critical passages about Islam and Muslims.[349]

The court said, "The messages have content that is clearly abusive to Muslims and it, therefore, expresses such inaccuracy as is required to be held liable for the crimes against ethnic groups." Except Muslims are not an ethnic group. Islam is a religion and ideology. People following Islam are called Muslim and Muslims come from all over the world, from many ethnic groups.

---

[349] Chris Tomlinson, "91-Year-Old Swede Convicted For Anti-Islam Hate Speech," Breitbart.com (Breitbart News, March 31, 2019), https://www.breitbart.com/europe/2019/03/31/91-year-old-swede-convicted-anti-islam-hate-speech/.

A Swedish online "social justice" group called Näthatsgranskaren, Swedish for "Network Examiner," comprised of lawyers, former police officers, and other professionals are said to be behind the rise of prosecutions against Swedes for "hate speech" on social media platforms. The organization gathers data on social media posts deemed to be breaking Sweden's hate speech laws and reports them to police. So far, the group has identified 800 or so "hate posts" which they have reported to authorities, though of these only 13 per cent have been acted upon.

The average age of the Facebook "haters" is 65.

Sweden is expected to receive another 7.5 million Swedish Kronor (£618,375/$807,150) from the European Union in 2019 to go towards hate crime projects. The more "hate" found the more money these organizations will receive. These projects seem to be directed at citizens commenting on Islam.

The Swedish government is worried about the rise in hate crimes. Would that all hate crimes around the world be as benign as these.

Whether by chance or design, Europe is importing Sharia Law regarding speech. In Islam, one cannot disparage Mohamed or Islam. We saw the results in France at Charlie Hebdo. Philippe Val, the former editor of the magazine *Charlie Hebdo*, declared "It is certain that no one today would publish the cartoons of Muhammad."[350]

---

[350] Elisabeth Lévy, ed., "[Translated] Philippe Val: 'Nobody Today Would Publish the Cartoons of Muhammad,'" Causeur.fr, August 5, 2019, https://www.causeur.fr/philippe-val-charlie-hebdo-gauche-163103.

CHAPTER 17: IS ISLAM COMPATIBLE WITH THE WEST?

"Tolerance becomes a crime when applied to evil."

~ Thomas Mann

While we are prepared to criticize other ideologies, governments, belief systems, our leaders in the West go out of their way to ingratiate themselves with Islam. We are told by Western leaders that Islam is compatible with the West. From Justin Trudeau to Theresa May, Barack Obama, and Angela Merkel.

Federica Mogherini, High Representative of the Union for Foreign Affairs and Security Policy and Vice-President of the European Commission since November 2014, said in 2016:

> *"The idea of a clash between Islam and "the West" – a word in which everything is put together and confused – has misled our policies and our narratives. Islam holds a place in our Western societies. Islam belongs in Europe. It holds a place in Europe's history, in our culture, in our food and – what matters most – in Europe's present and future."*

> *"Some people are now trying to convince us that a Muslim cannot be a good European citizen, that more Muslims in Europe will be the end of Europe. These people are not just mistaken about Muslims: these people are mistaken about Europe; they have no clue what Europe and the European identity are."*

"The so-called Islamic State is putting forward an unprecedented attempt to pervert Islam for justifying a wicked political and strategic project. ... Da'esh is Islam's worst enemy in today's world. Its victims are first and foremost Muslim people. Islam is a victim itself."

"I am not afraid to say that political Islam should be part of the picture. Religion plays a role in politics – not always for good, not always for bad. Religion can be part of the process. What makes the difference is whether the process is democratic or not."

In 2009, Barack Obama said in his Cairo speech "A New Beginning" that "America and Islam are not exclusive and need not be in competition. Instead, they overlap, and share common principles of justice and progress, tolerance and the dignity of all human beings."

In 2014 President Obama sent these wishes[351] to the Muslim community:

"While Eid marks the completion of Ramadan, it also celebrates the common values that unite us in our humanity and reinforces the obligations that people of all faiths have to each other, especially those impacted by poverty, conflict, and disease."

---

[351] Barack Obama, "Statement by the President on the Occasion of Eid-Al-Fitr," National Archives and Records Administration (National Archives and Records Administration), accessed September 2, 2021, https://obamawhitehouse.archives.gov/the-press-office/2014/07/27/statement-president-occasion-eid-al-fitr.

"In the United States, Eid also reminds us of the many achievements and contributions of Muslim Americans to building the very fabric of our nation and strengthening the core of our democracy. That is why we stand with people of all faiths, here at home and around the world, to protect and advance their rights to prosper, and we welcome their commitment to giving back to their communities."

Addressing the Islamic Society of Baltimore on February 3, 2016, former U.S. President Barack Obama declared:

"it is possible to be faithful to Islam and to be part of a pluralistic society... and to believe in democracy."[352]

Except, of course, that leading Muslim scholars have said otherwise as I explained in the chapter about Shirk.

President Obama said:

"So, let's start with this fact: For more than a thousand years, people have been drawn to Islam's message of peace. We are all God's children. We're all born equal, with inherent dignity."

---

[352] Barack Obama, "Remarks by the President at Islamic Society of Baltimore," National Archives and Records Administration (The White House Office of the Press Secretary, February 3, 2016), https://obamawhitehouse.archives.gov/the-press-office/2016/02/03/remarks-president-islamic-society-baltimore.

The Vatican's Pontifical Council for Interreligious Dialogue (PCID) made the exhortation in a message released on the occasion of Id al-Fitr in 2018:

"A spirit of competition has too often marked past relations between Christians and Muslims, the negative consequences of which are evident: jealousy, recriminations and tensions. In some cases, these have led to violent confrontations, especially where religion has been instrumentalized, above all due to self-interest and political motives."

"Such interreligious competition," the Council said, *"wounds the image of religions and their followers, and it fosters the view that religions are not sources of peace, but of tension and violence."*[353]

Recognize common values, respect differences

This message to Christians and Muslims to recognize the "religious and moral values they share" and respect their "legitimate differences" in order to bring about an "effective cooperation for the common good."

The Pontifical Council thus called on both communities to work together and honour each other in order to further peace and fraternal relations and promote harmony in society which is becoming increasingly multi-ethnic, multi-religious and multi-cultural.

---

[353] Robin Gomes, "Vatican's Message for Ramadan: 'Move from Competition to Collaboration,'" Vatican News, May 18, 2018, https://www.vaticannews.va/en/vatican-city/news/2018-05/vatican-dicastery-message-ramadan-competition-collaboration.html.

In 2014, Canada's Prime Minister, Justin Trudeau said:

"Muslim communities continue to make Canada stronger, more open, and more prosperous. Today, let's celebrate their major contributions to our country."[354]

Prime Minister Justin Trudeau has stated unequivocally that Islam is compatible with the west,[355] or as he puts it:

"Islam is not incompatible with the West."

In 2018, German Chancellor Angela Merkel said:

"But now four million Muslims are living in Germany, and they are practicing their religion here. These Muslims belong to Germany, and also their religion of Islam belongs to Germany."[356]

In 1933, Germany came under the rule of Adolf Hitler, the leader of the Nazi Party. The Germans had been ground down by the Versailles Treaty. The economy was in shatters. Inflation took every last dime. The people were ripe for a man who promised better times. Under Hitler, Europe was invaded. Swiftly. By 1939 the Nazis

---

[354] Justin Trudeau, "Statement by the Prime Minister of Canada on Eid Al-Fitr," Prime Minister of Canada, June 14, 2018, https://pm.gc.ca/en/news/statements/2018/06/14/statement-prime-minister-canada-eid-al-fitr.

[355] Jonathan D. Halevi, "Is Canada's Justin Trudeau the Great Reformer of Islam?," Jerusalem Center for Public Affairs, November 18, 2018, https://jcpa.org/is-canadas-justin-trudeau-the-great-reformer-of-islam/.

[356] Ayhan Simsek, "German Chancellor Merkel: 'Islam Belongs to Germany'," Anadolu Agency, March 16, 2018, https://www.aa.com.tr/en/europe/german-chancellor-merkel-islam-belongs-to-germany/1090930.

were ready to take Britain. And there were those in Britain who believed that it would be in the best interests of the Island to make a treaty with Hitler. Nazism wasn't all that bad, was it? There was a great deal of discussion about Nazism in parliament and on the streets and in the media.

Neville Chamberlain, the PM at the time, pushed for a treaty. And he came up against Winston Churchill who said "No."

> *"Nowadays we are assailed by a chorus of horrid threats. The Nazi Government exudes through every neutral State inside information of the frightful vengeance they are going to wreak upon us, and they also bawl it around the world by their leather-lunged propaganda machine. If words could kill, we should be dead already."*

Nazism was in no way compatible with the values of Britain. Those who wanted to appease the Nazis were pushed aside. Churchill and Britain prevailed.

"When I look round to see how we can win the war, I see that there is only one sure path . . . and that is absolutely devastating, exterminating attack by very heavy bombers from this country upon the Nazi homeland."

Now what of Islam? Is Islam compatible with the West?

Winston Churchill wrote about his experiences with Islam when he fought in the Middle East in the late 19th century.

> *"Indeed, it is evident that Christianity, however degraded and distorted by cruelty and intolerance, must always exert a modifying influence on men's passions, and protect them*

219

from the more violent forms of fanatical fever, as we are protected from smallpox by vaccination. But the Mahommedan religion increases, instead of lessening, the fury of intolerance. It was originally propagated by the sword, and ever since its votaries have been subject, above the people of all other creeds, to this form of madness. In a moment the fruits of patient toil, the prospects of material prosperity, the fear of death itself, are flung aside. The more emotional Pathans are powerless to resist. All rational considerations are forgotten. Seizing their weapons, they become Ghazis—as danger-ous and as sensible as mad dogs: fit only to be treated as such. While the more generous spirits among the tribesmen become convulsed in an ecstasy of religious blood-thirstiness, poorer and more material souls derive additional impulses from the influence of others, the hopes of plunder and the joy of fighting. Thus, whole nations are roused to arms. Thus, the Turks repel their enemies, the Arabs of the Soudan break the British squares, and the rising on the Indian frontier spreads far and wide. In each case civilisation is confronted with militant Mahommedanism. The forces of progress clash with those of reaction. The religion of blood and war is face to face with that of peace. Luckily the religion of peace is usually the better armed.[357]

---

[357] "Churchill on Islam," The Churchill Project - Hillsdale College (Churchill Literary Estate and Curtis Brown Ltd., London, March 5, 2019), https://winstonchurchill.hillsdale.edu/churchill-on-islam/.

~ The Story of the Malakand Field Force (1898)

He also stated in his book, The River War, published in 1899:

> "How dreadful are the curses which Mohammedanism lays on its votaries! Besides the fanatical frenzy, which is as dangerous in a man as hydrophobia in a dog, there is this fearful fatalistic apa-thy. The effects are apparent in many countries. Improvident habits, slovenly systems of agriculture, sluggish methods of commerce, and insecurity of property exist wherever the followers of the Prophet rule or live. A degraded sensualism deprives this life of its grace and refinement; the next of its dignity and sanctity. The fact that in Mohammedan law every woman must belong to some man as his absolute property—either as a child, a wife, or a concubine—must delay the final extinction of slavery until the faith of Islam has ceased to be a great power among men."[358]

The man who attacked Nazism attacked Islam as well, long before the rise of Hitler.

So, is Islam compatible with the West, today?

How many non-Muslims are aware of the teachings of Islam in mosques all over the world; including your local mosque? Let me share their teachings with you. I am not providing my views, my interpretations. I am sharing with you the words of the prominent leaders and books

---

[358] "Churchill on Islam," The Churchill Project - Hillsdale College (Churchill Literary Estate and Curtis Brown Ltd., London, March 5, 2019)

from all over the world. You decide. Is Islam compatible with Western values? Is the fear of Islam irrational?

Muslim leaders have told us over and over that Islam is not compatible with the West.

ICNA Canada is an Islamic nation-wide organization striving "to build an Exemplary Canadian Muslim Community" by "total submission to Him [Allah] and through the propagation of true and universal message of Islam." Its Amir (President) is Dr. Iqbal Massod Al-Nadvi also serves as the Chairperson of Canadian Council of Imams. An online book published by ICNA (Islamic Circle of North America) Canada contradicts Prime Minister Justin Trudeau that "Islam is totally incompatible with western democracy."[359] Who are we non-Muslims to argue that point?

Mazin AbdulAdhim is a prominent Canadian Muslim scholar and Imam of Iraqi descent who is affiliated with the pro-Caliphate Islamic global movement of Hizb ut-Tahrir. On January 17, 2019, Mazin AbdulAdhim posted the following on his Facebook page:

> "In terms of morality, the West is absolutely a cesspool of corruption and depravity. The Zina [fornication, adultery], pornography, homosexuality, drinking, drugs, etc., are not only widespread, but they are completely and totally accepted as normal – to the extent that anyone questioning or speaking out against these things are shunned and attacked. The Muslim lands are a saint-haven in comparison, except for

---

[359] Jonathan D. Halevi, "ICNA Canada Contradicts Trudeau: 'Islam Is Totally Incompatible with Western Democracy,'" CIJ News, February 25, 2016, https://archive.is/eHtz9.\

whatever has been influenced by the West's way of life."

"If a person is looking for something to be scared of, they will find it. We discuss the Khilafah [Caliphate, or Islamic State], we discuss the corruption of Western governments, we discuss "Shari'a [Islamic] law," we discuss many things that scares people due to the fear mongering by the media."[360]

On March 17, 2017, Mazin Abdul Adhim stated

"We need to understand that this is a struggle between two ideologies, not between countries or leaders or religions. It is a (mostly) silent war between secularism and Islam. Muslims win the moment they establish a true Khalifah [leader of the Caliphate] ... And as Muslims inch closer to breaking free from the political control of the colonial West, we should expect to see them become more vicious against political Islam, and more friendly towards Muslims who accept secularism and defend it (called "moderates")."

Mazin AbdulAdhim, posted a video April 15, 2018, entitled "10 Reasons Why the Khilafah" on his You Tube channel. In this video[361] Mazin Abduladhim explains the

[360] "Canadian Muslim Scholar: 'The West Is a Cesspool of Moral Corruption," Including Homosexuality," ACDemocracy (American Center for Democracy, January 22, 2019), https://news.acdemocracy.org/canadian-muslim-scholar-the-west-is-a-cesspool-of-moral-corruption-including-homosexuality.
[361] *10 Reasons Why the Khilafah, YouTube,* 2018, https://www.youtube.com/watch?v=VpsCsGSS4SY.

importance and the benefits of re-establishing the Caliphate or the Islamic State that will unite all Muslims under rule of Islam.[362] Here is an excerpt:

"In this video I'm going to give you ten reasons why the Khilafa [Caliphate or Islamic State].

"Reason number one – A better government. The world today is run by politicians who essentially rule according to their own whims and desires. They look after only the interests of their friends and their own economic interests and laws are enacted basically on nothing more than public opinion and whatever pressures are applied to them through lobbies. This is due to the fact that the laws that are enacted are man-made laws and human beings will always be corrupted by their personal interests and the environment that they live in. Under a Khilafa [Caliphate or Islamic State] system the laws are confined within the limits of what is in the Quran and Sunnah [Islamic teachings]."

In a series of lectures on the "Minor Signs of Qayamaah – The Last Day", Toronto Imam Said Rageah said that the Muslims will eventually defeat the Christians and take over Rome, the Capital of Italy where the Vatican City is located.

---

[362] Rachel Ehrenfeld, "Canadian Muslim Scholar Calls for Reestablishing the Islamic State, Rejecting Nation-States," ACDemocracy (American Center for Democracy, April 20, 2018), https://news.acdemocracy.org/canadian-muslim-scholar-calls-for-reestablishing-the-islamic-state-rejecting-nation-states/.

Rageah, who suggested that signs of the Last Day are already seen in our time, said in this regard the following (Published YouTube on January 12, 2013):

> "There would be a war [between Muslims and Christians] ... the third group would be victorious. They will win over the enemy [Christians]... and then the Muslims will go again to Constantinople, which is known as Istanbul today... Muslims will conquer that land without a fight. First time we did was with a fight. We fought them we won over them, but this time without a fight. Rome same thing. We'll go to Rome. We will not fight. The Muslim believers will pray Allah Akbar [Allah is the greatest] and then they will be victorious. Allah will them the victory over the enemy [Christians]."

On December 23, 2016, Sheikh Muhammad bin Musa Al Nasr (نصر آل موسى بن محمد) led the Friday prayer at Dar Al-Arqam Mosque (Mosquée Dar Al-Arqam) in Montreal.

In his sermon, Sheikh Muhammad bin Musa Al Nasr, a Jordanian cleric, called the Jews the "most evil of mankind" and "human demons" emphasizing that their fate was predetermined by Allah to be killed by the hands of the Muslims.

In Saskatchewan, Canada, Muhammad Mustafa Mustaan preaches,

> "I stand against the injustices happening because of the democracy, because of the capitalism, because of the invasion in our lands and because of the traitors and the rulers who we have on our lands who are brutal against us and who are the enemies."

"In Islam, this is, the freedom of choice that you talk about, is not the way it is in a democracy, because democracy comes from a belief that God does not have any right in our daily life. We are the ones who choose it."

"Democracy is nothing else but something which gives you the right to choose anything. The biggest shirk [Arabic term for idolatrous and heretical polytheism] is when you give your own self the right to choose whatever you want. So, democracy, in no terms, is compatible with Islam."

The booklet titled "Dispelling Misinformation About Islam"[363] has been handed out at the Islamic booth at Toronto's Dundas Square. Printed and distributed by the Walk-In Islamic InfoCenter[364] located in Toronto, the booklet introduces the daily prayers for Muslims.

In some of the supplications dealing with the "Kafiroun," the disbelievers or infidels, Muslims are ordained to ask Allah to help them overcome and defeat their enemies who are identified as the disbelieving people.

The book "Riyad us-Saliheen" ("The Paradise of the Pious") [365] posted on the ICNA Canada website adds modern commentary to the verses from the Qur'an and

---

[363] "Dispelling Misinformation About Islam." Toronto: Walk-In Islamic *Info*Center, August 29, 2016. http://islamicbooth.ca
[364] "Home: Walk-in Islamic Infocenter," collectfreequran.org (Walk-In Islamic InfoCenter (WIIC), 2021), https://www.collectfreequran.org/.
[365] *Riyad Us-Saliheen (The Paradise of the Pious)* (Calgary, AB: Islamic Information Society of Calgary, n.d.).

hadith. The following are excerpts from the book which deals with the question:

> "Is Islam compatible with the values of Western democracy?
>
> "[Hadith]: 673. Abu Bakrah (May Allah be pleased with him) reported: I heard Messenger of Allah (PBUH) saying, "He who insults the rulers Allah will insult him."
>
> [At-Tirmidhi].
>
> "Commentary: To affront and degrade the ruler means to disobey him and to by-pass his orders. This impairs his power, honour and dignity.
>
> "Believers have been told to obey and support rulers for the sake of national interest and welfare, understanding that they desist from committing an overt disbelief and maintain congregation Salat and other duties of religion.
>
> "The political system of Islam is totally incompatible with western democracy.
>
> "The concept of government party and the opposition is alien to Islam.
>
> "All belong to one Ummah with only one goal and pursue the same aims and objects of Islamic guidelines!"

The member states of the Organisation of Islamic Cooperation (OIC) called "to respect the freedom of religion of all Muslims and not to deny them the right to exercise their civil and cultural rights."[366] What are

---

[366] News Desk, "OIC Urges UN to Tackle Islamophobia, Declare It a Form of Racism," The Express Tribune Pakistan (The

those cultural and rights? Do they include following Shari'a Law?

I ask this question here because of the response to the actions of the Sultan of Brunei in April 2019. Brunei, a Muslim-majority former British protectorate with a population of around 400,000, implemented Sharia law beginning April 3, punishing sodomy, adultery and rape with the death penalty, including by stoning, and theft with amputation." The Sultan explained that Shari'a law "aims to educate, respect and protect the legitimate rights of all individuals, society or nationality of any faiths and race." Are these not their "civil and cultural rights?" Yet there were protests around the world against implementing these laws.[367]

Brunei is not alone. At an April 1996 conference, Canadian Imam Zafar Bangash was criticizing the West for being "proud of being homosexuals," and saying:

"It is time for us to pick up the stones to stone these people to death for [this] abomination... Allah imposes [this responsibility] upon us."[368]

Express Tribune, March 23, 2019),
https://tribune.com.pk/story/1935888/3-oic-urges-un-tackle-islamophobia-declare-form-racism.

[367] Reuters Staff, "Brunei Defends Tough New Islamic Laws against Growing Backlash," Reuters (Thomson Reuters, March 30, 2019), https://www.reuters.com/article/us-brunei-islamiclaws/brunei-defends-tough-new-islamic-laws-against-growing-backlash-idUSKCN1RB0E1.

[368] GrainOfTruth, "MEMRI TV Clip: Canadian Imam Calling for the Stoning to Death of Gays," Grain of Truth, March 7, 2019, https://web.archive.org/web/20190317232804/https://grainoftruth.ca/memri-tv-clip-canadian-imam-calling-for-the-stoning-to-death-of-gays/.

February 20, 2019, Mazin AbdulAdhim, a prominent Canadian Muslim scholar and Imam of Iraqi descent who is affiliated with the pro-Caliphate Islamic global movement of Hizb ut-Tahrir posted on his Facebook page the following:

> *"I've been asked many times about whether or not I believe that homosexuality is genetic.*[369] *And my answer is: I believe that homosexuality is absolutely not genetic in any way, shape, or form. It is entirely conceptual, period. It is no different from being sexually attracted to one's own siblings, or one's parents, or infants, or animals. None of those things are genetic, and neither is homosexuality... It is a sexual perversion, an illness of the desires, and it must be accepted as such, then suppressed and trained out of one's feelings through a positive process of correction of one's concepts, control of one's inner thoughts, positive reminders of the Islamic viewpoint on procreation and sexuality."*[370]

And cutting of limbs? This is taught in Canada[371] and America. Islam prescribes chopping off the hands of the convicted robber.

---

[369] Mazin AbdulAdhim, "I've Been Asked Many Times about Whether or Not I Believe That Homosexuality Is Genetic.," Archive Today (Facebook.com, 2019), https://archive.is/oGZjP.

[370] Rachel Ehrenfeld, "Canadian Muslim Scholar: 'Homosexuality Is a Sexual Perversion; It Can Also Be Reversed,'" ACDemocracy (American Center for Democracy, February 20, 2019), https://news.acdemocracy.org/canadian-muslim-scholar-homosexuality-is-a-sexual-perversion-it-can-also-be-reversed/.

[371] Rachel Ehrenfeld, "Salaheddin Islamic Centre: Chopping off

"As to the thief, male or female, cut off his or her hands: a punishment by way of example, from Allah, for their crime: and Allah is Exalted in power, full of wisdom." (Quran 5:38)

The non-Muslim may say, "Chopping off the hands in this 20th century. Islam is a barbaric and ruthless religion!"

America is supposed to be one of the most advanced countries in the world. Unfortunately, it also has one of the highest rates of crime, theft, and robbery.

Suppose the Islamic Law is implemented in America i.e., every rich person gives Zakat, (2.5% of his savings in charity above 85 grams of gold every lunar year) and every convicted robber has his or her hands chopped off as a punishment.

Will the rate of theft and robbery in America increase, remain same or decrease? Naturally it will decrease. Moreover, the existence of such a stringent law would discourage many a potential robber.

Daniel Haqiqatjou, about whom I wrote earlier, is a scholar of Islam. He attended Harvard University where he majored in Physics and minored in Philosophy. He was over the moon when Brunei announced that it would implement Sharia Law for all in that country.

On March 30, 2019, Daniel Haqiqatjou posted on his website The Muslim Skeptic an article titled *"Salute the*

Thieves' Hands in America Will Decrease Crime Rate," ACDemocracy (American Center for Democracy, December 27, 2018), https://news.acdemocracy.org/salaheddin-islamic-centre-chopping-off-thieves-hands-in-america-will-decrease-crime-rate/.

Sultan! Brunei Reinstates Hudud [fixed punishments] for Sexual Deviance."[372,373]

"If you have had a rough week or are feeling down in the dumps, I have just the news to cheer you up. The Muslim country of Brunei is implementing hudud [fixed punishments] to crack down on sodomites and fornicators!

"...This is exactly right. The Shari'a [Islamic Law] protects all our rights, individually and communally. When rectum-sex enthusiasts are allowed to promote their gender-bending degeneracy openly, that deeply harms all of us. That brings down the moral character of society. That destroys the sanctity of marriage. That teaches the world that sexual desire — no matter how base, how deviant, how contrary to God's will — is acceptable to pursue and, in fact, must be pursued.

"The LGBT indoctrination program, however, doesn't want you to recognize these harms. They want you to think gay sex acts are "victimless" and that marriage between men and women is not a sanctified institution. Rather, marriage, according to them, can be remolded into

---

[372] Rachel Ehrenfeld, "American Muslim Scholar Salutes Brunei for Reinstating Law on Stoning Gays," ACDemocracy (American Center for Democracy, March 31, 2019), https://news.acdemocracy.org/american-muslim-scholar-salutes-brunei-for-reinstating-law-on-stoning-gays/.
[373] Daniel Haqiqatjou, "Salute the Sultan! Brunei Reinstates Hudud for Sexual Deviance," The Muslim Skeptic, March 30, 2019, https://muslimskeptic.com/2019/03/30/salute-the-sultan-brunei/.

anything that society chooses: two men, two women, two men and one woman, three women and a horse, etc. There is nothing special or unique about the relationship between men and women that forecloses the possibility of LGBT marital options."

As Haqiqatjou said regarding the statements by the "celebrities."

"By the way, how silly that these Western politicians and celebrities can't stand it that a Muslim country implements the Sharia. They are frothing with anger. Isn't it great?"

When a leading Muslim organization, Hizb ut Tahrir in Britain says "Islam is the only system that united people of all races and religions in history and will unite them once more when it returns,"[374] who are we non-Muslims to disagree or push back?

On June 4, 2017 the Islamic organization Hizb ut Tahrir Britain posted on Facebook the following statement:[375]

"Islam is NOT only for Muslims, but for all mankind. If Islam is a religion, then it is only for Muslims. But if Islam is a deen as it was revealed, then it is for all mankind. "And we did not send

---

[374] Rachel Ehrenfeld, "Islamic Organization in Britain: 'Islam Is Not Only for Muslims, but for All Mankind,'" ACDemocracy (American Center for Democracy, September 19, 2018), https://news.acdemocracy.org/islamic-organization-in-britain-islam-is-not-only-for-muslims-but-for-all-mankind/.
[375] "Islam Is NOT Only for Muslims, but for All Mankind," Facebook.com (Hizb ut-Tahrir Britain, June 4, 2017), https://www.facebook.com/htbritain/photos/a.46591433684 3458/1077423705692515.

you (Muhammad) except as a mercy to mankind" [21: 107]

"When the Prophet migrated to Medina as its ruler, most of his subjects weren't Muslim yet all were governed by the justice and truth of Islam as citizens of its state.

"If we look to the universe, we see that everything is governed by the laws of its All Mighty Creator, except here on earth where Allah has allowed the children of Adam free will to choose the system by which they govern their lives.

"And He in His mercy also gave us the choice to follow the true system by which human society should be governed; Al-Islam. For all its people, all its races and all its religions to live in harmony under the system designed for them by their creator. "...and we made you peoples and tribes that you may get to know each other..." [49: 13] But if Islam is a religion, then it is only for Muslims.

"Secularism is therefore portrayed as the only way to govern over people of different religions and races. This is the lie we are fed to forget about our glorious history where all people flourished. Where there was a golden age of Jewish culture in Islamic Spain. Where the knowledge of all cultures were studied and preserved in Baghdad. Where Muslims, Christians and Jews lived in peace in Palestine.

"Islam is the only system that united people of all races and religions in history and will unite them once more when it returns."[376]

On March 8, 2019, Qatari sociologist Abd Al-Aziz Al-Khazraj Al-Ansari uploaded a video to the Al-Mojtama YouTube channel, which he runs, in which he mocked International Women's Day for being a celebration of women's freedom to "act like whores, to play around... and to do whatever they want."[377] Al-Ansari's Facebook page says that he is the manager of the Center for the Organization of Marriage Projects. The Al-Mojtama YouTube channel's "About" section says that the channel calls for a return to the instructions of Allah and the Prophet Muhammad.

He mocked Western criticism of the hijab and of the Muslim male chaperone system, alleging that the West tells women to act like sluts instead. He also mocked the West for turning women into "cheap merchandise" and encouraging them to dance, use Snapchat, work as TV hosts and actresses, and attend co-ed universities,

---

[376] Rachel Ehrenfeld, "Islamic Organization in Britain: 'Islam Is Not Only for Muslims, but for All Mankind,'" ACDemocracy (American Center for Democracy, September 19, 2018), https://news.acdemocracy.org/islamic-organization-in-britain-islam-is-not-only-for-muslims-but-for-all-mankind/.

[377] MEMRI TV Editors, "Qatari Sociologist Abd Al-Aziz Al-Khazraj Al-Ansari Mocks the West, International Women's Day: These Filthy Secular Dogs Celebrate Women's 'Freedom' to Act Like Whores," MEMRI TV (Middle East Media Research Institute, March 8, 2019), https://web.archive.org/web/20190713083125/https://www.memri.org/tv/qatari-sociologist-abd-alaziz-khazraj-ansari-mocks-west-womens-day-filthy-dogs-celebrate-freedom-slut-education-snapchat/transcript.

where male students fondle them behind the professors' backs during class. He mockingly said: "Bear him a bastard child!... Yes, freedom!" He also said that the West allows women to serve in the military and police in order to "provide comfort" to male service members and added that dogs are more honorable than the "filthy" secular people who fool women into driving cars, working as electricians, completing their education, and turning into prostitutes like in Europe, where he claimed 90 percent of children are bastards.

With all these facts from Muslim scholars and Imam, why do Western leaders fall all over themselves to protect and defend Islam; an ideology that is far more compatible with fascism, communism and Nazism than democracy?

CHAPTER 18: DOESN'T ISLAM SPEAK OF PEACE?

"Koran says whoever believes in God in the last day shall be saved. It is a religion whose very name, Islam, comes from the word Shalom, which means peace. It's about establishing peace. We greet each other with peace be upon you, which the Jews do in greeting each other."

~ Feisal Abdul Rauf

We are told that Islam is a religion of peace. That Islam wants peace. That's true. They do. But what does Islam mean when to refers to "peace"?

Words have different meanings through time and in different countries. Fag and gay are two words whose meanings have changed over time and in different countries. Peace is another. In the West peace means "a state or period of mutual concord between governments and a pact or agreement to end hostilities between those who have been at war or in a state of enmity."

In Islam peace has a different meaning. And it is important that we understand that meaning when we talk about peace with Muslim leaders.

Peace in Islam means submission to Allah. The ultimate meaning of Islamic peace is all of us living in Dar-al-Islam[378] — the house of submission. This is not a "radical" interpretation. Modern-day Islamic scholar, Ibrahim

---

[378] "Dār Al-Islam," Encyclopædia Britannica (Encyclopædia Britannica, inc., August 29, 2011), https://www.britannica.com/topic/Dar-al-Islam.

Sulaiman, says submission and peace can be very different concepts, even if a form of peace is often brought about through forcing others into submission.

> *"Jihad is not inhumane, despite its necessary violence and bloodshed, its ultimate desire is peace which is protected and enhanced by the rule of law."*

Armed responses are only permitted when all peaceful possibilities have failed. And once armed resistance begins it doesn't stop "until the war lays down its burden" as Allah has mentioned in the Qur'an 47.

The late Egyptian scholar, Sayyid Qutb, a prolific, well-respected author whose works are quoted in the Muslim world and influenced members of the Muslim Brotherhood has written:

> *"The theory that our religion is a peaceful and loving religion is a wrong theory. The Holy war as it is known in Islamic jurisprudence is basically an offensive war, and it is the duty of all Muslims of every age...because our prophet Muhammad said that he is ordered by Allah to fight all people until they say 'No God but Allah,' and he is his messenger."*

He also wrote that western democracy is infertile of life-giving ideas, that obedience to Shari'a is necessary to achieve harmony and peace for mankind. He preached:

> *"When Islam strives for peace, its objective is not that superficial peace which requires that only that part of the earth where the followers of Islam are residing remain secure. The peace which Islam desires is that the religion (i.e. the*

Law of the society) be purified for God, that the obedience of all people be for God alone."

Qutb specifically claims the conquest of non-Muslim states as "a movement to wipe out tyranny and to introduce true freedom to mankind."[379] A true Muslim not only has no loyalty to any country "where the Islamic Shari'ah is not enforced," but must be prepared to fight against such countries.

Translations of his work exist in every Arabic language, including Farsi, the language spoken in Iran. Ayatullah Seyyed Ali Khamenei, who was appointed as Iran's Supreme Leader after the death of Ayatollah Ruhollah Khomeini in 1989, did the translations.

The leaders of Iran are followers of Qutb.[380]

Anjem Choudary, the British Muslim cleric who has a very large following, clearly defines the meaning of peace in Islam:

> *"Contrary to popular misconception, Islam does not mean peace but rather means submission to the commands of Allah alone. Therefore, Muslims do not believe in the concept of freedom of expression, as their speech and actions are determined by divine revelation and not based on people's desires."*[381]

---

[379] Elmer Swenson, "Sayyid Qutb's Milestones," Sayyid Qutb's Milestones (Elmer Swenson, June 27, 2005), https://gemsofislamism.tripod.com/milestones_qutb.html.

[380] Juan Cole, "Iran and Islam," The Iran Primer (United States Institute of Peace, October 5, 2010), https://iranprimer.usip.org/resource/iran-and-islam.

[381] Anjem Choudary, "People Know the Consequences: Opposing View," USA Today (Gannett Satellite Information

Peace in Islam is submission to Islam and its laws.

Network, January 8, 2015),
https://www.usatoday.com/story/opinion/2015/01/07/islam-allah-muslims-shariah-anjem-choudary-editorials-debates/21417461/.

CHAPTER 19: IS ISLAM BENIGN?

"...Christians are being killed in the Islamic world because of their religion. It is a rising genocide that ought to provoke global alarm..."

~ Ayaan Hirsi Aly

Despite these worldwide teachings, the tribal warfare between Muslim groups, the attacks on Christians worldwide that barely make it into the media or shared by politicians, we are told that to criticize, compare and contrast Islam, the ideology, is frowned upon because it spreads the irrational fear of Islam. [382]

According to the Government of Canada, under PM Justin Trudeau and shared at the UN, White supremacism and Islamophobia are among "the gravest threats" facing the world.[383] This is based on a white supremacist's March 15 terrorist attack on two mosques in Christchurch, New Zealand, which claimed the lives of 50 worshippers, and the deaths of six people in another terrorist attack on a Quebec City Mosque in 2017. Canada warned these attacks needed to be at the top of the global agenda during discussions on confronting global terrorism.

---

[382] Editors, "List of Killings in the Name of Islam: 2020," What makes Islam so different? (TheReligionofPeace.com (TROP), 2021),
https://thereligionofpeace.com/attacks/attacks.aspx?Yr=2020.
[383] "Neo-Nazism and Islamophobia among the 'Gravest Threats' Facing the World, Freeland Tells UN," CBCnews (CBC/Radio Canada, March 28, 2019),
https://www.cbc.ca/news/politics/white-supremacist-nazi-islamophobia-1.5076033.

So, we are cautioned against saying anything negative about Islam after an attack by Muslims, while at the same time we are called together to stand against attacks on Muslims. We have witnessed a world-wide coming together following an attack on Mosques. The mosque attack in New Zealand was followed by "rings of peace" around the world protecting Mosques, and women told to share their pain by wearing a hijab, and in New Zealand the mosques were permitted to publicly announce the call to prayer. There was a great deal of *sturm and drang* over this event. But,what of the massacre of Christians by Muslims, or Yazidis by Muslims, or Muslims by Muslims?

The #IslamophobiaIndustry has been highly successful. We rarely hear about attacks on non-Muslims.

An estimated 9,900 members of the ethnic and religious minority, the Yazidis, were killed or captured in a matter of days in August 2014.[384] Of that figure 3,100 were murdered, with almost half executed by gunshot, beheading or being burned alive,[385] while the rest died from starvation, dehydration or injuries during the ISIS siege on Mount Sinjar. Do we stay quiet because it is ISIS

---

[384] Valeria Cetorelli et al., "Mortality and Kidnapping Estimates for the Yazidi Population in the Area of Mount Sinjar, Iraq, in August 2014: A Retrospective Household Survey," *PLOS Medicine* 14, no. 5 (May 9, 2017), https://doi.org/10.1371/journal.pmed.1002297.

[385] "ISIS Burns 19 Yazidi Women to Death in Mosul for 'Refusing to Have Sex with Fighters'," The Independent (Independent Digital News and Media, June 6, 2016), https://www.independent.co.uk/news/world/middle-east/isis-burn-19-yazidi-women-death-mosul-refusing-have-sex-isis-militants-a7066956.html.

doing the murdering? And somewhere along the way of history it was decided that ISIS is not Muslim. Nazis weren't German?

In 2012 Ayaan Hirsi Aly wrote:

"Christians are being killed in the Islamic world because of their religion. It is a rising genocide that ought to provoke global alarm."[386] *In recent years the violent oppression of Christian minorities has become the norm in Muslim-majority nations stretching from West Africa and the Middle East to South Asia and Oceania. In some countries it is governments and their agents that have burned churches and imprisoned parishioners. In others, rebel groups and vigilantes have taken matters into their own hands, murdering Christians and driving them from regions where their roots go back centuries."*

One hundred and sixty-four people were murdered by Muslims in Mumbai, India, between November 26-29, 2008.[387] Christians have been murdered in Nigeria.[388]

---

[386] Ayaan Hirsi Ali, "Ayaan Hirsi Ali: The Global War on Christians in the Muslim World," Newsweek.com (Newsweek Digital LLC, February 6, 2012), https://www.newsweek.com/ayaan-hirsi-alithe-global-war-christians-muslim-world-65817.

[387] CNN Editorial Research, "Mumbai Terror Attacks Fast Facts," CNN (Cable News Network, December 3, 2020), https://www.cnn.com/2013/09/18/world/asia/mumbai-terror-attacks/index.html.

[388] Emily Jones, "Radical Muslims Murder More than 30 Nigerian Christians, Torch Church in Brutal Attack," CBN News (CBN News, March 4, 2019),

In Jan 2019 in the Philippines, ISIS claimed responsibility for an attack that killed 20 churchgoers and soldiers at a Catholic church in the Philippines.[389]

More than 45 Christians murdered in Egypt by Muslims.[390] One hundred and ten Christian school girls were taken by Muslims and forced to convert, forced into marriages. And raped.[391] Michelle Obama started a campaign "Bring Back our Girls." Where is Ms. Obama, today?

Too often these egregious attacks are underreported, if reported at all.[392] And always with an admonition against Islamophobia.

---

https://www1.cbn.com/cbnnews/cwn/2019/march/radical-muslims-murder-32-nigerian-christians-torch-church-in-brutal-attack.

[389] Morgan Lee, "Why Islamist Terrorists Attacked Christians in the Philippines," ChristianityToday.com (Christianity Today, January 30, 2019), https://www.christianitytoday.com/ct/podcasts/quick-to-listen/islamist-terrorists-attacked-christians-philippines.html.

[390] Darren Boyle for MailOnline, "Cairo Church Bombing Kills 43 in Palm Sunday Massacre," Daily Mail Online (Associated Newspapers, April 9, 2017), https://www.dailymail.co.uk/news/article-4394838/Thirteen-killed-42-wounded-Cairo-church-bombing.html.

[391] Chika Oduah, "'She Refused to Convert to Islam,' 85 Days on, Kidnapped Schoolgirl Leah Sharibu Remains in Captivity," CNN (Cable News Network, May 15, 2018), https://www.cnn.com/2018/05/15/africa/boko-haram-lone-school-girl/index.html.

[392] "List of Islamic Terror Attacks on Christians" (The Religion of Peace (TROP), August 2021), https://www.thereligionofpeace.com/attacks/christian-attacks.aspx.

Where is the world-wide condemnation of Muslim terror attacks? Where is our world-wide angst? Our coming together against Islamic terrorism?[393]

Muslims in Kenya torched five separate churches between January 20 and January 24—the very same days Muslims twice firebombed an 800-year-old church in Sweden over the course of four days—once on January 20, 2021, and another on January 24.

February 4, 2021, a report came out saying that 829 "hate crimes" against churches in Sweden have been reported between 2012-2018, or about 138 attacks on average every year. The churches of Sweden join those of other Western European nations that have taken in sizeable Muslim migrants. In France two churches are vandalized every day. According to a 2019 PI-News report, 1,063 attacks on Christian churches or symbols (crucifixes, icons, statues) were registered in France in 2018. This represents a 17 percent increase compared to the previous year (2017), when 878 attacks were registered.

A German news site reported:

"In this country, there is a creeping war against everything that symbolizes Christianity: attacks on summit crosses, on holy figures on the way, on churches and recently also on cemeteries."[394]

---

[393] Raymond Ibrahim, "Desecrated and Defecated on: Churches in Europe under Islam," FrontPageMag.com (David Horowitz Freedom Center, March 11, 2021), https://www.frontpagemag.com/fpm/2021/03/desecrated-and-defecated-churches-europe-under-raymond-ibrahim/.
[394] Raymond Ibrahim, "European Churches: Vandalized, Defecated on, and Torched 'Every Day,'" Gatestone Institute,

In virtually every instance of church attacks, authorities and media obfuscate the identity of the vandals. In those rare instances when the Muslim (or "migrant") identity of the destroyers is leaked, the perpetrators are then presented as suffering from mental health issues. As read in a recent PI-News report,[395] hardly anyone writes and speaks about the increasing attacks on Christian symbols. There is an eloquent silence in both France and Germany about the scandal of the desecrations and the origin of the perpetrators. Not a word, not even the slightest hint that could in anyway lead to the suspicion of migrants. It is not the perpetrators who are in danger of being ostracized, but those who dare to associate the desecration of Christian symbols with immigrant imports. They are accused of hatred, hate speech and racism. This is the result of the industry - attacks on others are not as important and the fear of backlash against the perpetrators leads to silence. Name another group treated this way.

Muslim terrorists in Europe have murdered non-Muslims in attacks in Madrid, Barcelona, Paris (many times), Nice, Toulouse, Tours, St. Etienne-du-Rouvray, London (many times), Manchester, Brussels, Antwerp, Amsterdam, Rotterdam, Berlin, Munich, Hamburg, Frankfurt, Copenhagen, Oslo, Stockholm, Malmö, Helsinki, Turku, Moscow, St. Petersburg, Beslan. Those attacks should make a deep impression, even on the likes of Bernie

April 14, 2019, https://www.gatestoneinstitute.org/14044/europe-churches-vandalized.

[395] "[Translated] WamS: Two Church Desecrations Every Day in France," PINews.net (PINews - Politically Incorrect, March 24, 2019), http://www.pi-news.net/2019/03/wams-jeden-tag-zwei-kirchenschaendungen-in-frankreich/.

Sanders, Jeremy Corbyn, and Barack Obama. And what would they make of the fact that Muslim terrorists have been responsible for more than 35,000 terror attacks around the world since 9/11? [396]

Anything? Nothing?

We have heard nothing but silence from the media.

Why?

While the world gave 24/7 coverage to the Christchurch mosque massacre and white folks rightfully denounced one of their own sons, to embrace their Muslim citizens, there was almost no coverage of the Muslim massacre of Christians in Nigeria just a few days earlier on March 4.

Similarly, on January 27, 2019, Muslim jihadis bombed a Catholic church in Jolo, Philippines, killing 20 Christians, [397] yet this attack barely caused a ripple. No weeping politicians, no candlelit vigils and no public demonstration by Muslims in Canada denouncing the jihadi terrorists the way whites denounced a white nationalist.

Slaughter of Christians Since 2019

Sri Lanka

---

[396] Hugh Fitzgerald, "Bernie Sanders at the Islamic Society of North America," FrontPageMag.com (David Horowitz Freedom Center, September 20, 2019), https://www.frontpagemag.com/fpm/2019/09/bernie-sanders-islamic-society-north-america-hugh-fitzgerald.
[397] Al Jazeera, "Philippines Church Bombing: Twin Blasts Hit Jolo Cathedral," News | Al Jazeera (Al Jazeera, January 27, 2019), https://www.aljazeera.com/news/2019/1/27/philippines-church-bombing-twin-blasts-hit-jolo-cathedral.

On Easter Sunday, April 21, Islamic terrorists launched a bombing campaign on Christians;[398] the death toll reached 253,[399] with hundreds more wounded. Eight separate explosions took place, at least two of which were suicide bombings. Three targeted churches celebrating Easter Sunday Mass; four targeted hotels frequented by Western tourists possibly in connection with Easter holiday; one blast was in a house and killed three police officers during a security operation.[400] At least 39 foreigners - including citizens of the United States, Britain, Australia, Japan, Denmark, and Portugal - were among the dead.

Most of the fatalities occurred in the three church-bombings. The worst took place in St. Sebastian's, a Catholic church in Negombo; there, over 100 Christian worshippers were murdered. At St. Anthony's Shrine, another Catholic church in Colombo, the nation's capital, at least 52 were murdered; and at the evangelical Zion Church, at least 28 were murdered.[401]

---

[398] "Sri Lanka Attacks: Death Toll Soars to 290 after Bombings Hit Churches and Hotels," BBC News (BBC, April 22, 2019), https://www.bbc.com/news/world-asia-48008073.

[399] News Wires, "Death Toll in Sri Lanka Attacks Revised down to 253," France 24 (France 24, April 26, 2019), https://www.france24.com/en/20190426-death-toll-sri-lanka-attacks-easter-bombings-revised-down-253.

[400] The Hindu Net Desk, "Eight Blasts at Churches, Hotels across Sri Lanka Kill at Least 207; 13 Arrested," The Hindu (THG Publishing Pvt Ltd., April 22, 2019), https://www.thehindu.com/news/international/live-multiple-explosions-in-colombo-and-other-parts-of-sri-lanka/article26903170.ece

[401] "189 Killed in Easter Attacks on Churches and Hotels in Sri Lanka," Persecution.org (International Christian Concern, April

"I don't have words to express my pain," said a Christian man who survived the bombing at St. Sebastian's Church in Negombo:

> *"We lost so many people... The smell of flesh is all around me... We are a peace-loving community in this small city, we had never hurt anyone, but we don't know from where this amount of hate is coming. This city has become a grave with blood and bodies lying around... Since the past three years, we don't know why, but we see an extremist's mindset developing among the Muslims. I know many good Muslims, but there are also a lot who hate us, and they have never been so before. It is in these three years that we see a difference."[402]*

> *"People were in pieces," recalled Ms. Silviya, 26, concerning the bombing of St. Anthony's Shrine in Colombo. "Blood was everywhere. I closed my son's eyes, took him out, passed him off to a relative and ran back inside to look for my family."*

Nigeria

On Sunday, April 14, Muslim herdsmen slaughtered 17 Christians who had gathered after a baby dedication at a

---

21, 2019), https://www.persecution.org/2019/04/21/189-killed-easter-attacks-churches-hotels-sri-lanka/.

[402] Southern India Correspondent, "Unprecedented Suicide Bombing Attacks Shock Christians in Sri Lanka," Morning Star News, April 22, 2019, https://morningstarnews.org/2019/04/unprecedented-suicide-bombing-attacks-shock-christians-in-sri-lanka/.

church.[403] The infant's mother was among the slain; the father was left hospitalized in critical condition.

On April 17, 2019, Fulani militants launched an attack on a predominantly Christian village; four people were killed, six were injured; over one hundred homes and food storage barns burned down.[404]

On April 19, Muslim raiders killed 11 Christians returning from Good Friday church service;[405] they also kidnapped and slaughtered a female British aid worker.[406]

On Sunday, April 21, ten boys were killed while taking part in an Easter procession. Emmanuel Ogebe, a Nigerian human rights lawyer remarked in an email, "The Holy Week killings in Nigeria do not grab headlines like

---

[403] Nigeria Correspondent, "Muslim Fulani Herdsmen Massacre Christians after Baby Dedication in Nigeria," Morning Star News, April 18, 2019, https://morningstarnews.org/2019/04/muslim-fulani-herdsmen-massacre-christians-after-baby-dedication-in-nigeria/.

[404] "Fulani Militants Attack Another Christian Village in Nigeria," Persecution.org (International Christian Concern, April 24, 2019), https://www.persecution.org/2019/04/24/fulani-militants-attack-another-christian-village-nigeria/.

[405] Peter Duru, "11 Killed after Good Friday Church Service, Many Missing in Benue Community," Vanguard News (Vanguard Media Limited, Nigeria, April 20, 2019), https://www.vanguardngr.com/2019/04/11-killed-after-good-friday-church-service-many-missing-in-benue-community/.

[406] Mattha Busby, "British Woman Faye Mooney Killed by Kidnappers in Nigeria," The Guardian (Guardian News and Media, April 21, 2019), https://www.theguardian.com/world/2019/apr/21/british-woman-faye-mooney-killed-kidnappers-nigeria.

Sri Lanka but still Nigeria's Christians are dying the deaths of a 1000 cuts in as many installments!"

The author of a separate April 21 report,[407] a Nigerian Christian, spoke of the nonstop carnage of Christians there:

> *"In the course of investigating anti-Christian violence throughout Nigeria, I have seen things that drove me to tears. I have entered rooms and houses that were covered with blood. I have seen bodies that were shot and butchered; corpses of pregnant women who had their stomachs ripped opened [sic], the bodies of unborn babies strewn about; homes destroyed; mass graves. In some of these attacks, entire families were killed. In a visit to one state in northern Nigeria, I went to 13 villages that were desolate as a result of herdsmen attacks. In another state, I visited eight churches that were bombed in one day, and in one town I saw the only four Christians who survived a Boko Haram onslaught. They were in hiding after all other Christians fled."*

Another report quotes a local Nigerian pastor's reaction to another church attack in April:

> *"After that attack, I came to visit the villages in the two-mile area around my church, and it was like a cemetery, as dozens were killed. I have dozens of little children, with no school supplies,*

---

[407] Nigeria Correspondent, "Nigeria: Herdsmen Attacks, Boko Haram and the Cross," Morning Star News, April 21, 2019, https://morningstarnews.org/2019/04/nigeria-herdsmen-attacks-boko-haram-and-the-cross/.

no uniforms and no desks, and I need to create a school for them."[408]

United Kingdom

A court "sentenced a Muslim Iranian asylum seeker to jail," an April 5 report says, "for stabbing his wife to death, in part for her conversion to Christianity."[409] Dana Abdullah, 35, stabbed Avan Najmadiein, his estranged wife and 32-year-old mother of four, 50 times with a kitchen knife because she refused to support his asylum application. He was deported from the UK in 2013 for sexually assaulting a 13-year-old girl, had returned illegally, and was now "threaten[ing] to kill his wife because she 'dishonored' him by converting to Christianity, authorities said." One detective involved in the case characterized Abdullah as "an arrogant and controlling man," who "killed Najmadiein because he resented her rejection, her refusal to support his application and her conversion to Christianity." Abdullah was sentenced to a minimum of 18 years and one month in prison.

Attacks on Churches and Crosses April 2019

Italy

---

[408] "Group Claims Nigeria Has Become a War Zone for Christians," Persecution.net (International Christian Concern, April 22, 2019), https://www.persecution.org/2019/04/14/group-claims-nigeria-become-war-zone-christians/.

[409] Joshua Gill, "Muslim Asylum Seeker Imprisoned for Killing Wife Who Converted to Christianity," The Daily Caller, April 5, 2019, https://dailycaller.com/2019/04/05/muslim-asylum-seeker-imprisoned-for-killing-wife-who-converted-to-christianity/.

A 37-year-old Muslim migrant in Rome was recently arrested for attempted homicide after he stabbed a Christian man in the throat for wearing a crucifix around his neck.[410] "Religious hate" is cited as an "aggravating factor" in the crime.

Days earlier, a separate report noted that "crosses on graves in an Italian cemetery in Pieve di Cento have been covered with black cloth so as not to offend those who may come from another religion," an apparent reference to Muslim migrants, some of whom have been known to desecrate Christian cemeteries. [411] "The cemetery," the report adds, "has also installed motorised blackout curtains in a local chapel following renovations to hide Roman Catholic symbols during ceremonies involving other denominations."

Indonesia

Several crosses in the Bethesda Christian cemetery in Mrican, Indonesia were vandalized, broken, and burned[412] in the most populous Muslim nation. The cemetery

[410] "Man Wearing Crucifix Stabbed in Rome," ANSA.it, April 23, 2019, https://www.ansa.it/english/news/2019/04/23/man-wearing-crucifix-stabbed-in-rome_1eb22433-8089-449b-abdb-36221c7d2bac.html.

[411] Chris Tomlinson, "Crosses in Italian Cemetery Covered to Avoid Offence to Other Religions," Breitbart.com (Breitbart News, April 9, 2019), https://www.breitbart.com/europe/2019/04/09/crosses-italian-cemetery-covered-avoid-offence-other-religions/.

[412] Mathias Hariyadi, "Indonesia: Crosses Desecrated in a Christian Cemetery in Yogyakarta," AsiaNews.it (Fondazione PIME Onlus – AsiaNews, April 8, 2019), http://www.asianews.it/news-en/Crosses-desecrated-in-a-Christian-cemetery-in-Yogyakarta-46715.html.

keeper said that "in the ten years since he has held the job, he has never seen such vandalism." The report notes that:

> *"The incident joins a long list of cases of intolerance that have taken place in recent months.... In December 2018, some residents in Purbayan removed the upper part of a cross placed on the tomb of Albertus Slamet Sugihardi, after informing his widow, Maria Sutris Winarni, that the cemetery was 'for the exclusive use of Muslims.' Before that, the Catholic family was forced to hold a private funeral to avoid tensions with the Islamic community. A few weeks later, Christian tombs were vandalised in several cemeteries in Magelang, 30 kilometres north of Yogyakarta, Central Java."*

Germany

While cursing his "pig god," Muslim migrants beat and repeatedly stabbed a homeless man in Berlin for apparently displaying some Christian symbol. According to the report:[413]

> *"Arabic-speaking youths were caught on video assaulting and stabbing a homeless Berlin man is speculated in the German press to be an anti-Christian motivated attack.... After physically attacking the victim, one of the men then drew a knife and stabbed him several times, leaving him*

---

[413] Chris Tomlinson, "Homeless Berlin Man Stabbed in Alleged Anti-Christian Attack," Breitbart.com (Breitbart News, April 9, 2019), https://www.breitbart.com/europe/2019/04/09/watch-homeless-berlin-man-stabbed-alleged-anti-christian-attack/.

with severe injuries to the buttocks, thigh, and arm, according to investigators."

The Arabic words they yelled were translated as "We f*ck your sister, we'll finish you!" and "Your pig-God, we f *ck your pig-God!" The report adds that this "incident is not the first in which a migrant-background Christian has been physically attacked by Arabic-speaking young men for displaying Christian symbols in public in the German capital. Recently, a 39-year-old had been beaten for wearing a necklace with a cross on it."

Separately in Germany, a migrant man, apparently of Somali origin, entered a church in Munich during Easter Mass and threw dangerous objects at worshippers (variously described as stones or firecrackers) while shouting, "Allahu Akbar" ("Allah is the greatest").[414] Congregants hurled their Easter meal baskets on the ground and rushed out in a panic. Some were injured; children were left in a "state of shock." Authorities concluded that he was "mentally ill" and therefore not responsible for his actions.

Egypt

After a large Muslim mob beat two Christians, one a Coptic priest, in front of 200 terrified children who had gathered for Bible lessons, authorities responded by arresting the beaten Christian priest and shutting the church in compliance with the wishes of the mob.[415] On

---

[414] Croatian News Agency (HINA), "Croatian Mass in Munich Disrupted by Mentally Ill Person Shouting 'Allahu Akbar,'" Total Croatia News, April 21, 2019, https://www.total-croatia-news.com/the-croatian-diaspora/35455-allahu-akbar.

[415] Cairo Correspondent, "Church Closed in Egypt after Muslim Mob Frightens Children in Sunday School," Morning Star

the previous day, the mayor had gone to oversee ongoing reconstruction of the church. Angered at what he considered too much of an "add-on," he accused the church of "treason" and riled local Muslims against it. At that point, according to the report:

> "The city council immediately arrived, stopped the work and confiscated building materials, including the cement and the reinforced steel. The next day at 4 p.m., dozens of angry demonstrators tried to enter the church premises but were unable to get through a steel door. Carrying clubs and knives, they started shouting, cursing and pelting the building with rocks, according to Coptic Solidarity. Additional forces arrived, and Father Basilious was struck as he and another priest were escorted off the premises. Parents and church leaders were not able to move the 200 children away from the angry, chanting villagers until security forces dispersed the crowds. Though police witnessed the beating of the priest, no arrests were made. Both Father Basilious and Father Bakhoum were taken for questioning into the evening hours. Police issued an indefinite closure order, pending investigations, and froze all activities of the 10-year-old church, including its daycare and the Sunday School."

One local Christian woman said, "The hardest emotion in that incident is the kids lived the incident in the reality. They saw the extremists attacking the church and how

News, April 23, 2019, https://morningstarnews.org/2019/04/church-closed-in-egypt-after-muslim-mob-frightens-children-in-sunday-school/.

they injured the priests. This incident will hurt them psychologically in the future."[416] "This is a very hard situation," said another. "You can see kids praying in tears because of their feelings of fear ... that is very painful for us as Christians personally. I don't trust in the government promises, but we have to continue praying for [a] reopening [of] the church."[417]

United States of America

South Carolina's Anderson Co. Midway Presbyterian Church was vandalized, an act that included having its 125-year-old windows shattered. Spray-painted in black on the church's side were: "SUBMIT TO GOD THRU ISLAM" and "MUHAMMED IS HIS PROPHET."[418] "It was very disturbing because we feel like this was an individual act and we don't hold any religious group responsible for it," said Bob Harrell, a church leader. "We think it most likely was some misguided young people."

General Discrimination and Persecution

Palestinian Authority

---

[416] "Coptic Christians Without Church for Easter Following Mob Attack," Persecution.org (International Christian Concern, April 16, 2019), https://www.persecution.org/2019/04/16/coptic-christians-without-church-easter-following-mob-attack/.

[417] "Reconciliation Session Leads to Another Church Closure in Egypt," Persecution.org (International Christian Concern, May 3, 2019), https://www.persecution.org/2019/05/03/reconciliation-session-leads-another-church-closure-egypt/.

[418] WSPA Staff, "Vandals Spray Paint Messages, Break Windows at Anderson Co. Church," WSPA.com (WSPA 7 News, April 16, 2019), https://www.wspa.com/news/vandals-spray-paint-messages-break-windows-at-anderson-co-church/.

On April 25, "the terrified residents of the Christian village of Jifna near Ramallah," states a report, "were attacked by Muslim gunmen ... after a woman from the village submitted a complaint to the police that the son of a prominent, Fatah-affiliated leader had attacked her family. In response, dozens of Fatah gunmen came to the village, fired hundreds of bullets in the air, threw petrol bombs while shouting curses, and caused severe damage to public property. It was a miracle that there were no dead or wounded."[419] The "rioters" the report continues, "called on the [Christian] residents to pay jizya[420] - a head tax - that was levied throughout history on non-Muslim minorities under Islamic rule. The most recent victims of the jizya were the Christian communities of Iraq and Syria under ISIS rule." Moreover, as often happens when Muslims attack Christians in Islamic nations, "Despite the [Christian] residents' cries for help... the PA police did not intervene during the hours of mayhem. They have not arrested any suspects."

Malaysia

After moving to a Muslim village, Slamet Sumiarto, a Catholic artist and his family "were expelled from a

---

[419] Dr. Edy Cohen, "The Persecution of Christians in the Palestinian Authority," Begin-Sadat Center for Strategic Studies (Bar-Ilan University, May 27, 2019), https://besacenter.org/persecution-christians-palestinian-authority/.

[420] Raymond Ibrahim, "Islamic Jizya: Fact and Fiction," RaymondIbrahim.com, May 28, 2015, https://www.raymondibrahim.com/2015/05/28/islamic-jizya-fact-and-fiction/.

village because they are not Muslim."[421] Sumiarto made a video about the situation:

> *"I just moved here to Pleret and brought all my stuff and paintings to Karet. Today I am very sad to know that I do not have the 'right' to stay and live here simply because I am not a Muslim and my whole family is Catholic. From an emotional point of view, I am really exhausted from this unexpected experience. My poor wife, my children and I hope to soon find a good solution to this problem so that I could stay here, in this rented house in Pleret."*

Although some local officials tried to get involved after seeing his video, in the end, Sumiarto and his family chose prudence and moved.

Pakistan

Because of his Christian identity, Muslims attacked and beat Kenneth Johnson, a 27-year-old Christian, after he tried to open a small grocery store.[422] According to Johnson, a poor agricultural laborer who takes care of three children:

---

[421] Mathias Hariyadi, "Indonesia: Yogyakarta Catholic Family Expelled Because Non-Muslim," AsiaNews.it (Fondazione PIME Onlus – AsiaNews, April 2, 2019), http://www.asianews.it/news-en/Yogyakarta-Catholic-family-expelled-because-non-Muslim-%28video%29-46670.html.

[422] "Pakistani Christian Attacked and Beaten for Opening Small Grocery Store," Persecution.org (International Christian Concern, April 10, 2019), https://www.persecution.org/2019/04/10/pakistani-christian-attacked-beaten-opening-small-grocery-store/.

"It took about a year for me to save and arrange the required funds to establish a grocery store. However, Christians in this Islamic society are not allowed to initiate a business. I had customers in my shop when Fiaz Khattak led an armed group of about a dozen Muslim [sic]. They attacked my shop, damaged the stuff, thrashed me, passed derogatory remarks against Christians and Christianity. However, I managed to escape from the scene and protected myself from major injuries."

The Muslims made remarks to Johnson such as:

"How dare you, a Christian, initiate a business of a grocery store in the village. You are born to clean the roads and our houses, not to do businesses."

Johnson continued:

"The police did not reach the scene on time when we called the helpline. Instead of a legal course of action, the police officer referred the case to the community leader. However, the community leader is even more helpless in front of an influential Muslim, therefore, I have not got any relief. It is very hard for Christians to uplift themselves. They are deprived and discouraged at different levels and face discrimination. Muslims often resist to provide opportunities to Christians. Rather, they create hurdles to keep them at lower positions."

"What is done cannot be undone."

~ Shakespeare, Macbeth, Act 5 Scene 1

Let us hope that is not true.

CHAPTER 20: LAST THOUGHTS

"When people are forced to remain silent when they are being told the most obvious lies, or even worse when they are forced to repeat the lies themselves, they lose once and for all their sense of probity... A society of emasculated liars is easy to control."

~ Theodore Dalrymple

I have taken you on a journey into the #IslamophobiaIndustry. We have learned about the infiltration of Islam, the religion, ideology, and law into western culture. We are watching, standing idly by, while Western Culture's greatest gift, questioning, investigating, critiquing, has been taken away by Islam and Islamophobia.

We are at a crossroads, similar to the one in the 1930s, when Nazism reared its ugly head. It took the courage of those who would not be silenced to stop the appeasement of Hitler and his value system.

We are being inundated by a religion and ideology that is diametrically opposed to everything we believe in the West. Everything. And to say so is a crime, now, because of Islam and its propaganda.

While Christians all over the world are being attacked by Muslims, we hear silence rather the screams of those being butchered.

Our education system has been hijacked. Governments cower. Journalists are threatened. Think about that. Journalists are threatened by their governments not to report when a Muslim commits a crime. The fourth estate, the institution in a democracy that is called upon to hold all institutions to account, is allowing the government to stifle them. Mainstream media had no trouble calling out Saudi Arabia when journalist Jamal Khashoggi was murdered. Yet, they are silent about the infiltration of Islam into all of our institutions, including the fourth estate.

Why are we silencing ourselves?

Because we have failed to protect and defend our value system in the name of tolerance, inclusion and accommodation. We have succumbed to the slow drip, drip, drip of rules imposed upon us by Muslims in positions of power.

We are the lobster.

AFTERWORD

Editorial note: The following article[423] is reprinted with the kind permission of the author, Tarek Fatah.

Just one day after Kabul fell, Taliban 2.0 along with their American and Pakistani sponsors reassured us that the fresh version of the Islamist terrorist group was 'new and improved,' we witnessed the work of the barbarians.

After Taliban spokesman Zabihullah Mujahid claimed that his government would "honour women's rights, within Islamic law," Taliban fighters shot and killed a woman for not wearing a burqa.

A photo emerged of a woman in Takhar province lying in a pool of blood, with loved ones crouched around her, after she was killed by insurgents for being in public without a hijab, the so-called Islamic head covering.

For the Biden and Kamala Harris types of this world, beholden to the hijab-promoting 'Squad' in the U.S. Congress and among the guilt-ridden Feminists of the "Mee-Too" world, this "Islamic Sharia 101" lesson may yet escape their attention.

Behind the cause of the calamity in Afghanistan, one name stands out as one gambled the lives of tens of million while locked inside expensive conference halls of Doha in Qatar (Iran's closest ally in the region).

---

[423] Tarek Fatah, "FATAH: This Betrayal of Afghanistan Is beyond Belief," torontosun.com (Postmedia Network Inc., August 18, 2021), https://torontosun.com/opinion/columnists/fatah-this-betrayal-of-afghanistan-is-beyond-belief.

Experts on Afghan affairs in India believe that the biggest 'credit' for this plight of Afghanistan and the loss of the country to the Taliban goes to the shadowy American Afghan diplomat, Zalmay Khalilzad, better known for his pro-Pakistan policies.

As early as March 2019, the American news outlet 'Politico' ran a story with the sub-heading: "Under peace envoy Zalmay Khalilzad, the U.S. Administration seems poised to give away everything America has fought for in Afghanistan since 9/11".

An example of this was recently seen in April 2021. At a time when the Taliban were rampaging in Afghanistan through Pakistan's support, Khalilzad defended Pakistan during a hearing at the US Senate's Committee on International Relations, denying Pakistan's role in supporting the Taliban.

Khalilzad assured the Senate committee that the Pakistani leadership has given assurances that it does not support the Taliban and stressed, "I think Pakistan understands the implications of the civil war in Afghanistan."

Much has been written on the 'Fall of Kabul' and the 'Victory of Islam' over 'non-believers' such as the West and India, and celebrations have broken out among India's Muslim community as well as Pakistan's. However, these celebrations of Islam's victory over the 'kufaar' is not restricted to jihadis and their admirers in South Asia.

Sam Westrop in the Middle East Forum has listed major Muslim figures in the West who have expressed their joy at the Taliban victory in Kabul.

Among them is Yasir Nadeem Al Wajidi, Islamic cleric in the U.S. Director of Darul Uloom Online, and lead teacher of the Institute of Islamic Education Elgin IL. He tweeted: "Congratulations to #Taliban and the people of Afghanistan on the rebirth of the Islamic Emirate! Allah has once again given you the opportunity to present to the world the Islamic system based on justice and fairness. Your blessed entry into #Kabul is reminiscent of the Prophetic era."

Kamil Ahmad, a Canadian Islamic cleric who lectures at TV channels Peace TV and Huda TV, and teaches at the Islamic Online University, said: "Whether you like the #IslamicEmirateOfAfghanistan (aka #Taliban) or not, they are now in power. As long as their mandate is to rule by Islam and not man-made ideologies and systems of governance, they should be supported."

I asked the National Council of Canadian Muslims (NCCM) for their statement on the Taliban takeover of Kabul, since the Canadian Muslim community has a large Afghan population, but I received no response. There were other Canadian Islamic groups that did not release with their position on the Taliban takeover of Afghanistan.

On Tuesday, I sat on numerous Indian TV networks discussing Afghanistan and was shocked to see the glee and joy of Pakistanis and Indian Muslims celebrating the Taliban victory.

On the approaching 20th anniversary of 9/11 — while Joe Biden may not realize — the forces of Islamism will be celebrating the deaths in the United States, wherever proponents of Islamism reside, be it in Kabul, Karachi or Kashmir.

BIBLIOGRAPHY

"13 Confucius Institutes (CIs) in Canada." Confucius Institute of Toronto. Confucius Institute of Toronto, 2021. https://confuciusinstitutetoronto.weebly.com/.

"189 Killed in Easter Attacks on Churches and Hotels in Sri Lanka." Persecution.org. International Christian Concern, April 21, 2019. https://www.persecution.org/2019/04/21/189-killed-easter-attacks-churches-hotels-sri-lanka/.

Abdul-Adhim, Mazin. *10 Reasons Why the Khilafah*. *YouTube*, 2018. https://www.youtube.com/watch?v=VpsCsGSS4SY.

AbdulAdhim, Mazin. "I've Been Asked Many Times about Whether or Not I Believe That Homosexuality Is Genetic." Archive Today. Facebook.com, 2019. https://archive.is/oGZjP.

"About - Toronto Association for Democracy in China." Toronto Association for Democracy in China, 2021. https://www.tadc.ca/about/.

"About Shariah Finance." Shariah Finance Watch. Center for Security Policy. Accessed August 22, 2021. https://shariahfinancewatch.org/about-shariah-finance/.

"About 'Media Against Hate.'" #MediaAgainstHate. European Federation of Journalists (EFJ), 2016. http://europeanjournalists.org/mediaagainsthate/about/.

"Abu Bakar Ba'asyir: The Radical Indonesian Cleric Linked to Bali Bombings." BBC News. BBC, January 8, 2021. https://www.bbc.com/news/world-asia-pacific-10912588.

Aharony, Michal. "Why Does Hannah Arendt's 'Banality of Evil' Still Anger Israelis?" Haaretz.com, the online English edition of Haaretz Newspaper in Israel. Haaretz Daily Newspaper Ltd., May 11, 2019. https://www.haaretz.com/israel-news/.premium.magazine-why-does-hannah-arendt-s-banality-of-evil-still-anger-israelis-1.7213979.

Ahmed, Dr. Qanta. "My Grief for the Victims of the New Zealand Mosque Attack." The Spectator. The Spectator (1828) Ltd, March 14, 2019. https://www.spectator.co.uk/article/my-grief-for-the-victims-of-the-new-zealand-mosque-attack.

Ahuja, Gitika. "Saudi Prince Donates $40 Million to Harvard, Georgetown Universities." ABC news. ABC News Network, December 13, 2005. https://abcnews.go.com/International/story?id=140 2008.

Akram, Mohamed. "1991 Explanatory Memorandum on the General Strategic Goal for the Group [Muslim Brotherhood] in North America [Translated] Government Exhibit, U.S. v HLF, Et Al." U.S. Government, May 19, 1991. Document available at: http://www.investigativeproject.org/documents/mis c/20.pdf

"Al Jazeera Partners with Bloomberg to Expand Business Coverage." Reuters. Thomson Reuters, February 11, 2019. https://mobile.reuters.com/article/amp/idUSKCN1Q 00K3.

Al Jazeera. "Philippines Church Bombing: Twin Blasts Hit Jolo Cathedral." News | Al Jazeera. Al Jazeera, January 27, 2019. https://www.aljazeera.com/news/2019/1/27/philipp ines-church-bombing-twin-blasts-hit-jolo-cathedral.

Alhas, Ali Murat. "OIC Calls for Global Action against Islamophobia." Anadolu Ajansı. Anadolu Agency, March 22, 2019. https://www.aa.com.tr/en/middle-east/oic-calls-for-global-action-against-islamophobia/1426137.

Ali, Ayaan Hirsi. "Ayaan Hirsi Ali: The Global War on Christians in the Muslim World." Newsweek.com. Newsweek Digital LLC, February 6, 2012. https://www.newsweek.com/ayaan-hirsi-alithe-global-war-christians-muslim-world-65817.

Ali, Ayaan Hirsi. "Opinion | Can Ilhan Omar Overcome Her Prejudice?" The Wall Street Journal. Dow Jones & Company, July 12, 2019. https://www.wsj.com/articles/can-ilhan-omar-overcome-her-prejudice-11562970265.

Alshareef, Muhammad. *Christians, Jews and Kuffar*. *YouTube.com*. TIFRIBvideos, 2016. https://www.youtube.com/watch?v=42cSYW-P1iU.

"American Islamic Forum for Democracy." American Islamic Forum for Democracy | At Home with American Liberty and Freedom, 2016. https://aifdemocracy.org/.

"Amira Elghawaby: Authors: Toronto Star." thestar.com. Toronto Star Newspapers Ltd., 2021. https://www.thestar.com/authors.elghawaby_amira.html.

Anderlini, Jamil, Lucy Hornby, and James Kynge. "Inside China's Secret 'Magic Weapon' for Worldwide Influence." Financial Times. The Financial Times Ltd., October 26, 2017. https://www.ft.com/content/fb2b3934-b004-11e7-beba-5521c713abf4.

Anderson, Shane. "Critical Thinking in Religious Education." *Religious Educator* 18, no. 3 (2017): 69–

81. https://rsc.byu.edu/vol-18-no-3-2017/critical-thinking-religious-education.

Annan, Kofi. "Secretary-General Addressing Headquarters Seminar on Confronting Islamophobia, Stresses Importance of Leadership, Two-Way Integration, Dialogue." United Nations. United Nations, December 7, 2004. https://www.un.org/press/en/2004/sgsm9637.doc.htm.

Arab News Editors. "European-Islamic Media Forum Calls for Clampdown on Hate Speech in Western Press." Arab News. Saudi Research & Publishing Company, June 30, 2018. https://www.arabnews.com/node/1330536/saudi-arabia.

Armstrong, Amelia. "Police-Reported Hate Crime in Canada, 2017." Statistics Canada: Canada's national statistical agency / Statistique Canada : Organisme statistique national du Canada. Government of Canada, April 30, 2019. https://www150.statcan.gc.ca/n1/pub/85-002-x/2019001/article/00008-eng.htm.

Armstrong, Karen. Essay. In *A History of God: The 4000-Year Quest of Judaism, Christianity, and Islam*, 295. New York, NY: Alfred A. Knopf, 1993.

Awada, Dalila. "Society Must Fight Islamophobia, Says Awada." Edited by CUPE. Canadian Union of Public Employees, October 5, 2017. https://cupe.ca/society-must-fight-islamophobia-says-awada.

Barzegar, Dr. Abbas, and Zainab Arain. "Hijacked by Hate: American Philanthropy and the Islamophobia Network." Washington DC: Council on American-Islamic Relations (CAIR), May 6, 2019.

Bederman, Diane Weber. "#Rotherham: Where Are the #Metoo Feminists?" The Bederman Blog, January 11, 2018. https://dianebederman.com/rotherham-where-are-the-metoo-feminists/.

Bederman, Diane Weber. "#Rotherham: Where Are the #MeToo Feminists?" The Bederman Blog. Diane Weber Bederman, January 6, 2018. https://dianebederman.com/rotherham-where-are-the-metoo-feminists/.

Bederman, Diane Weber. "Hate Incidents All Start with Words." The Bederman Blog. Diane Weber Bederman, April 3, 2019. https://dianebederman.com/hate-incidents-all-start-with-words/.

Bederman, Diane Weber. "I Stand by Canadian Lauren Southern Because SILENCE IS COLLUSION." The Bederman Blog. Diane Weber Bederman, March 23, 2018. https://dianebederman.com/i-stand-by-canadian-lauren-southern-because-silence-is-collusion/.

Bederman, Diane Weber. "If Islam Is so Compatible with the West Why Is It That Western Culture Is Not Welcome in Muslim Countries?" The Bederman Blog, March 22, 2019. https://dianebederman.com/if-islam-is-so-compatible-with-the-west-why-is-it-that-western-culture-is-not-welcome-in-muslim-countries/.

Bederman, Diane Weber. "Is It Time to Repeal Islamophobia?" The Bederman Blog. Diane Weber Bederman, January 18, 2019. https://dianebederman.com/is-it-time-to-repeal-islamophobia/.

Bederman, Diane Weber. "Muslim Prayer in Public Schools." The Bederman Blog. Diane Weber

Bederman, February 5, 2018.
https://dianebederman.com/muslim-prayer-in-public-schools/.

Bederman, Diane Weber. "Muslim Students Insulted at Public Schools." The Bederman Blog. Diane Weber Bederman, January 8, 2017.
https://dianebederman.com/muslim-students-insulted-at-public-schools/.

Bederman, Diane Weber. "What Do Judaism Christianity and Islam Have in Common? Part 3." Diane Bederman - Your Passionate Voice of Reason, November 12, 2017.
https://dianebederman.com/what-do-judaism-christianity-and-islam-have-in-common-part-3/.

Bederman, Diane Weber. "Why Are Esteemed Jewish Elders Bending the Knee to Cancel Culture and the #IslamophobiaIndustry?" The Bederman Blog. Diane Weber Bederman, July 7, 2021.
https://dianebederman.com/why-are-esteemed-jewish-elders-bending-the-knee-to-cancel-culture-and-the-islamophobiaindustry/.

Bensman, Todd. "When Terrorists Learned 'Lawfare' Works: The Holy Land Foundation Trial's 10-Year Anniversary." pjmedia.com. PJ Media, May 19, 2020.
https://pjmedia.com/homeland-security/todd-bensman/2018/12/03/when-terrorists-learned-lawfare-works-the-holy-land-foundation-trials-10-year-anniversary.

Bergman, Judith. "Facebook Still Championing Blasphemy Laws." Gatestone Institute. Gatestone Institute, February 19, 2019.
https://www.gatestoneinstitute.org/13583/facebook-blasphemy-laws.

Bergman, Judith. "Facebook: More Government Censorship." Gatestone Institute, July 16, 2019. https://www.gatestoneinstitute.org/14293/faceboo k-government-censorship.

Bergman, Judith. "Germany: A Shocking Degree of Self-Censorship." Gatestone Institute, July 4, 2019. https://www.gatestoneinstitute.org/14362/germany -self-censorship.

Bergman, Judith. "Germany: Full Censorship Now Official." Gatestone Institute, October 21, 2017. https://www.gatestoneinstitute.org/11205/germany -official-censorship.

Bergman, Judith. "Killing Free Speech." Gatestone Institute, September 21, 2018. https://www.gatestoneinstitute.org/12975/killing-free-speech.

Bergman, Judith. "The EU Courts the Arab League." Gatestone Institute, May 7, 2019. https://www.gatestoneinstitute.org/14188/eu-courts-arab-league.

Bergman, Judith. "UK: The Push to End Free Speech." Gatestone Institute. Gatestone Institute, September 17, 2019. https://www.gatestoneinstitute.org/14329/britain-criticism-of-islam.

Bergstrom, Guy. "Understanding the Mechanisms of Propaganda." The Balance Small Business. Dotdash publishing family, August 29, 2019. https://www.thebalancesmb.com/what-is-propaganda-and-how-does-it-work-2295248.

Berns-McGown, Rima. "Day of Remembrance and Action on Islamophobia Act, 2019." Legislative Assembly of Ontario. Government of Ontario, 2019.

https://www.ola.org/en/legislative-business/bills/parliament-42/session-1/bill-83.

Besson, Sylvain. "L'argent Du Qatar Inonde L'islam Suisse Et Paie Tariq Ramadan." Tribune de Genève. Tamedia Publications romandes S.A., April 3, 2019. https://www.tdg.ch/suisse/argent-qatar-inonde-lislam-suisse-paie-tariq-ramadan/story/13748479.

Biography.com, ed. "Salman Rushdie - Biography." Biography.com. A&E Networks Television, May 21, 2021. https://www.biography.com/writer/salman-rushdie.

Black, Edwin. "When the Holocaust Came to the Middle East." History News Network, May 30, 2018. https://historynewsnetwork.org/article/169158.

Blackwell, Tom. "How China Uses Shadowy United Front as 'Magic Weapon' to Try to Extend Its Influence in Canada." thestarphoenix.com. The Star Phoenix, a division of Postmedia Network Inc., December 31, 2019. https://thestarphoenix.com/news/how-china-uses-shadowy-united-front-as-magic-weapon-to-try-to-extend-its-influence-in-canada.

Blackwell, Tom. "Open Letter from Chinese-Canadian Groups Boosts Hong Kong Government, Blasts Protesters." nationalpost.com. Postmedia Network Inc., July 9, 2019. https://nationalpost.com/news/open-letter-from-chinese-canadian-groups-boosts-hong-kong-government-blasts-protesters.

Blake, Dean. "Zeldin Calls for Firing of City University of New York Professor after Anti-Semitic Sermon." JNS.org. Jewish News Syndicate, July 30, 2021. https://www.jns.org/zeldin-calls-for-firing-of-city-university-of-new-york-professor-after-anti-semitic-sermon.

Bokhari, Kamran, and Farid Senzai. Essay. In *Political Islam in the Age of Democratization*, 194–94. Basingstoke, UK: Palgrave Macmillan, 2013.

Borger, Julian, ed. "French Media to Stop Publishing Photos and Names of Terrorists." The Guardian. Guardian News and Media, July 27, 2016. https://www.theguardian.com/media/2016/jul/27/french-media-to-stop-publishing-photos-and-names-of-terrorists.

"Boston Marathon Bombing of 2013." Encyclopædia Britannica. Encyclopædia Britannica, Inc., 2021. https://www.britannica.com/event/Boston-Marathon-bombing-of-2013.

Brady, Andrea. "Profile: The Council on American Islamic Relations." New York NY: Anti-Defamation League, August 21, 2015.

Breakenridge, Rob. "Commentary: Properly Describing the Terror Threat Means Acknowledging Religious Extremism Exists." Global News. Global News, a division of Corus Entertainment Inc., April 19, 2021. https://globalnews.ca/news/5238890/terror-threat-canada-shia-sunni/.

Brelet, Amaury. "Génération Identitaire Accuse Un Imam D'avoir Donné Le Nom Arabe De La Bataille De Poitiers à Sa Mosquée." Valeurs Actuelles, July 5, 2018. https://www.valeursactuelles.com/societe/generation-identitaire-accuse-un-imam-davoir-donne-le-nom-arabe-de-la-bataille-de-poitiers-a-sa-mosquee/.

Brenner, Yermi, and Katrin Ohlendorf. "Time for the Facts. What Do We Know about Cologne Four Months Later?" The Correspondent, May 2, 2016. https://thecorrespondent.com/4401/time-for-the-facts-what-do-we-know-about-cologne-four-months-later/1073698080444-e20ada1b.

Britannica, The Editors of. "Muslim Brotherhood." Encyclopædia Britannica. Encyclopædia Britannica, inc., September 11, 2020. https://www.britannica.com/topic/Muslim-Brotherhood.

Bruckner, Pascal. "There's No Such Thing as Islamophobia." Edited by Brian C. Anderson. Translated by Alexis Cornel. CityJournal.org. Manhattan Institute, January 8, 2020. https://www.city-journal.org/html/theres-no-such-thing-islamophobia-15324.html.

Busby, Mattha. "British Woman Faye Mooney Killed by Kidnappers in Nigeria." The Guardian. Guardian News and Media, April 21, 2019. https://www.theguardian.com/world/2019/apr/21/british-woman-faye-mooney-killed-kidnappers-nigeria.

"CAIR Civil Rights Reports." CAIR. Council on American-Islamic Relations (CAIR), August 26, 2020. https://www.cair.com/resources/cair-civil-rights-reports/.

"CAIR.CAN Evolves – Introducing the National Council of Canadian Muslims (NCCM)." NCCM. National Council of Canadian Muslims (NCCM) / Conseil National des Musulmans Canadiens (CNMC), July 6, 2013. https://www.nccm.ca/introducing-the-national-council-of-canadian-muslims-nccm/.

"CAIR: About Us." CAIR.com. Council on American-Islamic Relations (CAIR), May 6, 2020. https://www.cair.com/about_cair/about-us/.

Cairo Correspondent. "Church Closed in Egypt after Muslim Mob Frightens Children in Sunday School."

Morning Star News, April 23, 2019.
https://morningstarnews.org/2019/04/church-
closed-in-egypt-after-muslim-mob-frightens-
children-in-sunday-school/.

"Canadian Muslim Scholar: 'The West Is a Cesspool of
Moral Corruption," Including Homosexuality."
ACDemocracy. American Center for Democracy,
January 22, 2019.
https://news.acdemocracy.org/canadian-muslim-
scholar-the-west-is-a-cesspool-of-moral-corruption-
including-homosexuality.

CBN News. "EU: British Press Should Not Report When
Terrorists Are Muslim." CBN News. Christian
Broadcasting Network, Inc., October 6, 2016.
https://www1.cbn.com/cbnnews/world/2016/octob
er/eu-british-press-should-not-report-when-
terrorists-are-muslim.

Central Information Department. "JI Donates Rs. 6 m to
Palestinians - Internet Archive Wayback Machine." 'JI
donates RS. 6 M TO Palestinians' - JI media news.
Jamaat-e-Islami Pakistan, August 17, 2006.
https://web.archive.org/web/20071003065109/http
://www.jamaat.org/news/2006/aug/17/1001.html.

Cetorelli, Valeria, Isaac Sasson, Nazar Shabila, and
Gilbert Burnham. "Mortality and Kidnapping
Estimates for the Yazidi Population in the Area of
Mount Sinjar, Iraq, in August 2014: A Retrospective
Household Survey." PLOS Medicine 14, no. 5 (May 9,
2017).
https://doi.org/10.1371/journal.pmed.1002297.

Chang, Gordon G. "Opinion | Xi Changed My Mind about
Trump." The Wall Street Journal. Dow Jones &
Company, July 24, 2019.

https://www.wsj.com/articles/xi-changed-my-mind-about-trump-11564008053.

Chen, James. "Shariah-Compliant Funds Definition."
Edited by Gordon Scott. Investopedia, May 30, 2021.
https://www.investopedia.com/terms/s/shariah-compliant-funds.asp.

"Chinese Student and Scholars Association." Chinese
Student and Scholars Association at the University of
Calgary (UCCSSA). Campus Labs, 2021.
https://suuofc.campuslabs.ca/engage/organization/chinese-students-and-scholars-association.

Chinese Students and Scholars Association (CSSA).
Students' Society of McGill University, 2021.
https://ssmu.ca/clubs/religion-culture-clubs/chinese-students-and-scholars-association-at-mcgill-university-cssa/.

"Chinese Students and Scholars Association (UTCSSA)."
Ulife - Chinese Students and Scholars Association (UT
CSSA) - University of Toronto. Office of the Vice-Provost Students, University of Toronto, 2021.
https://www.ulife.utoronto.ca/organizations/view/id/1832.

Choudary, Anjem. "People Know the Consequences:
Opposing View." USA Today. Gannett Satellite
Information Network, January 8, 2015.
https://www.usatoday.com/story/opinion/2015/01/07/islam-allah-muslims-shariah-anjem-choudary-editorials-debates/21417461/.

"Churchill on Islam." The Churchill Project - Hillsdale
College. Churchill Literary Estate and Curtis Brown
Ltd., London, March 5, 2019.
https://winstonchurchill.hillsdale.edu/churchill-on-islam/.

CIRC Staff. "NCCM Once Again Calling for Resignation of Conservative Candidate." circanada.com. Centre for Investigative Research Canada, September 16, 2019. https://circanada.com/2019/09/15/nccm-once-again-calling-for-resignation-of-conservative-candidate/.

CJME News. "Sask. to Adopt Day against Islamophobia." 980 CJME. Rawlco Radio Ltd, March 20, 2019. https://www.cjme.com/2019/03/26/sask-to-adopt-anti-islamophobia-day/.

CNN Editorial Research. "Mumbai Terror Attacks Fast Facts." CNN. Cable News Network, December 3, 2020. https://www.cnn.com/2013/09/18/world/asia/mumbai-terror-attacks/index.html.

Cohen, Dr. Edy. "The Persecution of Christians in the Palestinian Authority." Begin-Sadat Center for Strategic Studies. Bar-Ilan University, May 27, 2019. https://besacenter.org/persecution-christians-palestinian-authority/.

Cole, Juan. "Iran and Islam." The Iran Primer. United States Institute of Peace, October 5, 2010. https://iranprimer.usip.org/resource/iran-and-islam.

Cole, Nicki Lisa. "Cultural Relativism Explains Why Breakfast Differs around the World." ThoughtCo.com. ThoughtCo, part of the Dotdash publishing family, August 17, 2019. https://www.thoughtco.com/cultural-relativism-definition-3026122.

"Cops: Killer Felt Stepdaughter Ignored Faith." https://www.inquirer.com. The Philadelphia Inquirer, May 4, 2011. https://www.inquirer.com/philly/news/nation_worl

d/20110504_Cops__Killer_felt_daughter_ignored_fa
ith.html.

"Coptic Christians Without Church for Easter Following
Mob Attack." Persecution.org. International
Christian Concern, April 16, 2019.
https://www.persecution.org/2019/04/16/coptic-
christians-without-church-easter-following-mob-
attack/.

"Council on American Islamic Relations (CAIR) (Profile)."
InfluenceWatch.org. Capital Research Center, April
24, 2020. https://www.influencewatch.org/non-
profit/council-on-american-islamic-relations-cair/.

"The Council on American-Islamic Relations (CAIR): CAIR
Exposed." Washington, DC: The Investigative Project
on Terrorism, April 8, 2008.

Croatian News Agency (HINA). "Croatian Mass in Munich
Disrupted by Mentally Ill Person Shouting 'Allahu
Akbar.'" Total Croatia News, April 21, 2019.
https://www.total-croatia-news.com/the-croatian-
diaspora/35455-allahu-akbar.

Daniels, J. "[Translation] EILT: Six Months Imprisonment
for PI-NEWS Author Michael Stürzenberger." PI-
NEWS (Politically Incorrect), August 18, 2017.
http://www.pi-news.net/2017/08/eilt-sechs-
monate-haft-fuer-pi-news-autor-michael-
stuerzenberger/.

Dathan, Matt. "European Human Rights Chiefs Order the
British Press NOT to Reveal When Terrorists Are
Muslims in Crackdown on Freedom of Speech." Daily
Mail Online. Associated Newspapers Ltd, October 5,
2016. https://www.dailymail.co.uk/news/article-
3823706/European-human-rights-chiefs-orders-
British-press-NOT-reveal-terrorists-Muslims.html.

David, Javier E. "Angela Merkel Caught on Hot Mic Griping to Facebook CEO over Anti-Immigrant Posts." CNBC. CNBC LLC, September 27, 2015. https://www.cnbc.com/2015/09/27/angela-merkel-caught-on-hot-mic-pressing-facebook-ceo-over-anti-immigrant-posts.html.

Dawidowicz, Lucy S. "The War against the Jews: 1933-1945." The War Against the Jews: 1933-1945. Amazon.ca, March 1, 1986. https://www.amazon.ca/War-Against-Jews-1933-1945/dp/055334532X.

Dhillon, Amrit. "Why Not a Museum for the Dalits of India?" The Globe and Mail. The Globe and Mail Inc., September 30, 2016. https://www.theglobeandmail.com/opinion/why-not-a-museum-for-the-dalits-of-india/article32150225/.

"Dispelling Misinformation About Islam." Toronto: Walk-In Islamic Info Centre, August 29, 2016. http://islamicbooth.ca

"Does Shariah-Compliant Finance Have the Power to Change the World? | Bloomberg Professional Services." Bloomberg.com, November 3, 2020. https://www.bloomberg.com/professional/blog/does-shariah-compliant-finance-have-the-power-to-change-the-world/.

Douglass-Williams, Christine. "Canada: Sharia Financing Rapidly Expanding with Increasing Sharia-Adherent Population." Jihad Watch, February 15, 2020. https://www.jihadwatch.org/2020/02/canada-sharia-financing-rapidly-expanding-with-increasing-sharia-adherent-population.

Douglass-Williams, Christine. "U.S., Canada's RCMP Team up with Islamists." Gatestone Institute,

October 13, 2014.
https://www.gatestoneinstitute.org/4768/us-
canada-islamists-nccm.

"Dow Jones Islamic Market Indexes." Dow Jones,
February 16, 2007.

Duniho, Fergus. "The Importance of Critical Thinking in
Religion." For the Love of Wisdom. Fergus Duniho,
May 26, 2019.
https://fortheloveofwisdom.net/57/religion/critical-
thinking/.

Duru, Peter. "11 Killed after Good Friday Church Service,
Many Missing in Benue Community." Vanguard
News. Vanguard Media Limited, Nigeria, April 20,
2019. https://www.vanguardngr.com/2019/04/11-
killed-after-good-friday-church-service-many-
missing-in-benue-community/.

"Dār Al-Islam." Encyclopædia Britannica. Encyclopædia
Britannica, inc., August 29, 2011.
https://www.britannica.com/topic/Dar-al-Islam.

Editor. "Can Ilhan Omar Overcome Her Prejudice? By
Ayaan Hirsi Ali (Wsj)." Israel Activist Alliance. Wall
Street Journal, July 12, 2019. http://israelaa.ca/can-
ilhan-omar-overcome-her-prejudice-by-ayaan-hirsi-
ali-wsj/.

Editorial Team. "Al-Azhar University."
MuslimHeritage.com. Foundation for Science,
Technology and Civilisation, UK (FSTCUK), April 10,
2001. https://muslimheritage.com/al-azhar-
university/.

Editors of Encyclopaedia Britannica, Thinley Kalsang
Bhutia, and Adam Zeidan. "Shirk." Encyclopædia
Britannica. Encyclopædia Britannica, Inc., April 23,
2020. https://www.britannica.com/topic/shirk.

Editors. "About ICNA." icnacanada.net. Islamic Circle of North America, 2020. https://icnacanada.net/about-2/.

Editors. "Canadian Islamic Organization Refutes Trudeau's Claim That Islam Is Compatible with Democracy." Centre for Investigative Research Canada, June 22, 2018. https://circanada.com/2018/06/21/canadian-islamic-organization-refutes-trudeaus-claim-that-islam-is-compatible-with-democracy/.

Editors. "Dr. Mohd Daud Bakar – 16th Kuala Lumpur Islamic Finance Forum." 16th Kuala Lumpur Islamic Finance Forum (KLIFF2021). CERT Centre for Research and Training, 2021. https://kliff.com.my/sp-datuk-dr-mohd-daud-bakar/.

Editors. "Dr. Omar Suleiman, Founder & President (CEO)." Yaqeen Institute for Islamic Research, 2021. https://yaqeeninstitute.ca/team/omar-suleiman.

Editors. "Global Islamic Finance Market - Growth, Trends, and Forecast (2018 - 2024)." Research and Markets - Market Research Reports, 2021. https://www.researchandmarkets.com/research/bq7pb4/global_islamic.

Editors. "History - Organisation of Islamic Cooperation (OIC)." The Organisation of Islamic Cooperation (OIC), 2021. https://www.oic-oci.org/page/?p_id=52&p_ref=26&lan=en.

Editors. "Holy Land Foundation Convictions." Federal Bureau of Investigation, November 25, 2008. https://archives.fbi.gov/archives/news/stories/2008/november/hlf112508.

Editors. "Home - Organization of Islamic Cooperation (OIC)." The Organization of Islamic Cooperation (OIC), 2021. https://www.oic-oci.org/home/?lan=en.

Editors. "Islamic Circle of North America (ICNA) Canada."
ICNACanada.net, 2020. https://icnacanada.net/.

Editors. "Jasmin Zine | Professor, Sociology and Muslim
Studies Option." Wilfrid Laurier University, 2021.
https://www.wlu.ca/academics/faculties/faculty-of-
arts/faculty-profiles/jasmin-zine/index.html.

Editors. "Le Qatar Envisage D'investir 10 Milliards
D'EUROS Dans Des Groupes Français."
nouvelobs.com, November 7, 2012.
https://www.nouvelobs.com/societe/20121106.AFP
4166/le-qatar-envisage-d-investir-10-milliards-d-
euros-dans-des-groupes-francais.html.

Editors. "List of Killings in the Name of Islam: 2020."
What makes Islam so different?
TheReligionofPeace.com (TROP), 2021.
https://thereligionofpeace.com/attacks/attacks.aspx
?Yr=2020.

Editors. "Muhammad Taqi Usmani." The Muslim 500.
Royal Islamic Strategic Studies Centre (MABDA المركز
الملكي للبحوث والدراسات الإسلامية,) 2021). Accessed
August 22, 2021.
https://themuslim500.com/profiles/muhammad-
taqi-usmani/. An independent research entity
affiliated with the Royal Aal al-Bayt Institute for
Islamic Thought, which is an international Islamic
non-governmental, independent institute
headquartered in Amman, the capital of the
Hashemite Kingdom of Jordan.

Editors. "New Building by Zaha Hadid Unveiled at Oxford
University's Middle East Centre." University of
Oxford, May 26, 2015.
https://www.ox.ac.uk/news/2015-05-26-new-
building-zaha-hadid-unveiled-oxford-
university%E2%80%99s-middle-east-centre.

Editors. "Nizam Yaquby." The Muslim 500. Royal Islamic
Strategic Studies Centre (MABDA المركز الملكي للبحوث
الإسلامية والدراسات,) 2021.
https://themuslim500.com/profiles/nizam-yaquby/.
An independent research entity affiliated with the
Royal Aal al-Bayt Institute for Islamic Thought, which
is an international Islamic non-governmental,
independent institute headquartered in Amman, the
capital of the Hashemite Kingdom of Jordan.

Editors. "OIC Charter." The Organization of Islamic
Cooperation (OIC), 2021. https://www.oic-
oci.org/page/?p_id=53&p_ref=27&lan=en.

Editors. Religious Accommodation. Pell District School
Board, 2021.
https://www.peelschools.org/about/inclusion/religi
ous-accommodation/Pages/default.aspx.

Editors. "Sayyid Abul A'la Maududi." Islam Times, May
16, 2009.
https://www.islamtimes.org/en/article/4995/sayyid-
abul-a-la-maududi.

Editors. "Sharia-Compliant Financial Assets Forecast to
Reach $3.8 Trillion by 2023." Weekly Blitz, April 14,
2020. https://www.weeklyblitz.net/economy/sharia-
compliant-financial-assets-forecast-to-reach-3-8-
trillion-by-2023/.

Editors. "What's Wrong with Sharia Compliant Finance?"
What's Wrong with Sharia Compliant Finance? Sharia
Watch UK Ltd., 2017.
https://web.archive.org/web/20171025134711/http
://www.shariawatch.org.uk/?q=content%2Fwhat-s-
wrong-sharia-compliant-finance-0.

Editors. "Who Is ICNA? Islamic Circle of North America
(ICNA)." ICNA.org. Islamic Circle of North America,

December 14, 2020. https://www.icna.org/about-icna/.

Editors. "Writings by Giulio Meotti." Gatestone Institute, 2021. https://www.gatestoneinstitute.org/author/Giulio+Meotti.

Editors. Yaqeen Institute for Islamic Research, 2021. https://yaqeeninstitute.ca/. URL https://yaqeeninstitute.org for Dallas TX -based parent institute connects to the Canadian branch's website.

Editors. "Yusuf Al-Qaradawi [- Profile]." Counter Extremism Project, 2021. https://www.counterextremism.com/extremists/yusuf-al-qaradawi.

EEAS Press Team. "Federica Mogherini's Remarks at 'Call to Europe V: Islam in Europe', FEPS Conference.'" EEAS10. European Union External Action Service (EEAS), June 25, 2015. https://eeas.europa.eu/headquarters/headquarters-homepage/6332/federica-mogherinis-remarks-at-call-to-europe-v-islam-in-europe-feps-conference_en.

Ehrenfeld, Dr. Rachel, and Alyssa A. Lappen. "Financial Jihad." ACDemocracy. American Center for Democracy, September 22, 2005. https://acdemocracy.org/financial-jihad-2/.

Ehrenfeld, Dr. Rachel, and Alyssa A. Lappen. "Tithing for Terrorists." American Center for Democracy, October 12, 2007. https://acdemocracy.org/tithing-for-terrorists/.

Ehrenfeld, Rachel. "American Muslim Scholar Salutes Brunei for Reinstating Law on Stoning Gays." ACDemocracy. American Center for Democracy,

March 31, 2019.
https://news.acdemocracy.org/american-muslim-scholar-salutes-brunei-for-reinstating-law-on-stoning-gays/.

Ehrenfeld, Rachel. "American Muslim Scholar Says Liberalism Is a Dangerous Religion, 'Distinct from Islam.'" The American Center for Democracy, April 18, 2018. https://news.acdemocracy.org/american-muslim-scholar-says-liberalism-is-a-dangerous-religion-distinct-from-islam/.

Ehrenfeld, Rachel. "Canada Officially Defines Islamophobia." ACD. American Center for Democracy and the Economic Warfare Institute, July 3, 2019. https://news.acdemocracy.org/canada-officially-defines-islamophobia.

Ehrenfeld, Rachel. "Canadian Imam Explains the Quranic Verse on the 'Internal Filth' of Non-Muslims." ACDemocracy. American Center for Democracy, September 2, 2018. https://news.acdemocracy.org/canadian-imam-explains-the-quranic-verse-on-the-internal-filth-of-non-muslims/. An excerpt from Yusuf Badat's Friday sermon delivered at the Islamic Foundation of Toronto, May 25, 2012.

Ehrenfeld, Rachel. "Canadian Muslim Scholar Calls for Reestablishing the Islamic State, Rejecting Nation-States." ACDemocracy. American Center for Democracy, April 20, 2018. https://news.acdemocracy.org/canadian-muslim-scholar-calls-for-reestablishing-the-islamic-state-rejecting-nation-states/.

Ehrenfeld, Rachel. "Canadian Muslim Scholar Explains the Islamic Perspective on Democracy." ACDemocracy. American Center for Democracy, May

19, 2018. https://news.acdemocracy.org/canadian-muslim-scholar-explains-the-islamic-perspective-on-democracy/.

Ehrenfeld, Rachel. "Canadian Muslim Scholar: 'Homosexuality Is a Sexual Perversion; It Can Also Be Reversed.'" ACDemocracy. American Center for Democracy, February 20, 2019. https://news.acdemocracy.org/canadian-muslim-scholar-homosexuality-is-a-sexual-perversion-it-can-also-be-reversed/.

Ehrenfeld, Rachel. "Daniel Haqiqatjou Says American Muslim Leaders Desecrate Image of Islam by Supporting LGBTQ." ACDemocracy. American Center for Democracy, September 13, 2020. https://news.acdemocracy.org/daniel-haqiqatjou-says-american-muslim-leaders-desecrate-image-of-islam-by-supporting-lgbtq/.

Ehrenfeld, Rachel. "Islamic Organization in Britain: 'Islam Is Not Only for Muslims, but for All Mankind.'" ACDemocracy. American Center for Democracy, September 19, 2018. https://news.acdemocracy.org/islamic-organization-in-britain-islam-is-not-only-for-muslims-but-for-all-mankind/.

Ehrenfeld, Rachel. "Salaheddin Islamic Centre: Chopping off Thieves' Hands in America Will Decrease Crime Rate." ACDemocracy. American Center for Democracy, December 27, 2018. https://news.acdemocracy.org/salaheddin-islamic-centre-chopping-off-thieves-hands-in-america-will-decrease-crime-rate/.

Ehrenfeld, Rachel. "What Are Praying Muslims Repeating 17 Times Daily?" ACDemocracy. American Center for Democracy, January 30, 2018.

https://acdemocracy.org/what-are-praying-muslims-repeating-17-times-daily/.

"Eight Blasts at Churches, Hotels across Sri Lanka Kill at Least 207; 13 Arrested." The Hindu. THG Publishing Pvt Ltd., April 22, 2019. https://www.thehindu.com/news/international/live-multiple-explosions-in-colombo-and-other-parts-of-sri-lanka/article26903170.ece.

"Establishment - Background." Islamic Financial Services Board (IFSB), June 2021. https://www.ifsb.org/background.php.

"The EU Code of Conduct on Countering Illegal Hate Speech Online." European Commission, June 25, 2021. https://ec.europa.eu/info/policies/justice-and-fundamental-rights/combatting-discrimination/racism-and-xenophobia/eu-code-conduct-countering-illegal-hate-speech-online_en.

"European Convention on Human Rights." European Convention on Human Rights - Official texts, Convention and Protocols. European Court of Human Rights, 2021. https://www.echr.coe.int/Pages/home.aspx?p=basic texts&c.

Expert Participation. "Equality Act 2010." Legislation.gov.uk. Statute Law Database, 2010. https://www.legislation.gov.uk/ukpga/2010/15/section/9.

"Fact Sheet - Race to the Top." Home. U.S. Department of Education, December 29, 2009. https://www2.ed.gov/programs/racetothetop/factsheet.html.

The Faith and Order Commission. "God's Unfailing Word - Theological and Practical Perspectives on Christian

– Jewish Relations." London: Church of England by Church House Publishing, November 13, 2019.

Fatah, Tarek. "FATAH: This Betrayal of Afghanistan Is beyond Belief." torontosun.com. Postmedia Network Inc., August 18, 2021. https://torontosun.com/opinion/columnists/fatah-this-betrayal-of-afghanistan-is-beyond-belief.

Fatah, Tarek. "Huffpost Exclusive: Sharia Banking Goes Bankrupt." HuffPost Canada. HuffPost Canada, December 17, 2011. https://www.huffingtonpost.ca/tarek-fatah/sharia-banking_b_1011704.html.

"Fifteen Men Charged over Beheadings of Female Hikers in Morocco." Sky News. Sky UK, December 31, 2018. https://news.sky.com/story/fifteen-men-charged-over-beheadings-of-female-hikers-in-morocco-11595382.

Finan, Victoria. "Bataclan Victims Castrated by ISIS Killers and Had Their Eyes Gouged Out." Daily Mail Online. Associated Newspapers Ltd., July 16, 2016. https://www.dailymail.co.uk/news/article-3692359/French-government-suppressed-gruesome-torture-Bataclan-victims-official-inquiry-told-castrated-eyes-gouged-ISIS-killers.html.

Fitzgerald, Hugh. "Bernie Sanders at the Islamic Society of North America." FrontPageMag.com. David Horowitz Freedom Center, September 20, 2019. https://www.frontpagemag.com/fpm/2019/09/bernie-sanders-islamic-society-north-america-hugh-fitzgerald.

Folkenflik, David. "Clinton Lauds Virtues of Al Jazeera: 'It's Real News'." NPR.org. National Public Radio, March 3, 2011. https://www.npr.org/sections/thetwo-way/2011/03/03/134243115/clinton-lauds-virtues-of-al-jazeera-its-real-news.

Foreign Staff. "Prophet Mohammed Cartoons Controversy: Timeline." The Telegraph. Telegraph Media Group, May 4, 2015. https://www.telegraph.co.uk/news/worldnews/europe/france/11341599/Prophet-Muhammad-cartoons-controversy-timeline.html.

Forrest, Maura. "M-103 Report Makes Few Recommendations about Islamophobia." nationalpost.com. National Post, February 1, 2018. https://nationalpost.com/news/politics/m-103-report-makes-few-recommendations-about-islamophobia.

"France Teacher Attack: Seven Charged over Samuel Paty's Killing." BBC News Europe. BBC News Services, October 22, 2020. https://www.bbc.com/news/world-europe-54632353.

Franceinfo with AFP, and France Televisions. "[Translated] Eric Zemmour Definitively Condemned for Anti-Muslim Remarks." Franceinfo, September 19, 2019. https://www.francetvinfo.fr/societe/justice/eric-zemmour-definitivement-condamne-pour-des-propos-anti-musulmans_3623557.html.

"Franklin Templeton Shariah Funds - Understanding Shariah Equity Investing, April 2017." Dubai: Franklin Templeton Investments, April 2017.

Frot, Mathilde. "Pearson to Review GCSE Textbook on Israel and Palestine after 'Bias' Claim." www.jewishnews.co.uk. Jewish News - Britian's Biggest Jewish Newspaper, October 21, 2019. https://jewishnews.timesofisrael.com/pearson-to-review-gcse-textbook-on-israel-palestine-conflict-after-bias-claim/.

"Fulani Militants Attack Another Christian Village in Nigeria." Persecution.org. International Christian Concern, April 24, 2019. https://www.persecution.org/2019/04/24/fulani-militants-attack-another-christian-village-nigeria/.

Furey, Anthony. "Pro-Shariah Caliphate Lecture Held at Ontario College." torontosun.com. Postmedia Network Inc., January 7, 2016. https://torontosun.com/2016/01/06/mohawk-college-distances-itself-from-refugee-crisis-speaker.

Gallo, Miranda, and Samer Majzoub. "When Will Canadians Get the Anti-Islamophobia Measures They Want?" HuffPost Canada. HuffPost Canada, February 8, 2018. https://www.huffingtonpost.ca/miranda-gallo/canadians-support-m-103-recommendations-why-wont-the-government_a_23355447/.

Ganley, Elaine. "French Muslims, Stigmatized by Attacks, Feel under Pressure." AP News. The Associated Press, November 1, 2020. https://apnews.com/article/paris-france-emmanuel-macron-islam-europe-ea5e15bb651bbe443b27bc19948cae6b.

Getz, Leonard. "Sharia Finances Are Being Used to Bolster American Islamist Organizations." JNS.org. Jewish News Syndicate, June 26, 2020. https://www.jns.org/opinion/sharia-finances-are-used-to-bolster-american-islamist-organizations/.

Getz, Leonard. "Shariah Finance Used to Fund American Islamist Organizations." Leonard Getz | The Blogs. The Times of Israel, July 1, 2020. https://blogs.timesofisrael.com/shariah-finance-used-to-fund-american-islamist-organizations/.

Ghose, Sagarika. "The Dalit in India." *Social Research* 70, no. 1 (2003): 83–109.

Gill, Joshua. "Muslim Asylum Seeker Imprisoned for Killing Wife Who Converted to Christianity." The Daily Caller, April 5, 2019. https://dailycaller.com/2019/04/05/muslim-asylum-seeker-imprisoned-for-killing-wife-who-converted-to-christianity/.

Gilmore, Rachel. "What Is the Government Doing about Islamophobia in Canada? Here's What We Know - National." Global News. Global News, June 9, 2021. https://globalnews.ca/news/7934835/london-attack-islamophobia-muslim-hate-government-action/.

Glavin, Terry. "Terry Glavin: It's Official – China Is a Threat to Canada's National Security." nationalpost.com. National Post, a division of Postmedia Network Inc., April 10, 2019. https://nationalpost.com/opinion/terry-glavin-its-official-china-is-a-threat-to-canadas-national-security.

Gomes, Robin. "Vatican's Message for Ramadan: 'Move from Competition to Collaboration.'" Vatican News, May 18, 2018. https://www.vaticannews.va/en/vatican-city/news/2018-05/vatican-dicastery-message-ramadan-competition-collaboration.html.

Goolam, Nazeem MI. "The Cartoon Controversy: a Note on Freedom of Expression, Hate Speech and Blasphemy." *The Comparative and International Law Journal of Southern Africa* 39, no. 2 (July 2006): 333–50. https://www.jstor.org/stable/23252640.

Goos, Sebastian, and Maja Kærhus Jørgensen. "[Translated] Shared Murder Video Online - Now

Authorities Want to Remove Danish Debater's Foster Child." nyheder.tv2.dk. TV 2 DANMARK, March 14, 2019. https://nyheder.tv2.dk/2019-03-14-delte-drabsvideo-paa-nettet-nu-vil-myndigheder-fjerne-dansk-debattoers-plejebarn.

Gorka, Katharine C. "The Flawed Science Behind America's Counter-Terrorism Strategy." Washington: Council on Global Security, October 2014.

Gorlinski, Virginia. "Ayaan Hirsi Ali - Biography." Edited by Encyclopaedia Britannica. Encyclopædia Britannica. Encyclopædia Britannica, inc., February 11, 2021. https://www.britannica.com/biography/Ayaan-Hirsi-Ali.

Graham, William A. "Why Study Religion in the Twenty-First Century?" Harvard Divinity Bulletin. Harvard Divinity School, Harvard University, 2012. https://bulletin.hds.harvard.edu/why-study-religion-in-the-twenty-first-century/.

GrainOfTruth. "MEMRI TV Clip: Canadian Imam Calling for the Stoning to Death of Gays." Grain of Truth, March 7, 2019. https://web.archive.org/web/20190317232804/http s://grainoftruth.ca/memri-tv-clip-canadian-imam-calling-for-the-stoning-to-death-of-gays/.

Green, Dominic. "Why Hitler Wished He Was Muslim." The Wall Street Journal. Dow Jones & Company, January 16, 2015. https://www.wsj.com/articles/book-review-ataturk-in-the-nazi-imagination-by-stefan-ihrig-and-islam-and-nazi-germanys-war-by-david-motadel-1421441724.

Green, Erica L. "U.S. Orders Duke and U.N.C. to Recast Tone in Mideast Studies." The New York Times. The

New York Times Company, September 19, 2019.
https://www.nytimes.com/2019/09/19/us/politics/a
nti-israel-bias-higher-education.html.

Greif, James. "George Mason University Receives $1.5
Million Gift from IIIT for an Endowed Chair in Islamic
Studies." Media and Public Relations. George Mason
University, November 3, 2008.
https://web.archive.org/web/20081224224717/http
://eagle.gmu.edu/newsroom/722/.

"Group Claims Nigeria Has Become a War Zone for
Christians." Persecution.net. International Christian
Concern, April 22, 2019.
https://www.persecution.org/2019/04/14/group-
claims-nigeria-become-war-zone-christians/.

Gubert, Romain. "Comment Le Qatar Finance L'islam De
France." Le Point International, April 4, 2019.
https://www.lepoint.fr/monde/comment-le-qatar-
finance-l-islam-de-france-04-04-2019-
2305782_24.php.

Gutfeld, Prof. Arnon. "The Saudi Specter over the
American Education System." Jerusalem Center for
Public Affairs, May 23, 2019.
https://jcpa.org/article/saudi-specter-over-
american-education-system/.

Gutfeld, Professor Arnon. "The Saudi Specter over the
American Education System." Jewish Political Studies
Review, Volume 29, Numbers 1-2. Jerusalem Center
for Public Affairs, September 3, 2018.
https://jcpa.org/article/saudi-specter-over-
american-education-system/.

Halevi, Jonathan D. "Al-Qaeda's Intellectual Legacy: New
Radical Islamic Thinking Justifying the Genocide of
Infidels." Jerusalem Viewpoints. Jerusalem Center

for Public Affairs, December 1, 2003.
https://www.jcpa.org/jl/vp508.htm.

Halevi, Jonathan D. "ICNA Canada Contradicts Trudeau:
'Islam Is Totally Incompatible with Western
Democracy.'" CIJ News, February 25, 2016.
https://archive.is/eHtz9.

Halevi, Jonathan D. "Is Canada's Justin Trudeau the Great
Reformer of Islam?" Jerusalem Center for Public
Affairs, November 18, 2018. https://jcpa.org/is-
canadas-justin-trudeau-the-great-reformer-of-
islam/.

Halevi, Jonathan D. "Where Is the Muslim Brotherhood
Headed?" Jerusalem Center for Public Affairs, June
20, 2012. https://jcpa.org/the-muslim-brotherhood-
a-moderate-islamic-alternative-to-al-qaeda-or-a-
partner-in-global-jihad/.

Haney, Philip. "DHS Ordered Me to Scrub Records of
Muslims with Terror Ties." TheHill.com. Nexstar
Media Inc., February 5, 2016.
https://thehill.com/blogs/congress-blog/homeland-
security/268282-dhs-ordered-me-to-scrub-records-
of-muslims-with-terror.

Haqiqatjou, Daniel. "Salute the Sultan! Brunei Reinstates
Hudud for Sexual Deviance." The Muslim Skeptic,
March 30, 2019.
https://muslimskeptic.com/2019/03/30/salute-the-
sultan-brunei/.

Hariyadi, Mathias. "Indonesia: Crosses Desecrated in a
Christian Cemetery in Yogyakarta." AsiaNews.it.
Fondazione PIME Onlus – AsiaNews, April 8, 2019.
http://www.asianews.it/news-en/Crosses-
desecrated-in-a-Christian-cemetery-in-Yogyakarta-
46715.html.

Hariyadi, Mathias. "Indonesia: Yogyakarta Catholic Family Expelled Because Non-Muslim." AsiaNews.it. Fondazione PIME Onlus – AsiaNews, April 2, 2019. http://www.asianews.it/news-en/Yogyakarta-Catholic-family-expelled-because-non-Muslim-%28video%29-46670.html.

Harrod, Andrew. "Abe Foxman Discovers Islamic Anti-Semitism." Jihad Watch, March 9, 2021. https://www.jihadwatch.org/2021/03/abe-foxman-discovers-islamic-anti-semitism.

Hartford Seminary Offers First Program to Educate Muslim Community Leaders. Hartford Seminary, October 11, 2011. Hartford Seminary. https://web.archive.org/web/20111217082144/http://www.hartsem.edu/pages/news-events/2011-Press-Release-Imam-Community-Program.aspx.

"Home Page | The New Arab." The New Arab. Fadaat Media Ltd., 2021. https://english.alaraby.co.uk/.

"Home: Walk-in Islamic Infocenter." collectfreequran.org. Walk-In Islamic InfoCenter (WIIC), 2021. https://www.collectfreequran.org/.

"HSBC Islamic Global Equity Index Fund." Global Asset Management from HSBC in the UK. HSBC Asset Management, 2021. https://www.assetmanagement.hsbc.co.uk/en/institutional-investor/investment-expertise/equities/islamic-global-eq-index-fund.

Ibrahim, Raymond. "Bribed: Subverting American Universities." Gatestone Institute, November 25, 2020. https://www.gatestoneinstitute.org/16786/subverting-american-universities.

Ibrahim, Raymond. "Desecrated and Defecated on: Churches in Europe under Islam."

FrontPageMag.com. David Horowitz Freedom
Center, March 11, 2021.
https://www.frontpagemag.com/fpm/2021/03/dese
crated-and-defecated-churches-europe-under-
raymond-ibrahim/.
Ibrahim, Raymond. "European Churches: Vandalized,
Defecated on, and Torched 'Every Day.'" Gatestone
Institute, April 14, 2019.
https://www.gatestoneinstitute.org/14044/europe-
churches-vandalized.
Ibrahim, Raymond. "Islamic Jizya: Fact and Fiction."
RaymondIbrahim.com, May 28, 2015.
https://www.raymondibrahim.com/2015/05/28/isla
mic-jizya-fact-and-fiction/.
"IIIT Advisory Council Member Dr. Ingrid Mattson Joins
Huron University College." IIIT News. International
Institute of Islamic Thought (IIIT), June 28, 2012.
https://web.archive.org/web/20140715220711/http
://iiit.org/NewsEvents/News/tabid/62/articleType/A
rticleView/articleId/262/Default.aspx.
"IIIT and Hartford Seminary Sign MOU." News.
International Institute of Islamic Thought (IIIT),
October 12, 2011.
https://web.archive.org/web/20111215092742/http
://www.iiit.org:80/NewsEvents/News/tabid/62/artic
leType/ArticleView/articleId/231/IIIT-and-Hartford-
Seminary-sign-MOU.aspx.
"IIIT Chair Inaugurated at Nazareth College." IIIT chair
inaugurated at Nazareth College > IIIT > NEWS.
International Institute of Islamic Thought (IIIT),
January 10, 2012.
https://web.archive.org/web/20120210070538/http
://iiit.org/NewsEvents/News/tabid/62/articleType/A

rticleView/articleId/244/IIIT-Chair-Inaugurated-at-Nazareth-College.aspx.

"IIIT Enters into Agreement with Shenandoah University." Shenandoah University. International Institute of Islamic Thought (IIIT), April 14, 2008. https://web.archive.org/web/20080414181150/http://iiit.org/AboutUs/Agreements/Shenandoah/tabid/111/Default.aspx.

"IIIT Hosts Friends of IIIT Iftar/Dinner." IIIT.org. International Institute of Islamic Thought (IIIT), August 26, 2011. https://web.archive.org/web/20111015143123/http://www.iiit.org/NewsEvents/News/tabid/62/articleType/ArticleView/articleId/228/IIIT-Hosts-Friends-of-IIIT-IftarDinner.aspx.

Imam Abu Zakaruya Yahya Bin Sharaf An-Nawawi. *Riyad Us-Saliheen (The Paradise of the Pious)*. Calgary, AB: Islamic Information Society of Calgary, n.d.

Imam Abu Zakaruya Yahya Bin Sharaf An-Nawawi. "Riyad-Us-Saliheen - The Paradise of the Pious." Oakville Ontario Canada: ICNA Canada, August 2012.

"Iman Fund - Shariah Mutual Fund and Investing." Shariah Investing | Mutual Fund | Iman Fund. Quasar Distributors, LLC, 2021. https://www.investaaa.com/.

Index on Censorship. "Thirty Years on: The Salman Rushdie Fatwa Revisited." Index on Censorship. Index on Censorship, June 9, 2021. https://www.indexoncensorship.org/2019/02/student-reading-list-salman-rushdie-fatwa/.

"Institutional Compliance with Section 117 of the Higher Education Act of 1965." Washington: United States Department of Education Office of the General Counsel, October 27, 2020.

"International Institute of Islamic Thought (IIIT)." Clarion Project, June 29, 2020. https://clarionproject.org/international-institute-islamic-thought/.

"International Institute of Islamic Thought (IITT)." iiit.org. International Institute of Islamic Thought (IITT), 2018. https://iiit.org/en/home/.

"ISIS Burns 19 Yazidi Women to Death in Mosul for 'Refusing to Have Sex with Fighters'." The Independent. Independent Digital News and Media, June 6, 2016. https://www.independent.co.uk/news/world/middle-east/isis-burn-19-yazidi-women-death-mosul-refusing-have-sex-isis-militants-a7066956.html.

"Islam Is NOT Only for Muslims, but for All Mankind." Facebook.com. Hizb ut-Tahrir Britain, June 4, 2017. https://www.facebook.com/htbritain/photos/a.465914336843458/1077423705692515.

Islam Religion Guardian. "Sharia Finances Are Used to Bolster American Islamist Organizations." Islamreligionguardian.com, June 26, 2020. https://www.islamreligionguardian.com/sharia-finances-are-used-to-bolster-american-islamist-organizations/.

"Islamic Finance Industry Mourns the Passing of Internationally Respected Shariah Scholar and Advisory Sheikh Dr. Abdul Sattar Abu Ghuddah." DDCAP Group, December 30, 2020. https://www.ddcap.com/islamic-finance-industry-mourns-the-passing-of-internationally-respected-shariah-scholar-and-advisory-sheikh-dr-abdus-sattar-abu-ghuddah/.

"Islamophobia." en-academic.com. Academic Dictionaries and Encyclopedias, 2021. https://en-academic.com/dic.nsf/enwiki/110470.

Jerusalem Post Staff. "CAIR Report Claims Jewish Funders Supporting 'Islamophobia Network'." The Jerusalem Post | JPost.com. Palestine Post Ltd., May 27, 2019. https://www.jpost.com/American-Politics/CAIR-report-claims-Jewish-funders-supporting-Islamophobia-Network-590747?fbclid=IwAR3lJ2LkjxIZdXl1HuYWrJeH7r3F98s FvtUOQpf_3hZvsqjMbcKqHSlbcXE.

"Jihad - Definition." Merriam-Webster.com dictionary. Merriam-Webster. Accessed August 9, 2021. https://www.merriam-webster.com/dictionary/jihad.

Johnson, Scott. "Is Islam a Religion of Peace?" Power Line. Power Line, August 25, 2013. https://www.powerlineblog.com/archives/2013/08/is-islam-a-religion-of-peace.php.

Jones, Bryony, and Susannah Cullinane. "What Is the Muslim Brotherhood?" CNN. Cable News Network, July 3, 2013. https://www.cnn.com/2013/07/03/world/africa/egypt-muslim-brotherhood-explainer/index.html.

Jones, Emily. "Radical Muslims Murder More than 30 Nigerian Christians, Torch Church in Brutal Attack." CBN News. CBN News, March 4, 2019. https://www1.cbn.com/cbnnews/cwn/2019/march/radical-muslims-murder-32-nigerian-christians-torch-church-in-brutal-attack.

Jovanovski, Kristina. "Canadian Groups Are Lashing out about Muslim Prayer in Schools." The World. PRX and WGBH Boston, May 24, 2017. https://www.pri.org/stories/2017-05-24/canadian-groups-are-lashing-out-about-muslim-prayer-schools.

JTA Staff. "Tainted Teachings, What Your Kids Are Learning about Israel, America, and Islam, Parts 1 through 4." Campus Watch. Middle East Forum, October 27, 2005. https://www.meforum.org/campus-watch/9987/tainted-teachings-what-your-kids-are-learning.

Kern, Soeren. "Britain's Back-Door Blasphemy Law." Gatestone Institute. Gatestone Institute, June 8, 2019. https://www.gatestoneinstitute.org/14351/britain-blasphemy-law.

Kern, Soeren. "Denmark Bans Foreign Funding of Mosques." Gatestone Institute, March 15, 2021. https://www.gatestoneinstitute.org/17167/denmark-mosques-foreign-funds.

Kern, Soeren. "Europe: Islamic Fundamentalism Is Widespread." Gatestone Institute, December 16, 2013. https://www.gatestoneinstitute.org/4092/europe-islamic-fundamentalism.

Kestler-D'Amours, Jillian. "Canada: The next Hub of Islamic Finance?" Middle East Eye, April 27, 2016. https://www.middleeasteye.net/news/canada-next-hub-islamic-finance.

Khan, Omar. "Islamophobia Is Anti-Muslim Racism." London UK: Runnymede Trust, 2018.

Klein, Morton A. "Written Testimony of Zionist Organization of America (ZOA) National President Morton A. Klein, Hearing Title: Hate Crimes and the Rise of White Nnationalism, before the U.S. House of Representatives Committee on the Judiciary, 116th

Congress." New York: Zionist Organization of America (ZOA), April 9, 2019.

Kocher, Renate. "Allensbach-Umfrage: Immer Mehr Tabuthemen." Faz.net. Frankfurter Allgemeine Zeitung GmbH, May 22, 2019. https://www.faz.net/aktuell/politik/inland/allensbac h-umfrage-ueber-meinungsfreiheit-und-kritische-themen-16200724.html.

Kuperwasser, Brig.-Gen. (res.) Yossi, Ehud Rosen, and Eitan Fischberger. "The Security Implications of Muslim Migration." Jerusalem Center for Public Affairs. Jerusalem Center for Public Affairs, March 26, 2019. https://jcpa.org/immigration-to-europe/the-security-implications-of-muslim-migration/.

Kuran, Timur. *Islam and Mammon: The Economic Predicaments of Islamism*. Princeton, NJ: Princeton University Press, 2006.

Kurtz, Stanley. "All Foreign Gifts Report: U.S. Department of Education." nationalreview.com. The National Review, March 31, 2008. https://web.archive.org/web/20080501093827/http ://www.nationalreview.com:80/kurtz/allforeigngiftsr eport.html. Title 20, Section 1011f of the U.S. Code, "Disclosures of foreign gifts"; all disclosure reports filed under Section 1011f are considered public records, as provided by National Review Online here.

Kurtz, Stanley. "Following the Foreign Money." National Review, March 26, 2008. https://www.nationalreview.com/2008/03/following -foreign-money-stanley-kurtz/.

Kurtz, Stanley. "Saudi in the Classroom." NationalReview.com. The National Review, July 29, 2020.

https://www.nationalreview.com/2007/07/saudi-classroom-stanley-kurtz/.

Lai, Amy Tak-Yee. "The Right to Parody: Comparative Analysis of Copyright and Free Speech." in SearchWorks catalog. Cambridge University Press, 2019. https://searchworks.stanford.edu/view/12863816.

Le Figaro with AFP and Reuters. "[Translated] Online Hate: The Assembly Votes on the Avia Bill at First Reading." Le Figaro, July 9, 2019. https://web.archive.org/web/20190709145543/http://www.lefigaro.fr/politique/haine-en-ligne-l-assemblee-vote-la-proposition-de-loi-avia-en-premiere-lecture-20190709.

Lee, Morgan. "Why Islamist Terrorists Attacked Christians in the Philippines." ChristianityToday.com. Christianity Today, January 30, 2019. https://www.christianitytoday.com/ct/podcasts/quick-to-listen/islamist-terrorists-attacked-christians-philippines.html.

Lehrer, Jim, and Ailsa Chang. "Shahzad 'Extremely Defiant' at Sentencing for Failed NYC Bombing." PBS.org. Public Broadcasting Service, October 5, 2010. https://www.pbs.org/newshour/show/shahzad-extremely-defiant-at-sentencing-for-failed-nyc-bombing.

Levin, Andy. "CAMERA Focuses on Newton Schools' Arab-Israeli Conflict Curriculum." Newton TAB. Garrett Co., November 21, 2017. https://newton.wickedlocal.com/news/20171121/camera-focuses-on-newton-schools-arab-israeli-conflict-curriculum.

Lewin, Tamar. "American Universities Create Partnerships in Saudi Arabia." The Tech. Massachusetts Institute of Technology, March 7, 2008. https://thetech.com/2008/03/07/saudi-v128-n10.

Lewis, Charles. "Muslim Prayers during Class Time Draws Fire at Toronto School." nationalpost.com. Postmedia Network Inc., July 5, 2011. https://nationalpost.com/holy-post/muslim-prayers-during-class-time-draws-fire-at-toronto-school.

Lewis, Elizabeth. "Franz Boas, Father of American Anthropology." ThoughtCo.com. ThoughtCo, part of the Dotdash publishing family, December 10, 2020. https://www.thoughtco.com/franz-boas-4582034.

Lindsay, Christopher. "The Problem with the Word 'Islamophobia'." American Thinker, April 3, 2019. https://www.americanthinker.com/blog/2019/04/the_problem_with_the_word_islamophobia.html.

"List of Islamic Terror Attacks on Christians." The Religion of Peace (TROP), August 2021. https://www.thereligionofpeace.com/attacks/christian-attacks.aspx.

Lum, Thomas, and Hannah Fischer. "IF11180 Confucius Institutes in the United States: Selected Issues - Version 5 (Updated)." Congressional Research Service - In Focus. Government of the United States, March 18, 2021. https://crsreports.congress.gov/product/pdf/IF/IF11180.

Lévy, Elisabeth, ed. "[Translated] Philippe Val: 'Nobody Today Would Publish the Cartoons of Muhammad.'" Causeur.fr, August 5, 2019. https://www.causeur.fr/philippe-val-charlie-hebdo-gauche-163103.

MacEoin, Denis. "Foreign Muslim Funding of Western Universities." Middle East Forum. Gatestone Institute, August 19, 2016. https://www.meforum.org/6205/foreign-muslim-funding-western-universities.

MacEoin, Denis. "Western Universities: The Best Indoctrination Money Can Buy." Gatestone Institute, June 26, 2016. https://www.gatestoneinstitute.org/8331/universiti es-indoctrination.

Magassa-Konaté, Maria. "Nantes: Assalam, Une Mosquée Ouverte Aidee Par Un Qatari." SaphirNews.com | Quotidien d'actualité sur le fait musulman en France, November 19, 2012. https://www.saphirnews.com/Nantes-Assalam-une-mosquee-ouverte-aidee-par-un-Qatari_a15716.html.

MailOnline, Darren Boyle for. "Cairo Church Bombing Kills 43 in Palm Sunday Massacre." Daily Mail Online. Associated Newspapers, April 9, 2017. https://www.dailymail.co.uk/news/article-4394838/Thirteen-killed-42-wounded-Cairo-church-bombing.html.

"Malaysia, Turkey and Pakistan to Jointly Launch Channel to Counter Islamophobia - Times of India." The Times of India. Bennett, Coleman & Co. Ltd., September 30, 2019. https://timesofindia.indiatimes.com/world/rest-of-world/malaysia-turkey-and-pakistan-to-jointly-launch-channel-to-counter-islamophobia/articleshow/71377023.cms.

"Man Wearing Crucifix Stabbed in Rome." ANSA.it, April 23, 2019. https://www.ansa.it/english/news/2019/04/23/man

-wearing-crucifix-stabbed-in-rome_1eb22433-8089-449b-abdb-36221c7d2bac.html.

Manthorpe, Jonathan. *Claws of the Panda: Beijing's Campaign of Influence and Intimidation in Canada.* Toronto, Ontario: Cormorant Books, 2019.

Manzo, Kathleen Kennedy. "Supplementary Text on Arab World Elicits Criticism." edweek.org. Editorial Products in Education Inc., March 1, 2005. https://www.edweek.org/teaching-learning/supplementary-text-on-arab-world-elicits-criticism/2005/03.

Marans, Daniel. "Al Jazeera Employees Fear Consequences of Qatar Crisis for Network." HuffPost Canada. BuzzFeed, Inc., June 9, 2017. https://www.huffingtonpost.ca/entry/al-jazeera-employees-fear-qatar-crisis-consequences_n_593a9ffee4b0c5a35c9ea755.

Marks, Anna. "When Artists Take the Piss out of Christ, It's Complicated." Vice.com. Vice Media Group, May 16, 2016. https://www.vice.com/en/article/8qv3gp/contemporary-controversial-artists-depictions-of-christ.

Maurice, Stéphanie. "Le Lycée Averroès S'accroche à Sa 'Normalité.'" Libération, February 24, 2015. https://www.liberation.fr/societe/2015/02/22/le-lycee-averroes-s-accroche-a-sa-normalite_1207940/.

Mauro, Ryan, and Alex Van Ness. "Clarion Exclusive Report: Foreign Influence Ops on US Universities [Incl. John Esposito]." Campus Watch. Clarion Project, September 6, 2019. https://www.meforum.org/campus-watch/59321/clarion-exclusive-report-foreign-influence-ops-on.

McCarthy, Andrew C. "In Europe, Free Speech Bows to Sharia." National Review. National Review Institute, October 27, 2018. https://www.nationalreview.com/2018/10/free-speech-sharia-european-court-of-human-rights-ruling/?fbclid=IwAR2U0X9Mk8rUkm3sEdeIk7BCHjJEf kqF7o2fh95ZQ8s6UweO0A44iyUB9oA.

McElroy, Damien. "Qatar 'Spent Huge Sums on Muslim Brotherhood Groups in Europe'." The National, July 5, 2021. https://www.thenationalnews.com/world/qatar-spent-huge-sums-on-muslim-brotherhood-groups-in-europe-1.845510.

MEMRI TV Editors. "Canadian Imam Younus Kathrada Calls for Support of the 'Mujahideen' In Afghanistan: The Jews and the Christians Are Our Enemies." MEMRI.org. Middle East Media Research Institute, August 24, 2021. https://www.memri.org/tv/canadian-imam-younus-kathrada-support-mujahideen-afghanistan-jews-christians-enemies.

MEMRI TV Editors. "Qatari Sociologist Abd Al-Aziz Al-Khazraj Al-Ansari Mocks the West, International Women's Day: These Filthy Secular Dogs Celebrate Women's 'Freedom' to Act Like Whores." MEMRI TV. Middle East Media Research Institute, March 8, 2019. https://web.archive.org/web/20190713083125/https://www.memri.org/tv/qatari-sociologist-abd-alaziz-khazraj-ansari-mocks-west-womens-day-filthy-dogs-celebrate-freedom-slut-education-snapchat/transcript.

Meotti, Giulio. "Erdoganistan: The New Islamic Superpower?" Gatestone Institute, March 28, 2021.

https://www.gatestoneinstitute.org/17202/erdogan-turkey-islamic-superpower.

Meotti, Giulio. "France Quietly Reintroducing the Crime of Blasphemy." Gatestone Institute. Gatestone Institute, February 9, 2020. https://www.gatestoneinstitute.org/15526/france-blasphemy-censorship.

Meotti, Giulio. "Is Radical Islam Horrifying the West into Paralysis?" Gatestone Institute, July 5, 2017. https://www.gatestoneinstitute.org/10603/radical-islam-west.

Meotti, Giulio. "Qatar: 'A Wolf in Sheep's Clothing'." Gatestone Institute, April 9, 2019. https://www.gatestoneinstitute.org/14042/qatar-europe-islamism-finance.

Meotti, Giulio. "The Religious Transformation of French Schools." Gatestone Institute. Gatestone Institute, January 23, 2021. https://www.gatestoneinstitute.org/16972/france-schools-religion.

Meotti, Giulio. "The West Needs to Wake up to China's Duplicity." Gatestone Institute. Gatestone Institute International Policy Council, March 28, 2020. https://www.gatestoneinstitute.org/15804/china-duplicity.

Mills, Jen. "Lib Dem Candidate Suspended over Comments about Muslims." Metro.co.uk, April 18, 2019. https://metro.co.uk/2019/04/18/lib-dem-candidate-suspended-comments-muslims-9243430/.

Minister of Public Safety and Emergency Preparedness, 2018 Public Report on the Terrorism Threat to Canada § (2019). https://www.publicsafety.gc.ca/cnt/rsrcs/pblctns/pblc-rprt-trrrsm-thrt-cnd-2018/index-en.aspx.

Mintz, Jason. "USA v. SAFA Group EDVA 02-MG-114 20 March Main Affidavit REDACTED Released Oct 31, 2017." Washington: Investigative Project on Terrorism (IPT), October 2003.

Mintz, John, and Douglas Farah. "In Search of Friends Among The Foes." The Washington Post. The Washington Post Company, September 11, 2004. http://www.washingtonpost.com/wp-dyn/articles/A12823-2004Sep10.html.

Mohamed, Shereen, Abdulaziz Goni, and Shaima Hasan. "Islamic Finance Development Report 2018." Thomson Reuters, 2018.

Motadel, David. "The Swastika and the Crescent." wilsonquarterly.com. Woodrow Wilson International Center for Scholars, December 2, 2014. https://www.wilsonquarterly.com/quarterly/fall-2014-the-great-wars/the-swastika-and-the-crescent/.

Mulholland, Rory. "Teacher Quits French Muslim SCHOOL Accusing It Of 'Promoting Islamism'." The Telegraph. Telegraph Media Group, February 8, 2015. https://www.telegraph.co.uk/news/worldnews/europe/france/11398672/Teacher-quits-French-Muslim-school-accusing-it-of-promoting-Islamism.html.

Mulroney, David. "Opinion: Ottawa Seems to Be out of Ideas on Devising a New Kind of China Policy." The Globe and Mail. The Globe and Mail Inc., June 20, 2019. https://www.theglobeandmail.com/opinion/article-ottawa-seems-to-be-out-of-ideas-on-devising-a-new-kind-of-china-policy/.

Mulroney, David. "Opinion: The NBA'S China Crisis Is Proof That Economic Diplomacy Is No Slam Dunk."

TheGlobeandMail.com. The Globe and Mail Inc.,
October 15, 2019.
https://www.theglobeandmail.com/opinion/article-
the-nbas-china-crisis-is-proof-that-economic-
diplomacy-is-no-slam/.
Murphy, Mary Alice, ed. "Does Anyone Believe That This
Was Just a Casual Partnership?" The Grant County
Beat, October 18, 2019.
https://www.grantcountybeat.com/columns/inform
ational/immigration-matters/53850-does-anyone-
believe-that-this-was-just-a-casual-partnership.
"Muslim Brotherhood (MB)." DiscoverTheNetwork.org -
A Guide to the Political Left. Internet Archive
Wayback Machine, April 23, 2020.
https://web.archive.org/web/20200423074744/http
://www.discoverthenetworks.com/groupProfile.asp?
grpid=6386.
"Muslim Brotherhood - Al-Ikhwan Al-Muslimin - Al-
Ikhwan ('The Brothers')." Muslim Brotherhood.
Federation of American Scientists (FAS), January 8,
2002. https://fas.org/irp/world/para/mb.htm.
"Muslim Brotherhood." Encyclopædia Britannica.
Encyclopædia Britannica, inc. Accessed August 9,
2021. https://www.britannica.com/topic/Muslim-
Brotherhood.
"Muslim Brotherhood." Wikipedia, the free
encyclopedia. Wikimedia Foundation, August 6,
2021.
https://en.wikipedia.org/wiki/Muslim_Brotherhood.
"NCCM Recommendations - National Summit on
Islamophobia." Ottawa: National Council of
Canadian Muslims (NCCM), July 19, 2021.
"Neo-Nazism and Islamophobia among the 'Gravest
Threats' Facing the World, Freeland Tells UN."

CBCnews. CBC/Radio Canada, March 28, 2019. https://www.cbc.ca/news/politics/white-supremacist-nazi-islamophobia-1.5076033.

News Desk. "OIC Urges UN to Tackle Islamophobia, Declare It a Form of Racism." The Express Tribune Pakistan. The Express Tribune, March 23, 2019. https://tribune.com.pk/story/1935888/3-oic-urges-un-tackle-islamophobia-declare-form-racism.

News Wires. "Death Toll in Sri Lanka Attacks Revised down to 253." France 24. France 24, April 26, 2019. https://www.france24.com/en/20190426-death-toll-sri-lanka-attacks-easter-bombings-revised-down-253.

Nigeria Correspondent. "Muslim Fulani Herdsmen Massacre Christians after Baby Dedication in Nigeria." Morning Star News, April 18, 2019. https://morningstarnews.org/2019/04/muslim-fulani-herdsmen-massacre-christians-after-baby-dedication-in-nigeria/.

Nigeria Correspondent. "Nigeria: Herdsmen Attacks, Boko Haram and the Cross." Morning Star News, April 21, 2019. https://morningstarnews.org/2019/04/nigeria-herdsmen-attacks-boko-haram-and-the-cross/.

Obama, Barack. "Remarks by the President at Islamic Society of Baltimore." National Archives and Records Administration. The White House Office of the Press Secretary, February 3, 2016. https://obamawhitehouse.archives.gov/the-press-office/2016/02/03/remarks-president-islamic-society-baltimore.

Obama, Barack. "Statement by the President on the Occasion of Eid-Al-Fitr." National Archives and Records Administration. The White House Office of the Press Secretary, July 27, 2014. https://obamawhitehouse.archives.gov/the-press-office/2014/07/27/statement-president-occasion-eid-al-fitr.

Oduah, Chika. "'She Refused to Convert to Islam,' 85 Days on, Kidnapped Schoolgirl Leah Sharibu Remains in Captivity." CNN. Cable News Network, May 15, 2018. https://www.cnn.com/2018/05/15/africa/boko-haram-lone-school-girl/index.html.

Omar, Ilhan. "PolitiFact - Ilhan Omar Misstates the Facts About CAIR's Founding." Edited by Angie Drobnic Holan. PolitiFact.com. The Poynter Institute, April 15, 2019. https://www.politifact.com/factchecks/2019/apr/15/ilhan-omar/ilhan-omar-misstates-facts-about-cairs-founding/.

Ortiz, Erik, Monica Alba, Tim Sandler, and Richard Esposito. "Man Beheaded Co-Worker in Moore, Oklahoma, Workplace Attack: Police." NBCNews.com. NBC Universal News Group, June 11, 2015. https://www.nbcnews.com/news/crime-courts/man-beheaded-co-worker-moore-oklahoma-workplace-attack-police-n212396.

"Our Corporate Partners." Silicon Valley Community Foundation. Silicon Valley Community Foundation, November 11, 2020. https://www.siliconvalleycf.org/our-corporate-partners.

"Pakistani Christian Attacked and Beaten for Opening Small Grocery Store." Persecution.org. International Christian Concern, April 10, 2019. https://www.persecution.org/2019/04/10/pakistani-christian-attacked-beaten-opening-small-grocery-store/.

Paldi, Camille. "Challenges for Islamic Finance in the USA." InternationalFinance.com. International Finance Publications Ltd., March 14, 2017. https://internationalfinance.com/challenges-for-islamic-finance-in-the-usa/.

Paul, Richard, Linda Elder, and Ted Bartell. A Brief History of the Idea of Critical Thinking. Foundation for Critical Thinking, 1997. https://www.criticalthinking.org/pages/a-brief-history-of-the-idea-of-critical-thinking/408.

Pearson, Allison. "Rotherham: In the Face of Such Evil, Who Is the Racist Now?" The Telegraph. Telegraph Media Group, August 27, 2014. https://www.telegraph.co.uk/news/uknews/crime/11059138/Rotherham-In-the-face-of-such-evil-who-is-the-racist-now.html.

PEN Canada. "Amy Lai Wins 2021 PEN Canada/Ken Filkow Prize for Freedom of Expression." PEN Canada, July 22, 2021. https://pencanada.ca/news/amy-lai-wins-2021-pen-canada-ken-filkow-prize-for-freedom-of-expression/.

"Peter Stockland - Senior Writer." Cardus.ca. Cardus Institute, August 6, 2021. https://www.cardus.ca/who-we-are/our-team/pstockland/.

Peters, Ralph. "How Saudi Arabia Dangerously Undermines the United States." New York Post. NYP Holdings, Inc., April 16, 2016. https://nypost.com/2016/04/16/how-saudi-arabia-undermines-the-united-states/.

Phillips, Melanie. "From Congress to Classrooms: Reframing the Israel Narrative." JNS.org. Jewish

News Syndicate, October 17, 2019.
https://www.jns.org/opinion/from-congress-to-
classrooms-reframing-the-israel-narrative.

Phillips, Melanie. "How Jews Claiming 'Islamophobia' Are
Helping Embolden Ant-Semitism."
MelaniePhillips.com, April 14, 2019.
https://www.melaniephillips.com/how-jews-
claiming-islamophobia-are-helping-embolden-
antisemitism.

Phillips, Melanie. "The Dangerous Drive to Correlate
Islamophobia with Anti-Semitism." JNS.org. Jewish
News Syndicate, July 4, 2019.
https://www.jns.org/opinion/the-dangerous-drive-
to-correlate-islamophobia-with-anti-semitism/.

Pipes, Daniel. "Examining Qatar's Influence."
DanielPipes.org, January 29, 2019.
http://www.danielpipes.org/18699/qatar-influence.

Pipes, Daniel. "Examining Qatar's Influence."
DanielPipes.org. Daniel Pipes, January 29, 2019.
http://www.danielpipes.org/18699/qatar-influence.

Pittman, Ken. "Obama 'Quid pro Quo' Revenge via
Impeachment? [Opinion]." 1420 WBSM, January 23,
2020. https://wbsm.com/obama-quid-pro-quo-
revenge-via-impeachment-opinion/.

Polege, Mark. "Sharia-Compliant Finance and How We
Are Funding Jihad in the Heartland." Breitbart News,
September 25, 2011.
https://www.breitbart.com/national-
security/2011/09/25/Sharia-Compliant-Finance-And-
How-We-Are-Funding-Jihad-in-the-Heartland/.

Poole, Patrick. "(PJM Exclusive) Holder's DOJ Scuttled
More Terror-Related Prosecutions." pjmedia.com. PJ
Media, April 28, 2011.
https://pjmedia.com/blog/patrick-

poole/2011/04/28/pjm-exclusive-holders-doj-
scuttled-more-terror-related-prosecutions-n11527.
"Preparing America's Students for Success." Home.
Common Core State Standards Initiative, 2021.
http://www.corestandards.org/.
Prof Heidi Hadsell Delivers Al Faruqi Memorial Lecture at
Friends of IIIT Iftar. International Institute of Islamic
Thought (IIIT), August 8, 2012.
https://web.archive.org/web/20120926205213/http
://iiit.org/NewsEvents/News/tabid/62/articleType/A
rticleView/articleId/268/Default.aspx.
"Profile: Nihad Awad`." The Investigative Project on
Terrorism. The Investigative Project on Terrorism,
2010.
https://www.investigativeproject.org/profile/113/ni
had-awad.
Public Safety Canada. "2018 Public Report on the
Terrorism Threat to Canada." Public Safety Canada.
Government of Canada, April 29, 2019.
https://www.publicsafety.gc.ca/cnt/rsrcs/pblctns/pb
lc-rprt-trrrsm-thrt-cnd-2018/index-en.aspx#s11.
"Public University Gives Chinese Communists Funding,
Exclusive Rights to Intellectual Concepts,
Trademarks, Inventions." Judicial Watch. Judicial
Watch, Inc., October 17, 2019.
https://www.judicialwatch.org/corruption-
chronicles/public-university-gives-chinese-
communists-funding-exclusive-rights-to-intellectual-
concepts-trademarks-inventions/.
"Qatar Foundation International." The Center for Citizen
Diplomacy. PYXERA Global, 2019.
https://www.centerforcitizendiplomacy.org/network
/qatar-foundation-international/.

"Qatar Has given $1.5 Billion to U.S. Universities in the Form of Monetary Gifts and Contracts." Qatarileaks.com, June 13, 2019. https://qatarileaks.com/en/leak/qatar-has-given-15-billion-to-us-universities-in-the-form-of-monetary-gifts-and-contracts.

Quiggin, Tom. "Muslim Brotherhood Front Organizations, U.S. and Canada." Gatestone Institute. Gatestone Institute, January 31, 2017. https://www.gatestoneinstitute.org/9770/muslim-brotherhood-front-organizations.

Ramadan Tafseer in Five | Surah Fatihah - V.7 Part A - "The Path of Favour". YouTube.com. Mathabah, 2015. https://www.youtube.com/watch?v=CP_9fZC1KjI&t=9s.

Raza, Raheel. "Raheel Raza: M-103 Won't Build a More United CANADA. It Will Turn Canadians against Each Other." nationalpost.com. National Post, February 27, 2017. https://nationalpost.com/opinion/raheel-raza-m-103-wont-build-a-more-united-canada-it-will-canadians-against-each-other.

Rebel Editors. "Muhammad Mustafa Mustaan." The Rebel. The Rebel Media, September 6, 2015. https://web.archive.org/web/20150906183217/http://www.therebel.media/muhammad_mustafa_mustaan.

"Reconciliation Session Leads to Another Church Closure in Egypt." Persecution.org. International Christian Concern, May 3, 2019. https://www.persecution.org/2019/05/03/reconciliation-session-leads-another-church-closure-egypt/.

"The Research Center for Islamic Legislation and Ethics (CILE)." CSIA-Oxford.org. University of Oxford, 2015.

https://www.csia-oxford.org/research-center-islamic-legislation-and-ethics-cile.html.

Reuters Staff. "Brunei Defends Tough New Islamic Laws against Growing Backlash." Reuters. Thomson Reuters, March 30, 2019. https://www.reuters.com/article/us-brunei-islamiclaws/brunei-defends-tough-new-islamic-laws-against-growing-backlash-idUSKCN1RB0E1.

Revel Jean François. *How Democracies Perish: Jean-Francois Revel; with the Assistance of Branko Lazitch; Trans. from the French by William Byron*. London: Weidenfeld and Nicolson, 1983.

"Riyad-Us-Saliheen (2 Vol. Set)." Dar-us-Salam Publications, 2020. https://dar-us-salam.com/english/hadith-sunnah/h04-riyad-us-saliheen-2-vol-set.html.

"The Road Traveled: 9th Annual International Islamophobia Conference." University of Canlifornia at Berkley (UCB) Center for Race & Gender, 2018. https://www.crg.berkeley.edu/events/the-road-traveled-9th-annual-international-islamophobia-conference/.

Robson, John. "John Robson: YES, Offending Muslim Sensibilities Is RUDE. but It Shouldn't Be Dangerous." nationalpost. National Post, May 16, 2019. https://nationalpost.com/opinion/john-robson-yes-offending-muslim-sensibilities-is-rude-but-it-shouldnt-be-dangerous?fbclid=IwAR0f4P_AVkjZmN-ea2cl2qvUI1RNC4RZrtGfNltX45MAtShvZOHrzBV4iEg.

"The Role of Socratic Questioning in Thinking, Teaching, and Learning." The Role of Socratic Questioning in Thinking, Teaching, and Learning. Foundation for Critical Thinking, 2019. https://www.criticalthinking.org/pages/the-role-of-socratic-questioning-in-thinking-teaching-amp-learning/522.

"Rotherham Child Sexual Exploitation Scandal." en.wikipedia.org. Wikipedia, the free encyclopedia, August 7, 2021. https://en.wikipedia.org/wiki/Rotherham_child_sexual_exploitation_scandal.

Rovner, Ilana Diamond. "FindLaw's United States Seventh Circuit Case and Opinions." Global Relief Foundation Incorporated v. New York Times Company. FindLaw, December 1, 2004. https://caselaw.findlaw.com/us-7th-circuit/1308560.html.

Sacks, Rabbi Jonathan. "Biblical Insights into the Good Society." *Ebor Lectures 2011*. Lecture presented at the Biblical Insights into the Good Society, November 30, 2011. http://www.rabbisacks.org/biblical-insights-into-the-good-society-ebor-lecture-2012/.

Safa TV (Saudi Arabia). "Egyptian Researcher Mohamed Gad El-Zoghby: We Should Erect a Statue of Hitler Because of What He Did to the Jews." MEMRI.org. Middle East Media Research Institute (MEMRI), February 15, 2019. https://www.memri.org/tv/egyptian-researcher-gad-zoghby-should-erect-statue-hitler-because-did-jews-holocaust-khomeini-worse.

"Sahih Bukhari: Book Of 'Merits of Al-Ansaar.'" Sahih Bukhari : Book Of "Merits of Al-Ansaar". Accessed September 6, 2021. https://www.sahih-bukhari.com/Pages/Bukhari_5_58.php.

Said, Edward W. "Orientalism Reconsidered." *Cultural Critique*, no. 1 (1985): 89–107. https://doi.org/10.2307/1354282.

Salaam Gateway Editors. "State of the Global Islamic
Economy 2020/2021 Report." Salaam Gateway -
Global Islamic Economy Gateway, 2020.
https://www.salaamgateway.com/specialcoverage/S
GIE20-21.

Sarah. "Challenges of Countering Islamophobia - The OIC
Initiative." IqraSense.com | Islamic Blog. Unknown,
February 16, 2018.
http://www.iqrasense.com/islamic-
outreach/challenges-of-countering-islamophobia-
the-oic-initiative.html. Extract from "The Journal"
Issued by the Organization of the Islamic Conference
(OIC) — Professor Ekmeleddin Ihsanoglu (Secretary-
General of the Organization of the Islamic
Conference)

Sauvaget, Bernadette, and Willy Le Devin. "Le Qatar
Verserait 35,000 Euros Chaque Mois à Tariq
Ramadan." Libération, April 5, 2019.
https://www.liberation.fr/france/2019/04/05/le-
qatar-verserait-35-000-euros-chaque-mois-a-tariq-
ramadan_1719428/.

Schmidt, Susan. "Saudi Money Shaping U.S. Research."
The National Interest. The Center for the National
Interest, February 11, 2013.
https://nationalinterest.org/commentary/saudi-
money-shaping-us-research-8083.

Scriven, Michael, and Richard Paul. Defining Critical
Thinking. Foundation for Critical Thinking, 1987.
https://www.criticalthinking.org/pages/defining-
critical-thinking/766. A definition of Critical Thinking
by Michael Scriven & Richard Paul, presented at the
8th Annual International Conference on Critical
Thinking and Education Reform, Summer 1987.

"Second Annual ISNA Conference on Economic
Development Sponsored by the Islamic Society of
North America (ISNA), Kansas City, Missouri, May 28-
30, 1988." Washington: Investigative Project on
Terrorism (IPT), 1988. Extract from declassified FBI
investigative records on the North American Islamic
Trust (NAIT).

"Sheikh Dr. Mohammed Ali Elgari." Islamic Finance
House, 2021. https://www.ifh.ae/sharia-
supervisory/sheikh-dr-mohammed-ali-elgari/.
Islamic Finance House (IFH) is a private joint stock
company.

Shideler, Kyle. "Another Jihad Attack, Another MB
Mosque - Will There Be an Investigation?" Center for
Security Policy, July 17, 2015.
https://centerforsecuritypolicy.org/another-jihad-
attack-another-mb-mosque-will-there-be-an-
investigation/.

Shinal, John. "When Silicon Valley Execs Suddenly Make
Billions, They Turn to This Man to Help Them Give It
Away." CNBC.com. CNBC LLC, June 10, 2017.
https://www.cnbc.com/2017/06/10/silicon-valley-
community-foundation-got-huge-on-tech-industry-
giving.html.

Silva, Dennis, and Iqbal J. Unus. "MOU between Center
for Interfaith Studies and Dialogue (CISD) at
Nazareth College, Rochester NY and The Fairfax
Institute (TFI) at International Institute of Islamic
Thought (IIIT) Herndon VA." Agreements.
International Institute of Islamic Thought (IIIT),
January 13, 2006.
https://web.archive.org/web/20080414181652/http
://www.iiit.org/Portals/0/agreements/CISD.pdf.

Simpson, James. "CAIR's New 'Islamophobia' Report: A Partnership with the SPLC." Capital Research Center. Capital Research Center, July 1, 2019. https://capitalresearch.org/article/cairs-new-islamophobia-report-part-1/?fbclid=IwAR22sHdXccQMBu_vc9OczgSJd0NPKOPt QeC_rPLQ-UhmrbsnYTSdWwH3Tag.

Simsek, Ayhan. "German Chancellor Merkel: 'Islam Belongs to Germany'." Anadolu Agency, March 16, 2018. https://www.aa.com.tr/en/europe/german-chancellor-merkel-islam-belongs-to-germany/1090930.

Smith, Adam. "Erdoğan's American Mosque Spreads Islamism." Middle East Forum, July 29, 2021. https://www.meforum.org/62539/turkish-regime-mosque-near-dc-spreads-islamism.

Smith, Cliff. "'Steele Dossier' Law Firm Peddles Misinformation for Jamaat-e-Islami Linked Charity." The Sunday Guardian Live. Information TV Pvt Ltd., June 27, 2020. https://www.sundayguardianlive.com/news/steele-dossier-law-firm-peddles-misinformation-jamaat-e-islami-linked-charity.

"Socially Responsible Investing." RBC Wealth Management. RBC Dominion Securities Inc., 2021. https://ca.rbcwealthmanagement.com/web/abbas.f azal/sri.

"Socratic Questions." Socratic Questioning. Changing Works, 2021. http://changingminds.org/techniques/questioning/s ocratic_questions.htm.

Sones, Mordechai. "Philadelphia Imam: 'The Jews Are the Vilest People'." Israel National News. Arutz Sheva, March 7, 2019.

https://www.israelnationalnews.com/News/News.as
px/260054.

Southern India Correspondent. "Unprecedented Suicide
Bombing Attacks Shock Christians in Sri Lanka."
Morning Star News, April 22, 2019.
https://morningstarnews.org/2019/04/unprecedent
ed-suicide-bombing-attacks-shock-christians-in-sri-
lanka/.

Spencer, Robert. "Canada: Muslim Professor Who Claims
She Was Assaulted at Conference Has Long Record
of 'Islamophobia' Propagandizing." Jihad Watch,
April 15, 2019.
https://www.jihadwatch.org/2019/04/canada-
muslim-prof-who-claims-she-was-assaulted-at-
conference-has-long-record-of-islamophobia-
propagandizing.

Spencer, Robert. "Canada's Jihad Denial." FrontPageMag
Archive. Frontpagemag.com, October 23, 2014.
https://archives.frontpagemag.com/fpm/canadas-
jihad-denial-robert-spencer/.

Spencer, Robert. "In Wake of Ottawa Shootings, Police
Chiefs Send Letters to Muslim Leaders Inviting
Muslims to Contact Them If They Fear 'Backlash.'"
Jihad Watch, October 22, 2014.
https://www.jihadwatch.org/2014/10/in-wake-of-
ottawa-shootings-police-chiefs-send-letters-to-
muslim-leaders-inviting-muslims-to-contact-them-if-
they-fear-backlash.

"Sri Lanka Attacks: Death Toll Soars to 290 after
Bombings Hit Churches and Hotels." BBC News. BBC,
April 22, 2019. https://www.bbc.com/news/world-
asia-48008073.

Staff Writer. "Italy Sold Its Education System to Qatar."
TheArabPosts.com. The Arab Posts, May 28, 2020.

https://thearabposts.com/italy-sold-its-education-system-to-qatar/.

Starnes, Todd. "School Apologizes after Students Pray to Allah on Field Trip to Mosque." Fox News. FOX News Network, LLC, November 3, 2015. https://www.foxnews.com/us/school-apologizes-after-students-pray-to-allah-on-field-trip-to-mosque.

Statistics Canada. "Canada Day... by the Numbers." Statistics Canada. Government of Canada, September 28, 2017. https://www.statcan.gc.ca/eng/dai/smr08/2017/smr 08_219_2017.

Steiner, George. Essay. In *In Bluebeard's Castle: Some Notes towards the Redefinition of Culture*, 47. New Haven, CT: Yale University Press, 1971.

Stern, Marilyn. "Martha Lee: Is France Getting Serious about Islamism?" MEForum.org. The Middle East Forum, August 30, 2021. https://www.meforum.org/62603/lee-is-france-getting-serious-about-islamism.

Stern, Marilyn. "Morten Uhrskov Jensen on Denmark's Cap on Non-Western Immigration." Middle East Forum, August 5, 2021. https://www.meforum.org/62551/jensen-denmarks-cap-on-non-western-immigration.

Stinson, Scott. "Stinson: NBA's Adam Silver Tries Compromise to Smooth Things over with China over pro-Hong Kong Tweet." torontosun.com. Postmedia Network Inc., October 9, 2019. https://torontosun.com/sports/basketball/nba/stins on-nbas-adam-silver-tries-compromise-to-smooth-things-over-with-china-over-pro-hong-kong-tweet.

Swenson, Elmer. Sayyid Qutb's Milestones. Elmer Swenson, June 27, 2005.

https://gemsofislamism.tripod.com/milestones_qut b.html.

Tafsir Suratul Fatiha 04. YouTube.com. ibndaqeeq, 2012. https://www.youtube.com/watch?v=Q8U4UUrca9Y.

Taher, Abul. "Disturbing Secret Government Report Exposes Extremist Alert in 48 British Islamic Schools." Daily Mail Online. Associated Newspapers, May 4, 2019. https://www.dailymail.co.uk/news/article-6993333/Disturbing-secret-Government-report-exposes-extremist-alert-48-British-Islamic-schools.html.

Tomlinson, Chris. "91-Year-Old Swede Convicted for Anti-Islam Hate Speech." Breitbart.com. Breitbart News, March 31, 2019. https://www.breitbart.com/europe/2019/03/31/91-year-old-swede-convicted-anti-islam-hate-speech/.

Tomlinson, Chris. "Crosses in Italian Cemetery Covered to Avoid Offence to Other Religions." Breitbart.com. Breitbart News, April 9, 2019. https://www.breitbart.com/europe/2019/04/09/crosses-italian-cemetery-covered-avoid-offence-other-religions/.

Tomlinson, Chris. "Homeless Berlin Man Stabbed in Alleged Anti-Christian Attack." Breitbart.com. Breitbart News, April 9, 2019. https://www.breitbart.com/europe/2019/04/09/watch-homeless-berlin-man-stabbed-alleged-anti-christian-attack/.

"Tommy Robinson's Facebook, Instagram Pages Removed FOR 'Organised Hate'." The Irish Times, February 26, 2019. https://www.irishtimes.com/news/world/uk/tommy

-robinson-s-facebook-instagram-pages-removed-for-
organised-hate-1.3807426.

Trudeau, Justin. "Statement by the Prime Minister of
Canada on Eid Al-Fitr." Prime Minister of Canada,
June 14, 2018.
https://pm.gc.ca/en/news/statements/2018/06/14/
statement-prime-minister-canada-eid-al-fitr.

Turley, Jonathan. "France Has Turned into One of the
Worldwide Threats to Free Speech." TheHill.com.
Nexstar Media Linc., July 7, 2019.
https://thehill.com/opinion/civil-rights/451813-
france-has-turned-into-one-of-the-worldwide-
threats-to-free-speech.

Turner, Camilla. "Pearson Launches Urgent Review of
GCSE Textbook after Complaints That It
'Whitewashed' Jewish History." The Telegraph.
Telegraph Media Group, October 26, 2019.
https://www.telegraph.co.uk/news/2019/10/26/pea
rson-launches-urgent-review-gcse-textbook-
complaints-whitewashed.

U.S. Attorney's Office, Eastern District of Virginia.
"Virginia Man Sentenced to 30 Years in Prison for
Plot to Carry out Suicide Bomb Attack on U.S.
Capitol." archives.fbi.org. Federal Bureau of
Investigation, September 14, 2012.
https://archives.fbi.gov/archives/washingtondc/pres
s-releases/2012/virginia-man-sentenced-to-30-
years-in-prison-for-plot-to-carry-out-suicide-bomb-
attack-on-u.s.-capitol.

Vadum, Matthew. "Lifting the Veil on the 'Islamophobia'
Hoax." Capital Research Center. Capital Research
Center, November 30, 2015.
https://capitalresearch.org/article/islamophobia-
hoax/.

325

Vahid, Mojtaba Amiri. "The OIC/NGOs Cooperation in Combating Islamophobia." Istanbul: International Conference on Islamophobia, December 8, 2007.

valeursactuelles.com. "800 Signalements Pour 'Radicalisme Islamiste' à L'ÉCOLE Depuis L'assassinat De Samuel Paty." Valeurs actuelles, December 16, 2020. https://www.valeursactuelles.com/societe/800-signalements-pour-radicalisme-islamiste-a-lecole-depuis-lassassinat-de-samuel-paty/.

Valinsky, Jordan. "How One Tweet Snowballed into the NBA's Worst Nightmare." CNN. Cable News Network, October 11, 2019. https://www.cnn.com/2019/10/09/business/nba-china-hong-kong-explainer/index.html.

VanNess, Alex. "DOE Launches Investigations into Harvard and Yale." Clarion Project. Clarion Project Inc., February 13, 2020. https://clarionproject.org/harvard-and-yale-doe-launches-investigations/.

Vela, Justin. "Qatar to Launch Al Jazeera Counterweight." The National. The National, June 17, 2021. https://www.thenationalnews.com/world/qatar-to-launch-al-jazeera-counterweight-1.244186.

Vidino, Lorenzo. The Muslim Brotherhood in the United Kingdom. Program on Extremism at George Washington University, December 2015. https://extremism.gwu.edu/sites/g/files/zaxdzs2191/f/downloads/MB%20in%20the%20UK.pdf.

Wallström, Margot, and Morgan Johansson. "Ändrade Mediegrundlagar Proposition 2017/18:49." Sveriges Riksdag, November 30, 2017. https://www.riksdagen.se/sv/dokument-

lagar/dokument/proposition/andrade-
mediegrundlagar_H50349/html.

Wang, Fei-Ling. *The China Order: Centralia, World
Empire, and the Nature of Chinese Power.* Albany,
NY: State University of New York Press, 2017.

Watson, Lani. "Good Democracy Needs Good
Questions." Open for Debate. Cardiff University,
October 9, 2017.
https://blogs.cardiff.ac.uk/openfordebate/2017/09/
25/good-democracy-needs-good-questions/.

The Way of Jihad : Complete text by Hassan Al-Banna,
founder of the Muslim Brotherhood. Militant Islam
Monitor, January 16, 2005.
http://www.militantislammonitor.org/article/id/379.

Weinthal, Benjamin. "Oberlin College's 'Professor of
Peace' Urged Elimination of Jewish State."
JPost.com. The Jerusalem Post, February 27, 2021.
https://www.jpost.com/diaspora/antisemitism/ober
lin-colleges-professor-of-peace-urged-elimination-
of-jewish-state-660298.

"Western Canadian University Introduces Islamic
Studies." IIIT News. International Institute of Islamic
Thought (IIIT), December 20, 2010.
https://web.archive.org/web/20140530025135/http
://iiit.org/NewsEvents/News/tabid/62/ArticleType/A
rticleView/ArticleID/202/PageID/192/Default.aspx.

"What Is a Fatwa?" Islamic Supreme Council of America.
Islamic Supreme Council of America, 2021.
https://wpisca.wpengine.com/?p=106.

Wilson, Tucker. "Pro-Sharia Law Group Banned by
Mohawk College." CBCnews. CBC/Radio Canada,
January 8, 2016.
https://www.cbc.ca/news/canada/hamilton/headlin

es/pro-sharia-law-group-banned-by-mohawk-college-1.3393605.

World Israel News Staff. "Trump Administration Targets Duke, UNC-Chapel Hill for Biased, Pro-Islamic Middle East Studies Program." worldisraelnews.com. World Israel News (WIN), September 22, 2019. https://worldisraelnews.com/trump-administration-targets-duke-unc-chapel-hill-for-biased-pro-islamic-middle-east-studies-program/.

WSPA Staff. "Vandals Spray Paint Messages, Break Windows at Anderson Co. Church." WSPA.com. WSPA 7 News, April 16, 2019. https://www.wspa.com/news/vandals-spray-paint-messages-break-windows-at-anderson-co-church/.

Zenishek, Steven G. "Sayyid Qutb's 'Milestones' and Its Impact on the Arab Spring." Edited by CDR Youssef Aboul-Enein. Sayyid Qutb's "Milestones" and Its Impact on the Arab Spring. Small Wars Journal, May 9, 2013. https://smallwarsjournal.com/jrnl/art/sayyid-qutb%E2%80%99s-%E2%80%9Cmilestones%E2%80%9D-and-its-impact-on-the-arab-spring.

zhyntativ. "Hasan Al-Banna and His Political Thought of Islamic Brotherhood." Ikhwanweb: The Muslim Brotherhood official English website, May 13, 2008. https://web.archive.org/web/20100107010100/http:/www.ikhwanweb.com/article.php?id=17065.

Zilber, Ariel. "Disturbing Video Shows Young Muslim Children at a Philadelphia Islamic Center Singing about 'Chopping off Heads', Martyrdom and 'Defending Palestine with Our Bodies'." Daily Mail Online. Associated Newspapers Ltd, May 6, 2019. https://www.dailymail.co.uk/news/article-

6994509/Muslim-children-Philadelphia-school-sing-chopping-heads-army-Allah.html.

"ZOA: Fire Four Imams Who Called for Murder of Jews." *Zionist Organization of America (ZOA)*, January 15, 2018. Zionist Organization of America (ZOA). https://zoa.org/2018/01/10377423-zoa-fire-four-imams-calling-for-murdering-jews/.

"[Report] Islamophobia: A Challenge for Us All." Runnymede Trust, 1997. https://www.runnymedetrust.org/companies/17/74/Islamophobia-A-Challenge-for-Us-All.html.

"[Translated] WamS: Two Church Desecrations Every Day in France." PINews.net. PINews - Politically Incorrect, March 24, 2019. http://www.pi-news.net/2019/03/wams-jeden-tag-zwei-kirchenschaendungen-in-frankreich/.

INDEX

338

339

343

ABOUT THE AUTHOR

Diane Weber Bederman is an author, chaplain, journalist, blogger and speaker who is passionate about religion, ethics, politics, and mental health. She has been published in many media outlets including Huffington Post Canada, Times of Israel and Canada Free Press. She is a contributor to Arutz Sheva.

Made in the USA
Las Vegas, NV
02 December 2021

35825934R00207